**Langston
University**

Langston University

A HISTORY

By Zella J. Black Patterson

with Lynette L. Wert

University of Oklahoma Press

The views and opinions expressed herein are solely those of the individual author(s) and do not reflect the policy, opinions, or positions of the University of Oklahoma its regents, officers, or employees.

Library of Congress Cataloging in Publication Data

Patterson, Zella J. Black, 1909-
Langston University.

ISBN 978-0-8061-9663-3 (paper)

Bibliography: p. 305
Includes index.
1. Langston, Okla. University — History.
I. Wert, Lynette L., joint author. II. Title.
LC2851.L23P37   378.766'33   79-1208

Copyright 1979 by the University of Oklahoma Press, Norman, Publishing Division of the University. Manufactured in the U.S.A. First edition. Paper back published 2026.

The manufacturer's authorized representative for product safety in the EU is Mare Nostrum Group B.V., Mauritskade 21D, 1091 GC Amsterdam, The Netherlands, email: gpsr@mare-nostrum.co.uk

The photograph on the title page is an aerial view of Langston University and the town of Langston, 1969.

*To my dear Father and Mother,
the late Thomas Black, Sr., and the late Mary E. Black,
who provided me every opportunity
during my youth for spiritual,
intellectual, social, and
personal development,
this book is lovingly dedicated*

Contents

Preface			Page xiii
Acknowledgments			xv
Chapter	1	The City of Langston	3
		John Mercer Langston	11
	2	Legislation and the College	13
	3	The Presidents and the University	26
	4	Vice-Presidents and Academic Deans	73
	5	The Normal (Teacher's) Department	75
	6	The High School Department	77
	7	Only Yesterday: Memories of Early Days	80
		Commencement, 1927	107
	8	Enrollment	110
	9	Expenses	118
		School Days, School Days, 1915	123
	10	Student Organizations	125
	11	The Student Strike of 1928 and Other Protests	131
	12	The Library	141
	13	The Struggle for Accreditation	146
		Frederick D. Moon and the Langston Alumni Association	151
	14	Agriculture	154
	15	Art	164
	16	Athletics	172
		Footballl Fever: The Wonder Team of 1924	185
		Caesar Felton ("Zip") Gayles: A Man for All Sports Seasons	191

17	Community Service	195
18	The Cooperative Extension Service	206
19	English, Ancient Languages, and Modern Languages	213
	Melvin B. Tolson: The Subject Is Poetry	223
20	Home Economics	226
21	The School of Law	233
22	Music	238
	Sam Sadler and His Song	245
23	Research	248
24	Science	251
	The Dean: LeRoy G. Moore	259
25	Trades and Mechanical and Industrial Arts	262
26	Langston Today — and Tomorrow	273

Appendices

A	Chronology	279
B	Oklahoma Governors and Langston University Presidents	283
C	Presidents	284
D	Vice-Presidents and Academic Deans	288
E	Enrollment, 1898-1978	290
F	Appropriations to Langston University, 1897-1975	292
G	The Land-Grant College	294
H	Langston High School Diploma, Normal Certificate, and University Diploma	297
I	University Publications	300
J	Degrees Conferred by the Oklahoma Institutions of Higher Education, by Race, Age, 1975-79	302
K	Organizational Chart, 1978-79	303
L	Faculty and Research Staff, 1978-79	304

Notes on Sources   305
Index   311

Illustrations

Aerial view, campus and town, Frontispiece
John Mercer Langston, Page 11
Inman E. Page, 27
Presbyterian Church, Langston, 28
First Main Building, 29
Attucks Hall, 29
Industrial Building, 30
First boys' dormitory, 30
First president's home, 31
Page Hall, 32
University Museum, 33
Isaac Berry McCutcheon, 35
John Miller Marquess, 37
Phyllis Wheatley Dormitory, 38
Second president's home, 38
Gymnasium, 39
Isaac William Young, M.D., 40
First Home Management House, 41
Campus laundry, 41
Zachary Taylor Hubert, 43
New Home Management House, 43
J. W. Sanford, 44
Sanford Hall, 45
Benjamin F. Lee, 47
Albert Louis Turner, 47
G. Lamar Harrison, 48
Harrison Library, 49
Young Auditorium, 50
"White House," 51
Jones Hall, 52
William Henri Hale, 53
Larzette Golden Hale, 53
Gandy Hall, 55
Brown Hall, 55
Hale Student Center, 56
Faculty apartments, 56
Wreckage of Old Page Hall, 57
New Page Hall, 58
Hargrove Hall Library Annex, 59
Hamilton Hall, 59
Third president's home, 60
Breaux Hall for Men, 61
Young Hall for Women, 62
William E. Sims, 63
Research Center, 64
Kerr Plaza, 65
James L. Mosley, 66
Thomas E. English, 67
Swimming-pool annex, 68
Ernest Holloway, 69
Samuel J. Tucker, 70
W. Bruce Jones, 73
Inman A. Breaux, 74
Joseph Roberts, 81
A. H. Fuhr, 82
Page Hall, 83
South Entrance, 85
Water-storage tank, 89
Thomas H. Black, Jr., 91
McKinley Fondren, 91
Girl in school uniform, 93

Flora Mae Johnson, 93
Mable Walker, 93
Hazel Folks in school uniform, 93
Weekly flag review, 94
Allie B. Jones, R.N., 97
Commencement program, 1927, 99
Graduation procession, 1964, 116
Theresa A. Black, 124
Thomas A. Black, Jr., 124
Spartan Club charter members, 127
Temporary recreation hall, 128
Sadie Waterford Jones, 129
J. S. Thomas, 132
Ella P. Baker, 133
Moxye Weaver King, 134
Roosevelt T. Gracey, 136
Theresa A. Black, 137
Roosevelt T. Gracey, 139
Harrison Library and Young Auditorium, 144
Elmyra Richardson Todd Davis, 145
Officers of Parents' Association, 1963, 149
Frederick D. Moon, 151
Agricultural field work, 155
Michigan barn, 156
1924 graduation announcement, 157
D. C. Jones, 159
Jimmie L. White and students, 159
A. B. Prewitt and head feed, 161
Livestock-judging arena, 161
Student with lamb, 162
The Reverend Richmond Kinnard, 163
Eugene E. Brown, 166
Jackie Jordan, 167
Painting by Eugene E. Brown, 168
Painting by Eugene E. Brown, 169
Mayhugh Sneed, 170

Wallace Owens, 171
Juanita Cotton, 171
Moses F. Miller, 177
Langston coaching staff, 178
Edison ("Hercules") Harrington, 179
W. E. Anderson, 182
Lawrence Cudjo, 183
Albert Schoats, 183
Wonder Football Team, 1923-24, 186
Booker T. Robinson, 189
John ("Big John") Williams, 189
C. Felton ("Zip") Gayles, 191
One of "Zip" Gayles's teams, 192
Gayles Gymnasium, 192
Oldest house in Langston, 197
Old Meeks Store, Langston, 198
Ulysses Cumby home, Langston, 204
Owens home, Langston, 204
Low-rent houses in Langston, 204
Old Morten home, Langston, 205
J. E. Taylor, Sr., 209
Visiting 4-H Club girls, 1948, 211
Joy Flasch, 218
Keith Slothower, 218
Language Laboratory, 218
Elwyn B. Welch, 220
Dust Bowl Players, 1976, 221
Melvin B. Tolson and Karl Shapiro, 224
Home-economics class, 1923, 226
Mrs. J. West, 227
Garvis Sparks Ricks, 229
Home Management House seniors, 1927, 229
Lenoliah E. Gandy, 231
Sadie G. Washington, 231
Ella M. Washington, 231
Odie Waller, 232
Ada Lois Sipuel Fisher, 235
Ada Fisher, 236

ILLUSTRATIONS

Early-day band, 239
Amelia R. Taylor, 243
Mitchell B. Southall, 243
Band and Chorus recital, 244
Samuel Levi Sadler, 245
"Dear Langston," 246
H. W. Conrad, M.D., 253
R. P. Perry, 256
Gomez C. Hamilton, 258
LeRoy G. Moore, 259
Early blacksmith shop, 263
Machine shop in the 1930s, 265
Tailoring class, 266
E. A. Miller, 267
Mrs. A. B. Cotton, 267

Nelle B. Dillon, 269
Radio class and H. Hendricks, 269
T. G. Green in laboratory, 271
Electronics class, 1968, 271
John Grayson and students, 272
Aerial view of campus, 1969, 276
Langston University
   of the future, 278

Maps

Oklahoma Territory and
   Langston University, 14
Langston University today, 24

Preface

THE PURPOSE of this book is to depict the growth and development of Langston University from its establishment to the present time. Langston University began in 1897 as the Colored Agricultural and Normal University following enactment of Oklahoma Territorial House Bill 151. In 1941 the name was officially changed to Langston University.

I have attempted to describe the many facets of the school, as well as to present material concerning the history of the village of Langston. Changes resulting from legislation, finance, politics, and presidential tenure are covered. How and when the normal, preparatory, and elementary divisions functioned are detailed. There are chapters dealing with enrollment trends and expenses, the student strike of 1928, and the individuals who have served as president, The struggle for accreditation is noted, as well as the growth of the library.

I have also taken into consideration the revision of the curriculum to meet changing needs. Athletics, course offerings, and student life and organizations are covered.

Through the years Langston University has developed slowly but surely. Some of the most serious problems have been political influences, financial stresses, and lack of adequate space and equipment. During the 1960s the campus underwent a complete facelifting. New buildings appeared, and additions were made to the library and the auditorium. Thus, despite the problems, Langston has braved the storms and produced outstanding graduates. Langston alumni are scattered throughout the nation and are serving humanity with pride.

Through the entire existence of the school there have been

rumors about either closing it or moving its campus. But always the clouds roll away, and Langston endures.

I do not fear for Langston's future. Instead, I can see it growing, increasing in enrollment with adequate percentages of all races. Future needs will continue to include buildings, faculty, and finance.

I was born near Langston village, attended both high school and college at the university, and was an employee there from 1937 until 1974. This long association has made it possible for me to undertake this book. It seemed fitting that a Langston graduate should undertake the responsibility of preserving the school's history. With the help of God, the writing of this book has been a pleasure.

Langston, Oklahoma   ZELLA J. BLACK PATTERSON

Acknowledgments

THIS PROJECT was a voluntary venture. As a Langston graduate, I felt that someone should record the various stages of the institution's development. For help in completing this huge piece of research, I am indebted to many people.

First, acknowledgement is due my parents, the late Thomas and Mary E. Black, who provided education, guidance, encouragement, and finance.

I would like to thank my grade school teachers and my secondary English teacher, Mrs. Leonelle Young Hargrove, who manifested interest in my writing during high school days.

David H. Morgan, my major professor at Colorado State University, gave me the foundation and principles of research. Larry K. Hayes, who conducted an in-service research seminar on the Langston campus in 1966-67, encouraged me to continue my historical research. The research adviser from Oklahoma State University, Donald E. Allen, and the Cooperative State Research Team director, Richmond E. Kinnard, also assisted me in that capacity.

The Oklahoma State Board of Regents for Higher Education also assisted by allowing me to excerpt data from biennial reports and other periodicals. I wish especially to express my thanks to E. T. Dunlap, chancellor of the regents. The project was also aided by the genuine interest of Melvin Todd, of the regents' office.

The Oklahoma Land Commission authorized the use of reports concerning land assignments held by Langston.

Joy Flasch, of the Langston Communications Department, gave me encouragement during the writing of the manuscript. Most of the information in the chapter on the town of Langston came from Kenneth Hamilton. Nedra Johnson, of the Oklahoma State Vocational Home Economics Education Office, and Willia Combs, of the

Langston Home Economics Department, offered their files for my research.

A. H. Fuhr and the late Booker Robinson contributed to the sections on early-day athletics. Roosevelt T. Gracey and Ira Hall assisted in the stories of the student strike of 1928 and the beginnings of student government at Langston. Material concerning the extension program was gathered from James L. Mosley, from Hazel King, retired human resources development specialist, and from a folder of historical documents loaned by the Oklahoma State University Cooperative Extension Office.

I interviewed Dean LeRoy G. Moore several times.

Dr. Louise Coleman assisted in obtaining materials concerning accreditation of Langston. Some of the data about Inman Page and Lincoln University, of Jefferson City, Missouri, was supplied by Sherman Savage.

The staff of the Langston Public Relations Department was supportive of all my efforts. Special thanks go to James A. Simpson, director, and to the Development Foundation.

Much of my research was aided by the staffs of Langston Library, the State Library, and the Oklahoma Historical Society Library.

Keith Northington was my accurate and patient typist. Lynette L. Wert helped me condense the manuscript to publishable length.

One of my original supporters in this extensive project was my late husband, George W. Patterson, who shared both business and home responsibilities with me in order that I might undertake the research.

Many others contributed to the making of this book. Original contributions are acknowledged in the footnotes and are on file with the original research materials.

Langston
University

CHAPTER ONE

The City of Langston

LANGSTON, Oklahoma Territory, was billed by its promoters as "the only distinctively Negro city in America." It was established twelve miles northeast of Guthrie, on the Cimarron River in Logan County, exactly one year after the opening of Oklahoma Territory to settlement. On April 22, 1890, Langston City was officially born. It was named for John Mercer Langston, a nationally known black leader, about whom more will be said in the pages that follow.

The town was the product of advance planning by two men, one white and one black. Charles H. Robbins, a white, had spent the previous year (1889) buying land from homesteaders. This area, "on the summit of the first hill two miles south of the Cimarron River" was systematically surveyed, platted, and owned by Robbins. The land was at the edge of the Unassigned Indian Lands, which were soon to be opened for settlement. Because Robbins saw a trend in Negro migration to the new territories, he promoted his town as a black settlement.

The principal agent of Robbins in this venture was a black man, Edward P. McCabe. In the heavy advertising campaign to promote the town, McCabe was listed on flyers as the founder of Langston.

The geographic location of the new town showed good pre-planning. The Cimarron River was flood-prone, and the town was laid out well above the possible high-water zone. It was in a favorable position to draw settlers interested in homesteading the new Indian lands. Robbins and McCabe envisioned Langston City as a supply base for settlement of much of Northern Oklahoma by blacks. Thus the town was founded as much on hard-headed economics as on ideals of promoting a "distinctively all-black city."

McCabe was just the man for the job of promoter and developer. He was born in Troy, New York, in 1850, attended public schools in Newport, Rhode Island, and Bangor, Maine, worked as a clerk on Wall Street in New York City, and eventually migrated to Chicago, where he was a clerk at the Palmer Hotel. While living in Chicago, he became the first black man to work in the Cook County treasurer's office. He remained in this job for eighteen months and then ventured west again, this time to Kansas.

Among McCabe's friends was Abraham T. Hall, who had been city editor of the *Chicago Conservator*. The two men struck out for Kansas, became interested in land-promotion schemes, and signed up as "town agents" for the new city of Nicodemus, Kansas.

In Nicodemus, McCabe did land surveying, legal business, and real estate speculating. He was appointed county clerk by the governor of the state and was then elected to the position. In 1882 he ran for state auditor of Kansas. His election to the post marked the first time a Negro had been elected to a statewide office in the North.

After two terms in office McCabe lost a bid for a third-term nomination. He moved to Topeka and after two years was again deep in promotion schemes. He and several other black men founded the Oklahoma Immigration Society. In his mind he saw Oklahoma as a frontier for Negro settlement, and he dreamed of establishing enough blacks in the new lands to ensure control of the political system. In 1890, McCabe visited Washington, D.C., supposedly in hopes of being appointed territorial governor of Oklahoma. He reportedly received a promise that "if he could prove... a majority of people in Oklahoma were Negroes that a Negro would be appointed governor." Population statistics put McCabe on very shaky grounds, however, for, in comparison to whites, there were few blacks in Oklahoma.

On a local level McCabe and his friends lobbied for his appointment as Oklahoma secretary of state. Through other connections he was offered the post of immigrant inspector of Key West, Florida. He refused the offer and finally gained the position of deputy auditor of Logan County, Oklahoma.

In addition to his official duties McCabe engaged in town building and newspaper publishing. He promoted the two towns Langston City and Liberty, Oklahoma, and while his name is indelibly linked with Langston, he never made his home in the city.

Throughout his career McCabe's basic philosophy was that Negroes' opportunities lay on the frontier. He was convinced that whites in the West had fewer rigid social ideas and that economic development would be unhampered. He insisted that Oklahoma, being a territory and subject to regulation by the federal government, gave blacks further opportunities. He recruited heavily, throughout the South especially, urging blacks who were "visionary and industrious" to head for Langston.

An example of his inspired editorializing is found in his paper, the *Langston City Herald*, in the issue of March 30, 1892. He asserted that "active, energetic men and women with some money and plenty of push... are wanted here. Come to our rescue, moneyed Negros, and we will demonstrate a fact long, oh so long questioned, touching our capacity to build a city." He made clear that money was a prerequisite for immigration, saying, "The facts are that we do not invite any to come here who have not sufficient means to bring themselves until such time as they can raise a crop. ... we think it is a mistake for any but self supporting people to come here."

Nevertheless, trainloads of blacks came to Oklahoma, both men of means and those without. Most of the immigrants came from Kansas, Arkansas, Louisiana, Missouri, Mississippi, Tennessee, and Texas. Some came as members of colonies; others as individuals; they came by train, horseback, or wagon or on foot. Under the auspices of the Oklahoma Immigration Association, McCabe and his officers sent new promotional propaganda throughout the South, declaring that "the soil, climate, and condition in Oklahoma is more favorable and evitable to the Negro race than any part of the Union that has been opened for settlement since the emanicipation of the Race."

The emphasis in the propaganda was on money — both bringing it to Oklahoma and making it after arrival. The *Herald* at one time insisted that "a conservative estimate of the amount of wealth acquired by the colored people in Oklahoma by securing homesteads is placed at from $250,000 to $450,000." McCabe ended his editorials with impassioned pleas for settlement in the new city of

Langston: "What will you be if you stay in the South? Slaves, liable to be killed at any time, and never treated right; but if you come to Oklahoma you have equal chances with the white man."

The late decades of the 1800s were the heyday of Jim Crow legislation, and McCabe and his followers had to overcome both anti-immigration efforts and hostile acts by whites. On one occasion a black preacher in Arkansas commented in discouragement: "The Oklahoma boom is getting feebler day by day and soon our people will begin to realize after all that it is best to leave well enough alone." The *Memphis Commercial* expected anti-immigration societies to spring up, persuading blacks to stay put and prove that Negroes were better off in the South "than anywhere else." Even Ida B. Wells, editor of the *Memphis Free Speech* and later a founder of the National Association for the Advancement of Colored people (NAACP), warned against indiscriminate haste in moving to the new territory.

In Oklahoma itself there was growing hostility by whites to the idea that blacks might succeed in making the new territory into an "all-black state." The *Kansas City Times* reported efforts to have 100,000 blacks in Oklahoma by the end of 1890. The *Hennessey Clipper* wailed that, between Indian allotments and the quantity of colored people waiting to "pounce" on new lands, there would be little chance for white men in the vicinity. It was rumored that the massive migration by blacks was the result of a conspiracy. The leaders were thought to be P. B. S. Pinchback, former acting governor of Louisiana; J. R. Lynce, former speaker of the Mississippi House of Representatives; and T. Thomas Fortune, editor of the *New York Age*. When McCabe was actively campaigning to be appointed territorial governor, he did little to quell whites' fears. In some towns blacks were asked to leave. They were physically driven out of Norman, Tecumseh, and other racially mixed towns. White terrorists called the White Cappers (an offshoot of the Ku Klux Klan) worked in Oklahoma and Indian territories, as well as in Missouri.

These conditions aided McCabe and Robbins in their drive to establish an all-black town. By January, 1891, Langston had a population of six hundred. The business section consisted of six retail groceries, two liquor stores, two smithies, two barbershops, and a feed store.

Apparently every early resident became a town promoter. The entire settlement joined in a cooperative truck patch. They used the eighty-acre garden to feed the inhabitants through the first long winter. Later they established a volunteer fire department, built a bridge across the creek, and were so cooperative in establishing religious organizations that the two Sunday schools scheduled services at different times so that citizens could attend both.

By 1892 four hacks were commuting daily between Langston and Guthrie. The number of retail businesses had grown to a value of $85,000, and the citizens began trying to make Langston a railroad point. An executive commission was appointed, which included McCabe, and the town lobbied for a railhead. Right of way was granted, $1,500 voted, and negotiations conducted, principally concerning the need for a shipment point for cotton. It was predicted that every farmer in eastern Logan County was planting twenty to one hundred acres in cotton. Moreover, in the preceding year over fifteen hundred bales had been ginned. Nevertheless, the railroad did not come to Langston.

Langston continued to boom, partly through the guidance of the City Board of Trade. Twenty-five retail businesses were operating by fall, 1892, among them an ice-cream parlor, a gristmill with a steam corn sheller, an opera house, a watch shop, a two-story bank, two hotels, and a broom factory. Editorials of the period downplayed the addition of three more saloons, one of which featured an icehouse. Telephone lines came to the city in 1895.

Under the crusading banner of the *Herald,* Langston's moral structure was kept straight and narrow. Editorial wars were conducted for cleanliness, godliness, and unity. McCabe promoted what was popularly known as "the gospel of the toothbrush." He urged pride in appearance, clean hands, faces, clothes, and living. The paper's wide circulation and moral crusading led the governor of Oklahoa to state in 1889 that "Langston has prospered, is well behaved and one of the modern communities of the territory."

The criminal code during the early era had fifteen sections, nine of which dealt with improper gambling or sexual behavior. Apparently the crusading was effective, for from the time of its inception thrugh 1893 there were no murders in Langston and only two cases of theft — one involving the removal of a door from a house being built in the country and the other the pocketing of a ring by a young lady's suitor. The assault cases were rare: a man named Walter Todd assaulted an elderly woman and was fined twenty-five dollars. Two white men engaged in fisticuffs, also ending up with a fine of twenty-five dollars. There were a few cases of drunkenness or disorderly conduct, but in the first six months after the jail was built, only three inmates had been incarcerated.

Along with McCabe's paper Langston had three churches to keep it in line: Baptist, Methodist, and Christian (Disciples of Christ). There was a chapter of the Knights of Pythagoras, a seventy-five-man militia, and a Catholic seminary founded by Belgian missionaries.

In the realm of social activities horse racing had many proponents. Expensive trotters and runners were brought to the territory, and such leading citizens as B. H. Hooks, the deputy sheriff and the outstanding attorney, purchased fine horses. Some of the animals sold for as much as a claim — approximately $1,000 to $1,700.

Politically, the citizens of Langston registered entirely Republican. By August, 1892, the town had a Republican club. Five men were sent to the 1892 Republican County Convention, and one, D. J. Wallace, was elected temporary clerk. The blacks of Langston managed to elect several officers in Logan County. Wallace went to the territorial legislature.

Langston, the "all-black city," had three white businessmen. Their presence was counter to McCabe's early propaganda. When agents of the town sold lots to prospective emigrants in the South, the settlers were told that title could never pass to any white man and that no white man was ever to reside or conduct business in the city. This misrepresentation was not the only one perpetrated on the unsuspecting settlers. The newspaper printed pictures of massive buildings, purportedly to show how Langston was expected to develop. Many immigrants thought that the buildings already existed and were disappointed to find only tents and prairie.

The nearest railway point to Langston was Guthrie. In the early days the Santa Fe would pull into Guthrie with "day cars" filled with blacks. Langston was twelve miles away, over nearly impassable roads. While most settlers continued the journey by foot or wagon, some remained in the railway cars and went farther on or returned to the South.

News of the new town spread as far as New York City. In 1891 the *New York Times* called it a "black Mecca." At that time the population was said to be two hundred people, with thirty residences and a hotel in the town. A black doctor, a black preacher, and a black schoolteacher were already at work, and the school was dignified by the title "the Academy."

The idea of a "little Africa" persisted. Notice was taken in a Catholic newspaper of the city's founding and religious offerings. The *Little Star of the Black Belt* spoke of the founding of the Catholic mission in 1895 by Sisters Beatrice, Genevieve, and Alphonse. At the time of their endeavor the city had "no railroads or even a horse and buggy." The sisters had to contend with "all kinds of snakes, prairie coyotes and wild cats, cyclones and tornadoes." Despite these hardships the paper was full of hope for a "Little Africa."

The crusade for good schools began early. With a property tax of five mills, the city completed a common school in February, 1892. Naturally the newspaper published the names of the best students in the seventh and eighth grades, giving their names and averages (three of the honorees were children of school-board members; one was the child of the *Herald's* owners).

The first school had a capacity of 200 children. Initially 135 enrolled. Six months after the common school opened, a boarding high school was built. The cost of board was eight to ten dollars a month. Segregation was not an issue, the board proclaiming the school open to "as many students as will attend, regardless of race, color or number."

Already looking ahead, the citizens organized a committee to secure higher education for the area. In July, 1892, three leading citizens, Edward Robinson, R. E. Stewart, and D. J. Wallace, appeared before the Oklahoma Industrial School and College Commission to petition that Langston have a college.

For the next two years the college became the town's goal. In his Thanksgiving Day speech of 1895, Mayor A. A. Williams issued a special proclamation entitled "Langston Must Have a Good School."

During this time of politicking for the new college, a row developed over location of the school and whether it should be for blacks only. The *City Herald* argued, "Give us a separate Normal of our own!" The *Guide* published an editorial entitled "From Regents to Janitor," apparently pointing out that the Catholic school was open to all. On one point, all citizens agreed: Langston needed a college. On March 12, 1897, the dream came true with the enactment of the Oklahoma Territorial House Bill 151 establishing the Colored Agricultural and Normal University at Langston, Oklahoma.

John Mercer Langston

John Mercer Langston, 1829-1897.

John Mercer Langston, the man for whom both Langston City and the university were named, was prominent in education and public affairs for a generation after the Civil War. He was born in Virginia in 1829. Both of his parents died when he was five, and he became the ward of a Colonel Gooch, of Chillicothe, Ohio, in accordance with his father's wishes. He moved to Ohio and entered the Preparatory Department of Oberlin College at age fifteen. Later he attended the college and Oberlin Law School, being admitted to the Ohio bar in 1854.

During the Civil War, Langston served as an agent for Negro troops and helped recruit men for Ohio and Massachusetts regiments. He served twice as a member of the Oberlin City Council and was a member of the Oberlin Board of Education for eleven years.

In 1868 he went to Washington, D.C., as inspector general of the Freedmen's Bureau schools. This federal agency included among its programs the supervision of an educational system for blacks. His work in the national capital brought him in close contact with General O. O. Howard, founder and first president of Howard University. Langston organized the first Department of Law at Howard and later served as vice-president and acting president of the university.

President Ulysses S. Grant appointed Langston to the Board of Health for the District of Columbia in 1871. In 1877, President Rutherford B. Hayes asked Langston to be resident minister to Haiti and charge d'affaires in Santo Domingo. Langston served in the diplomatic corps until 1885.

Upon his return to the States in 1885, he became president of Virginia State College for Negroes. He relinquished this post in 1888 to run for Congress. He was the Republican Nominee from his Virginia District. Elected to the House of Representatives, he served from 1890 to 1891. He was unsuccessful in a reelection bid. Langston retired in Washington, D.C., and wrote a book entitled From the Virginia Plantation to the National Capitol.

Though the university of Langston, Oklahoma, was legally named the Colored Agricultural and Normal University when it came into being, it was always popularly called Langston, after the man who had become a symbol of the highest form of educational leadership. The name was officially changed in 1941 by act of the Oklahoma Legislature. The bill changing the name was introduced in the House by Carl Morgan and in the Senate by Louis Ritzhaupt, both of Logan County. The bill was enacted by the Eighteenth Legislature and signed by Governor Leon C. Phillips on May 11, 1941. The pen was presented to Langston University President G. L. Harrison. A portrait of John Mercer Langston hangs in the foyer of the auditorium of Langston University.

CHAPTER TWO

Legislation and the College

LANGSTON CITY and Langston University take their names from educator John Mercer Langston. During his lifetime (1829-97) Langston became a symbol of the highest form of educational leadership. He attended Oberlin College in Ohio, practiced law, served for eleven years on the Oberlin Board of Education, and was twice elected to the Oberlin City Council.

He served as supervisor of the Ohio Negro schools and inspector general of the Freedmen's Bureau schools, and he was the first dean of the Howard University School of Law, in Washington, D.C. Later he became president of Virginia State College. He served as consul general to the Republic of Haiti from 1877 to 1885. He was elected to the United States Congress from the state of Virginia in 1889, where he served for one term. A portrait of John M. Langston hangs in the foyer of the Auditorium of Langston University.

Although the college was officially named the Colored Agricultural and Normal University, it was always popularly called Langston University. In 1941 the name of the institution was officially changed.

Despite the pleas of the citizens of Langston from as early as 1893, the college was not established until Charles Henry William Murce Sulcer carried the fight to the Resolutions Committee of the Oklahoma Territorial Convention of 1894. Sulcer introduced a plank in the statehood platform asking for the establishment of a school of higher education for Negroes. Sulcer was a religious leader, politician, and educator and the first Negro to serve as a delegate to the territorial governing bodies.

In his biennial message in January, 1895, Territorial Governor William Gary Renfrow proposed a reform program. One section of the program recommended the establishment of a territorial uni-

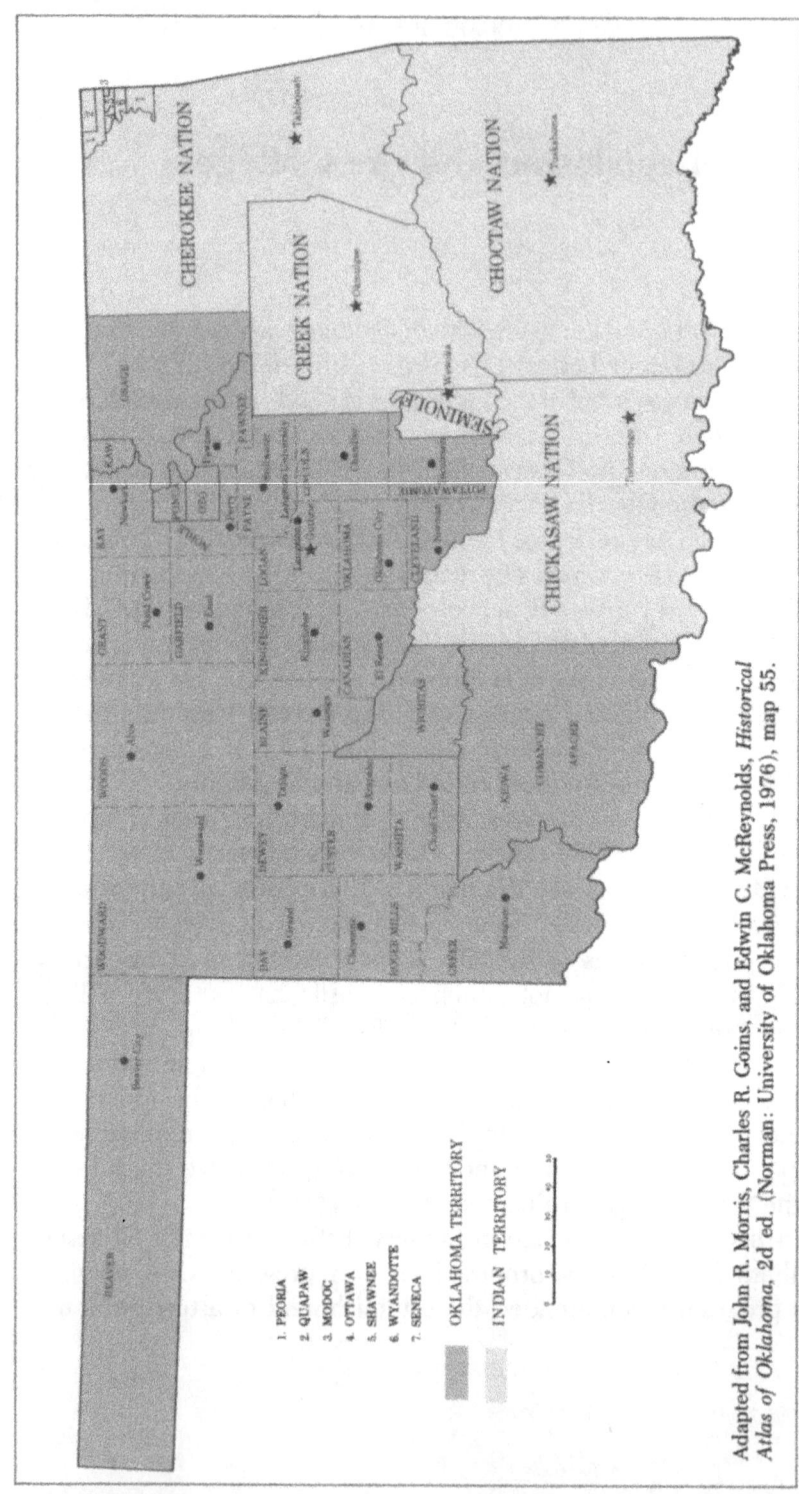

Oklahoma Territory and location of Logan County, Langston, and Langston University.

versity for Negroes. Renfrow vetoed a civil-rights bill that would have disregarded racial segregation.

After two years of politics and compromise, House Bill 151 was finally introduced in the territorial council on February 4, 1897. J. W. Johnson, president of the council and an eminent Oklahoma City lawyer, presented the legislation. Johnson personally shepherded the bill through legislative channels to its final adoption on March 12, 1897. It was thereupon signed by Johnson as president of the council, approved by J. C. Tulsley, speaker of the house, and signed into law by Governor Renfrow.

The bill set forth the purpose of the institution:

... the instruction of both male and female colored persons in the art of teaching various branches which pertain to a common school education and in such higher education as may be deemed advisable, and the fundamental laws of the United States in the rights and duties of citizens in the agricultural, mechanical and industrial arts."

The bill also named the site: "within a convenient distance from Langston in Logan County, Oklahoma Territory." It was to be called the Colored Agricultural and Normal University of Oklahoma. Thus Langston University came into being with the objectives of training teachers and offering agricultural, mechanical, and industrial training.

Throughout the struggle to obtain the college for Langston, the town's physician, Dr. A. J. Alston, wielded much influence among both blacks and whites.

Once the territorial legislature had established the school, the citizens of Langston went to work to turn the dream into books, papers, buildings, and students. The townspeople were to provide the land — forty acres. By March the regents had been appointed. The crusading *Langston City Herald* was eager to begin work by May. In an editorial it proclaimed, "It now becomes the duty of every citizen in Oklahoma to go to work and at once raise two or three dollars to purchase this acre tract." The newspaper ended its exhortations with the cry, "Let us awake from our drowsy slumber and go forth and capture our success!"

Money was raised by midsummer. Picnics, auctions, public meetings, and bake sales were held. Women of the town sold sandwiches, cakes, pies, and dinners to raise funds. Within a year the land had been secured, the Board of Regents had approved the final plans, and a president had been called for the institution.

The Board of Regents of Langston University was set up as a five-man board made up of three whites and two blacks. The territorial superintendent of public education and territorial treasurer were automatic members of the board. The others were to be appointed by the governor. They were to serve four-year terms, report to the legislature, and appoint the college president. The regents held the power to establish admissions standards and set salaries, as well as to issue teaching certificates to graduates of the Normal (Teacher's College) Department.

The first members of the Board of Regents were the Reverend L. H. Holt, of Guthrie, President; E. O. Tyler, of Kingfisher; S. N. Hopkins, of El Reno, state superintendent of education; Francis Thompson, of Pawnee, state treasurer; and P. F. Tyler, of the Manese settlement. The black members were E. O. Tyler and P. F. Tyler. E. O. Tyler was an attorney, and his wife was a schoolteacher. Tyler traveled in a horse and buggy from Kingfisher to Langston and Oklahoma City to attend board meetings.

In early action the Board of Regents set up annual inspection visits, established twenty-two-week terms for students seeking teaching certificates, and set up procedures for certifying teachers. The regents allowed themselves three dollars a day and five cents a mile for attending meetings and decided to meet four times a year. Five thousand dollars was to be appropriated from the territorial treasury so that the school could build one wing of a suitable building and begin classes.

The legislature duly appropriated the $5,000, but it was to cover all costs, including construction of the building, teachers' salaries, and other expenses for two years. The funding was quickly discovered to be grossly inadequate. Territorial Governor Cassius M. Barnes solved the problem by dividing land-lease money among the territorial institutions. Langston's share was $4,000, which made a total of $9,000. When the legislature met in the 1899 session, Langston's funding was increased to $10,000. The actual appropriation for 1898-99 amounted to nearly $23,000, when a one-tenth-mill tax was levied, one-fifth of the land-lease money was earmarked for Langston, and the school was ruled eligible to receive one-tenth of the accrued federal funds coming to the state from the second Morrill Act (see Appendix G for a discussion of the funding of land-grant colleges).

The school opened on September 3, 1898, though the building had not yet been erected. The first classes were held in the Presbyterian church and in the village school. Joseph Roberts, who had moved to Langston in March, 1897, recalled "a scramble among young men to be the first to register." The first three names on the university roll were Arthur Wallace, Thomas Slaughter, and Joseph Roberts.

The first main building was planned as a fourteen-room stone structure. A contract for the construction was let by the Board of Regents to John Henderson, of Kingfisher. Much of the labor on the new building was donated by the citizens of Langston.

The financing of the school was dependent for many years on the territorial and state legislatures. Eventually a formula was reached whereby Langston received money from four sources. Legislative appropriations continued, and after statehood one-third of one-tenth of the school-township lands were assigned to Langston, as well as one-tenth of the New Morrill Act funds and rental proceeds from an Enabling Act land grant of 100,000 acres. In making the permanent distribution of funds from the Morrill Act, the legislature moved to separate the funding of Langston from that of the college at Stillwater. With the Enabling Act for statehood 100,000 acres of land were set aside for Langston as of 1906. Under the legislation the school received title to various tracts, mostly in western Oklahoma. The value of the land acquired was approximately $374,955. Since that time some of the land has been sold and some has been leased outright, leased for royalties, and bonus-leased, all to provide income for the school.

For over a quarter of a century before Oklahoma became a state, the federal government had pursued the policy of making land grants to the states for the support of both common school and higher education. These monies were known as "Section 13" (the section of land set aside in each township for schools) and "New

College" funds. From the beginning appropriation of $5,000, the amount of money granted to Langston in the biennial state legislative appropriations varied widely. It was as high as $185,000 in 1907-1908 and was down to half that amount eight years later. A high of $397,000 was appropriated in 1929-30 and halved again the next biennium.

During the early years most of the funds were used to establish a physical plant. The first main building was used for classrooms and offices. In the second year, (1899) Attucks Hall Dormitory for Young Women was built. The next appropriation brought a mechanical-arts building, which was constructed of native stone. It was two stories high and built in a Gothic shape. With the blessing of the $15,000 appropriation from the Morrill Fund, a library and agricultural and mechanical departments were established. By 1901 the legislature had provided for an addition to the Main Building, a boy's dorm, and a president's home.

The first president's home was a two-story white frame house with a hip roof and a large front porch. In 1920 a new, red-brick home was built about a block south of the original residence.

Among the first campus improvements were a barn and agricultural tools. For many years students worked for two-week stretches at campus jobs. The jobs were rotated except for hauling wood and coal, working in the kitchens, and tending the boiler room and barns, for which a small credit toward room and board was allowed. Only students who could pay an additional four dollars above full board were exempted from "duty work." Jobs with no pay included sweeping halls, cleaning bathrooms, scrubbing steps, cleaning the grounds, and washing dishes.

In November, 1907, Main Building was destroyed by a fire of undetermined origin. Theories were put forth that arson was involved and that politics was the motive behind the trouble. The event came in the year of Oklahoma statehood. Whatever the cause, the new state legislature appropriated $100,000 for reconstruction of a new main building and other campus improvements. The new building was completed in 1909. It was a modern two-story pressed-brick structure with a basement. It contained twenty-seven rooms, nineteen of which were used for classes. The assembly hall seated four hundred people. The building also housed four labs, the Home Economics Department, a reception hall, and the President's office. The entire building had marble floors and hallways. The fireproof roof was of red tile.

By 1912 the university had six principal buildings, including two women's dorms. All buildings were heated by steam from a central plant. One of the girl's dorms, the main building, and the grounds were lighted by electricity. The steam plant also furnished water for labs and for toilets and baths in all buildings. It was not until 1923 that all buildings had steam heat, power, and sewer lines.

An important change in institutional funding came about with the enactment of vocational education bills by the federal government. In 1917 the United States Congress passed the Smith-Hughes Act. This provided federal funds to states for use in vocational training of students at the secondary level. President Woodrow Wilson signed the bill in February, 1917. Eventually the funding reached the level of seven million dollars a year nationwide. The

President Page's Summary of Disbursements 1911-12:

Cost of Improving Buildings and Grounds C.A.&N. University, July 1, 1911-June 30, 1912

Repairing Stairway Boys' Dormitory	$ 14.25
Brick Work on barn well	11.00
Concrete floor in engine room	64.90
Drainage	48.50
Repairing roof Mechanical Building	50.00
Building tool rooms in Mechanical Building	30.00
Building Pump House at pond	18.00
Building Chicken House at barn	2.50
Papering rooms in Nurse Training Dept.	14.00
Fencing Lawn	3.50
Putting in screens	5.20
Pruning trees on University grounds	12.00
Repairing Main Building	145.00
Repairing barns	45.00
Keeping Campus in proper condition	202.95
Drilling one well	75.75
Total	$742.55

thrust was toward agricultural, industrial, and home-economics training. Langston shared proportionately in the funds available.

Supplements to the vocational-training bills were embodied in the George-Reed Act. Passed by Congress in 1929, this act divided the funds equally between agriculture and home economics. Appropriations rose to the level of twenty-five million dollars a year. The act provided funds in Oklahoma between 1929 and 1934. The effect of the legislation was to encourage more rural girls and Negro girls in the study of domestic arts.

In 1937 the George-Deen Act became effective, making vocational home economics recognized in day schools. Until then most of the federal funds allocated to Negroes had been spent for evening classes. After that date Negro vocational day schools were reimbursed, provided they upheld standards. Langston used federal funds to train teachers for vocational agriculture and vocational home economics.

As with all other funding, the operations of Langston were shifted to reflect the good or bad times of the state and federal economies. For example, the library received one thousand dollars for books in 1936, nothing in 1937. Dormitories in the 1930s were financed by bonds in denominations of one hundred to sixteen hundred dollars bearing 5 percent interest for twenty-five years. In general, Langston's appropriations depended on funds from general revenue, new college, Section 13, and public building funds.

In the postwar boom of the late 1940s, Langston began upgrading its physical plant. Six new buildings were on the drawing boards, a stadium had been proposed as a self-liquidating project costing ninety thousand dollars, and long-range improvements were planned for heat, water, and grounds. Eventually self-liquidating projects came to be used extensively, providing a physical-education plant, a student center, and an administration building in the 1930s, four new dorms for men and women in the 1960s, and repairs.

In 1941 the funding changed. The regents received earmarked monies and allocated them to the colleges. More than thirty years later, in 1973-74, a study by the state regents resulted in an experimental basis for budgeting. Each institution of higher education was to be surveyed according to (1) instruction, (2) research, and (3) public service. Each area was to have a separate budget. Needs for college-trained manpower were to be considered in establishing priorities for funding at all state colleges. The regents hoped to establish a "cost per instructional program" figure at each institution. Appropriations were to be made by the legislature directly to the regents as a lump sum, which they would allocate to "each institution according to its needs and functions."

Revol-fund applications were also in effect from 1941. Proceeds from war orphans' legislation and Veteran's Administration laws were considered part of the revolving fund. Langston, like all other colleges, had a postwar surge of veteran enrollment, which reached a peak in 1947, when 402 students enrolled.

Langston shared in the programs of the 1960s that encouraged student loans. Federal guarantees were added in 1966. By 1973, Langston had 214 loans outstanding in the amount of $173,815.

The budgets, appropriations, and accounting sheets for each biennium are public records. By 1974 assets and liabilities for the institution included $1.7 million in permanent funds.

The 100,000-acre land grant to Langston University was established by the Department of the Interior in 1906. The first selection list amounted to 4,092.63 acres and was certified by the Land Office of Guthrie, under the authorization of Territorial Governor Frank Frantz. An additional 90,000 acres were selected in the Woodward Land District in 1908. Another approximately 3,000 acres in the same area of western Oklahoma was selected the same year, bringing the total to 97,649.31 acres.

It took many years to obtain the additional 2,400 acres still available under the original grant. It was annexed in tracts of 160 acres, 2,199 acres and finally, in 1969, 30 acres in New Mexico. This last tract reserved to the federal government all minerals and rights to prospect, mine, and remove deposits. The value of the grant land as of 1974 was estimated by commissioners of the Land Office at $435,211.92.

The low income from rental of lands owned by the university has caused controversy over the years. Much of the land held by Langston is in far-western Oklahoma, largely in Cimarron, Ellis, and Woodward counties. The tracts range in size from 40 to 640 acres. The rental has been figured on a formula involving the appraised land value. On an appraised value of $12,800 for 640 acres of Cimarron County, the rental in 1967 was $640, or $1.00 an acre. Some leases brought $0.75 an acre, others $1.50. Many adjoining tracts were leased by the same ranchers or farmers. One person in Cimarron County leased a total of 16,800 acres at an annual rent of $16,300. Leases are held by estates and by ranchers in Kansas, Texas, and Oklahoma.

Langston University shared in the civil-rights funds appropriated by the Federal Higher Education Act of 1965. The basic purposes of the funds were community-service, library-system training, aid to developing institutions, student assistance, teacher training, improvement of undergraduate instruction, and amendments to the facilities act. Each of these areas came to be known popularly as Title I, Title III, Title V, and so on, in reference to the sections of the act. Thus under Title I funds amounting to fifty million dollars were made available nationwide to attack problems of poverty and housing, provide for youth opportunities and transportation, and improve land use through college service programs. Title III funds were provided to help strengthen and develop higher-education institutions.

With the availability of federal program money the shift in funding of Langston University began to approach one-half state funds and one-half nonappropriated funds. In 1966-67 the funds amounted to $720,000 in state monies and $335,000 in nonstate funds. By 1973-74 the available money was $1,112,000 from the state and $690,000 from outside Oklahoma.

Coordination of all legislation under a central board of regents was proposed as early as 1911 by Governor Lee Cruce. Nothing happened, however, until May, 1929, when Governor William J. Holloway again recommended a central coordinating board. After concentrated effort, the proposal was finally acted upon by the legislature. Unfortunately, no real power was given to the body. As a matter of fact, no meeting was ever called to organize the board.

In 1933, under Governor William H. Murray, the State Board of Regents for Higher Education was finally created, but no appropriation was made for it. Individuals appointed to serve on the board went to work, however, and in 1940 a special constitutional amendment providing for the nine-member board was submitted to the people. It passed in a special election held on March 11, 1941.

Until July, 1944, the Oklahoma State Board of Agriculture administered all agricultural and mechanical colleges, including Langston. Langston came under the governance of this board, as well as of the Control and Education Board, the State Department of Education Board, and the Board of Regents of Oklahoma Colleges. Membership on the boards varied, some having as many as nine members. Agreement was hard to come by.

The nine-member Board of Regents for Oklahoma Agricultural and Mechanical Colleges retained control of the colleges at Stillwater, Goodwell, Langston, Lawton, Warner, Wilburton, Miami, and Tishomingo through the 1950s. With the expansion of Oklahoma A&M (Oklahoma State University) into extension and technical schools, the board also became responsible for them in the 1960s.

The first black woman to serve on the Board of Regents is Rubye M. Hall, whose term expires in 1980. She was elected chairman of the board in 1978. She is a graduate of Langston University.

In November of 1977, the report of a special interim legislative committee was presented to the state regents. This report projected that a Tulsa branch of Langston could expect to draw 2,000 undergraduate and 1,000 graduate students within "a reasonable period." The cost of such a campus was estimated at $15 million with an annual upkeep cost of approximately $10 million. Regents voted six to two to approve the report, which did not favor the Tulsa plan. The report cited as Langston's main problems the lack of continuity in the presidency of Langston, the lack of upgraded physical facilities, and lack of coordination with the Agricultural and Mechanical Board of Regents. The chief strengths of the university were reported as continuing pride and sense of unity and the maintenance of academic accreditation.

Early in 1978 the state legislature again faced the "Langston problem" as a result of increased pressure by activists in the student body, who camped on the legislative doorstep during a sit-in aimed at increased support funding.

Amendments to state-sponsored legislation calling for the closing of Langston were defeated, as were attempts to cut funding drastically.

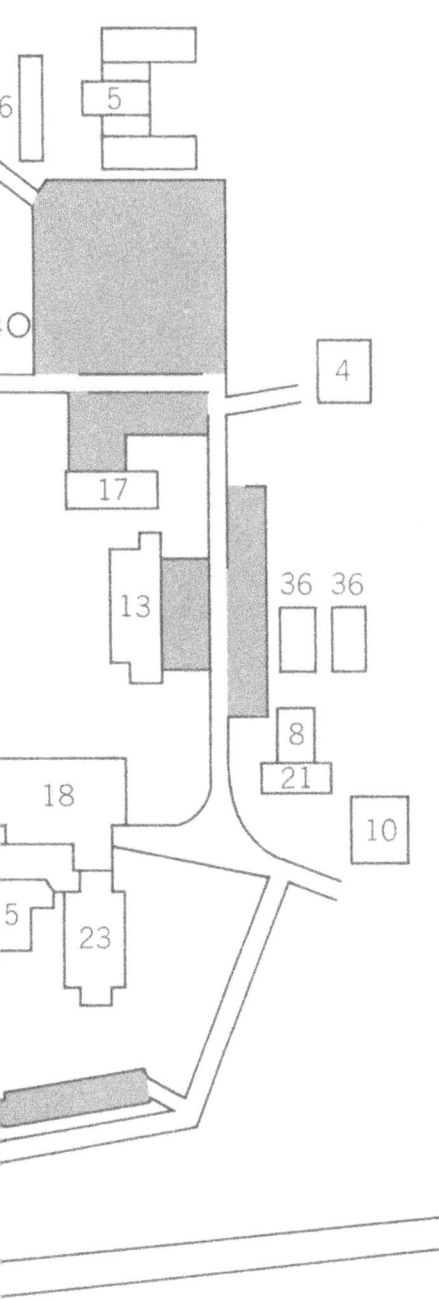

1. Agricultural facilities
2. Anderson Field
3. Baseball field
4. Boiler room
5. Breaux Hall
6. Brown Hall
7. Cimarron Garden Apartments
8. CSRS Research
9. Faculty Lounge
10. Faculty duplex
11. Gandy Hall
12. Gayles Gymnasium and Pool
13. Hamilton Hall
14. Hargrove Hall
15. Harrison Library
16. Infirmary
17. Jones Hall
18. Kerr Plaza
19. Moore Hall
20. Nursery
21. Old University of Men
22. Old University of Women
23. Page Hall
24. Physical plant
25. President's home
26. Sanford Hall
27. Student Government Association Cottage
28. Hale Student Union
29. Tennis courts
30. University faculty cottages
31. University faculty apartments
32. I. W. Young Auditorium
33. Young Hall
34. Water tower
    General parking
36. Agriculture and Research greenhouses
    Visitor parking

CHAPTER THREE

The Presidents and the University

SINCE 1898 thirteen men have served as presidents of Langston, and five have served as interim presidents. During its eighty years of existence Langston has had presidents who served as long as twenty years (G. L. Harrison) and as briefly as a few days (Albert Turner). A complete list of presidents and their dates of service is given in the Appendices. This chapter summarizes the changes in the institution under each president.

INMAN EDWARD PAGE
First President, 1898-1915

Inman Edward Page was born on a plantation in Warrenton, Virginia, on December 29, 1952. His first job was as horse boy on the plantation, a job he disliked intensely. Page's father, although a slave, established a livery stable. This occupation was highly successful, and the elder Page was able to purchase his own freedom and that of his wife, his daughter, and his young son, Inman. Because his father was a free man, Inman was able to attend the private schools of Washington, D.C. His education began at F. R. Clark's and George B. Vashon's private schools and continued at Howard University. As a young man Page helped clear ground for the erection of Howard University. He also worked in the Freedmen's Bureau under General O. O. Howard, for whom the university was named.

In 1873, Page transferred from Howard to Brown University in Providence, Rhode Island. He was elected class orator and spoke at the graduation ceremonies in 1877. Because of his speaking ability Page was offered a position as teacher at Natchez Seminary,

Inman E. Page, the first president of Langston University, 1898-1915. Photographs of all the presidents courtesy of Joe Jordan, Cooperative Extension Service communications specialist, 1973-75.

in Mississippi. He accepted the job and became the only black teacher at the school.

After a year in Mississippi, Page returned to Rhode Island to marry Zelia R. Ball, a graduate of Wilberforce University. Shortly after his marriage he received two job offers, one as principal of an Alabama school and the other as vice-president of Lincoln Institute, a predominantly black school in Missouri. Because a yellow-fever epidemic had broken out in the South, Page decided to move to Missouri. The offer from Lincoln had stated that the trustees hoped to elevate him from vice-principal to principal if his work proved satisfactory.

Presbyterian Church, Langston, the first building used by Langston University.

When Page arrived in Jefferson City, Missouri, he became assistant to Principal Henry Smith and the only black faculty member at Lincoln. After a year the trustees decided not to promote Page because of his youth (he was then twenty-six), and instead named A. C. Clayton principal. Page continued to work under the new appointee and in 1888 became principal. During his first year he informed the white teachers that their services would no longer be needed, for "educated Negro teachers would serve as a greater inspiration to Negro youth."

Page remained at Lincoln as principal from 1888 to 1898. During that time the school was attached to the Missouri state university system, and a manual-training section was established. During this period the New Morrill Land Grant Act for establishing agricultural and mechanical colleges was implemented, and Lincoln established a college department under Page.

First Main Building, 1899

Attucks Hall for Young Ladies, as shown in the 1904-1905 catalogue.

Industrial Building, Langston University, 1900.

The first boys' dormitory, 1898. Courtesy of Mrs. E. W. Whitlow.

The first president's home.

Meanwhile, in Oklahoma, the territorial legislature established the Colored Agricultural and Normal University in Langston, and on May 1, 1898, Inman Page was called to be its president, at a salary of $2,500 a year.

In hiring Page, the regents gave him power to "act as he saw fitting and proper and in the school's best interest." Page accepted the challenge of starting a school in a windswept prairie town where the population was both poor and uneducated. He opened the doors of the new school in the fall of 1898 in the Presbyterian Church of Langston with a total budget of $9,000.

As mentioned earlier, in the following year a building appropriation of $10,000 was made by the legislature, and the university also received money from the accrued Morrill Fund levies. Two new buildings were built, a dorm for young women and a mechanical-

Page Hall Administration Building, completed in 1909.

arts building. The acreage owned by the school increased from 40 to 160 acres.

Though the new school had no money for "public relations," the enrollment grew rapidly. Page suggested that the faculty members go throughout the state, lecturing and recruiting students. Since railroads were few and far between, most of these publicity jaunts were made in buggies, spring wagons, and surreys.

In the second-biennium appropriation for the school the legislature provided money for a president's home, a men's dorm, and an addition to the Main Building. The school continued to grow.

During Page's administration there was continuing conflict over the type of education that was suitable for Negro youth. Page believed that industrial and agricultural courses offered the most opportunity. He strengthened the farming, blacksmithing, and carpentry curricula. At the same time he was instrumental in establishing the College Department, and he listed this as one of

University Museum as shown in the 1905 catalogue.

his major accomplishments. During his tenure as president the faculty increased from four to thirty-five, and the student body climbed to 650.

None of the original campus buildings remains today. The first Main Building was destroyed by fire and replaced by the first Page Hall in 1909. That building was torn down during President William H. Hale's administration in the 1960s. Modern Page Hall now stands near the location; it is sometimes referred to as the Library Annex. (Many Langston supporters felt that the removal of the original Page Hall was a mistake, for it had marble steps and hallways and sturdy, fireproof construction. However, the ten-year physical-plant upgrading plan called for removal of old structures.)

The oldest building on the campus is the "White House." The house, which was originally red brick, was stuccoed during G. L. Harrison's administration. It was built in the early 1920s as the second president's residence. In the 1960s a new home was built, and the white stucco house served as a faculty activity and reception hall. It is still in use.

Of the original dormitories Attucks Hall was replaced by Sanford Hall. Phyllis Wheatley Dorm occupied the space where the Hale Student Center now stands. A stone dorm for men was later replaced by Marquess Hall (no longer standing). During Page's first years the museum collection, the library, and the dairy were begun.

Page resigned in 1915 to become president of Macon College in Missouri. Later he served as supervising principal of Oklahoma City's separate schools. He died on December 21, 1935, and is buried on the Langston University campus.

Isaac Berry McCutcheon
Second President, 1915-16

Isaac Berry McCutcheon was a native of Nashville, Tennessee, where he attended public grade schools and high schools. His college work was at Walden University, Fisk University, and the University of Chicago. His teaching career included posts in Clarksville, Tennessee, and in Atoka, Bristow, Depew and Pawhuska, Oklahoma. His wife, Blanche Lee Warfield McCutcheon, was also from Tennessee.

McCutcheon became president of Langston in August, 1915. He remained only six months. During that brief period there was considerable turmoil on the campus. McCutcheon later recalled, "...the atmosphere of discord prevailed. Dr. I. E. Page, the retiring president, was permitted to occupy the president's home for one month after my arrival, and I had to find sleeping quarters at other places and eat food in the dining room."

During McCutcheon's short stay the University switched from kerosene lighting to electricity. Running water, instead of galvanized tubs, was installed for bathing. The Music Department was able to obtain songbooks. Enough dishes and silver were finally bought to set the tables in the dining hall.

There was a cloud of discord at the time McCutcheon left. He had fired a dissident history professor, John Hogan. Several nights

Isaac Berry McCutcheon, the second president, 1915-16.

later five shots were fired at McCutcheon by "persons unknown." Hogan was arrested and held on $1000 bond. Charges and counter-charges were filed by both parties. At one point Mrs. McCutcheon carried her husband's pistol for defense, but it was soon taken away from her.

After the incident Hogan left for Chicago. McCutcheon quit office on June 30, 1916, and moved back to Atoka, where he became principal of the black high school.

Despite the drama surrounding McCutheon's leavetaking, more serious and underlying turmoil at the school involved whether the institution was to be an industrial-manual training center or a liberal-arts college. A bitter argument was going on among Negro proponents of both sides. Many believed that the teachings of Booker T. Washington, advocating close allegiance to the soil of the South and use of Negro talents in the domestic and manual areas was the prime purpose of Langston University. Others, equally adamant, wanted to follow the teachings of W. E. B. DuBois, who sought political and social equality with the whites. An impassioned article appeared in the *Black Dispatch* during this era, arguing against the "blanket rule" of industrial education for everyone enrolled at Langston.

The article, entitled "Negroes Not Satisfied with Langston School," maintained that industrial training "could do justice only to a bunch of cattle." The writer asked, "Do you not know that there are hordes of ambitious black boys who never intended to enter the trades or seek the farm?" A compromise proposition was offered: Langston would be an all-industrial school provided that "on another hill in Oklahoma" would be established a black school "where we may get everything that the intellect of the twentieth century offers."

As a result of this controversy Page left the presidency, and McCutcheon inherited a stack of problems he was unable to solve. The Board of Regents spent six months looking for another president for the school.

R. E. BULLITT
Interim President, 1916

R. E. Bullitt served as successor to McCutcheon for approximately five months during the early part of 1916. The Board of Regents met in March and appointed a new president, who took over in June.

JOHN MILLER MARQUESS
Third President, 1916-23

John Miller Marquess went to Langston at a troubled time. He was offered the presidency in the spring of 1916. A native of Arkansas,

John Miller Marquess, the third president, 1916-23.

born at Helena in 1882, Marquess attended Fisk University and graduated from Dartmouth. He was married to Anna M. Dickson.

When Marquess arrived at Langston in June, 1916, he inherited the controversy over industrial versus liberal-arts education. His position was to try to make friends of both sides. He was, first of all, a good businessman, and he tried to put the school on a paying basis. He made the boarding system a source of revenue and later boasted that the gymnasium had been built entirely from such funds. He was a good mixer, a shrewd politician, and an excellent orator. Eventually, however, he let Langston slide in the direction of industrial education. During most of his tenure the four-year college course was dropped entirely (1917-22).

Phyllis Wheatley Dormitory.

The second president's home, built in 1920.

The "new" gymnasium, 1921-22.

Some of the improvements completed under Marquess included the addition of electricity, steam heat, and running water in all campus buildings. Dorms for men and women were built, and a gym, a laundry, and the new red-brick president's home was finished.

Marquess resigned the presidency of Langston in 1923 and moved to Philadelphia, where he died in 1936.

ISAAC WILLIAM YOUNG
Fourth and Sixth President, 1923-27, 1931-35

The only man to serve two different times as president of Langston was Isaac William Young. He was born in 1874 in Glencoe, Louisiana, attended grammar school there, and then went to Gilbert College. After graduation in 1891 he studied medicine at New Orleans University. He graduated from medical school in 1900 and married Adelia Amber, of Alexandria, Louisiana.

After practicing medicine in the South for ten years, Dr. Young moved to Boley, Oklahoma, where he served as a physician and was elected mayor. He moved to Oklahoma City in 1917 and became active in Democratic party politics. It was his close association

LANGSTON UNIVERSITY

Isaac William Young, M.D., the fourth president, 1923-27, and sixth president, 1931-35.

with Governor-elect Jack Walton that led to his appointment as president of Langston in 1923. With a change of governors four years later, Dr. Young resigned and moved to Oklahoma City. He was subsequently reappointed for a second term by Governor William H. Murray in 1931.

When Dr. Young first became president in 1923, $1,000 was spent on library improvements — the first money, Young stated, spent on that facility in many years. The Science Department was renovated, and more than $40,000 went for campus repairs. The College Department was restored and began granting its first official undergraduate degrees. Through 1926 the school had a total of more than 15,000 students. The degree statistics through 1926 showed conferrals of 33 bachelor's degrees, 722 junior-college normal diplomas, 46 vocational-agriculture certificates, 31 home-

The first Home Management House.

The campus laundry, built during the Marquess administration.

economics diplomas, 11 trades certificates, and 3 commercial diplomas. The graduating class grew to 105 in 1925.

The school owned 320 acres in 1926. The valuation of the school was $326,267, most of that value being in the nine principal buildings.

During Dr. Young's second term at Langston the student enrollment again increased. Dr. Young established correspondence and extension courses for those who could not attend school on campus. He is credited with obtaining from the legislature the first substantial building appropriations, which were spent to equip the dorms and build the new Administration Building, a one-story, white-frame home-economics cottage, a dairy barn, a poultry plant, and a laundry.

Under Dr. Young a shift was made from manual and technical training to more emphasis on arts-and-science courses. Both the library and the science labs were upgraded during his time in office. In addition he was instrumental in establishing such industrial-arts courses as tailoring, auto mechanics, plumbing, printing, and landscaping. A park was built, and improvements were made in the campus grounds.

Dr. Young, a lifelong Methodist, received the highest award his church bestows on a layman. He served as delegate to two national church conferences.

After moving to New Mexico for his health, Dr. Young died in Clovis, New Mexico, on June 8, 1937. His body was interred on the Langston campus but later was moved to Guthrie.

ZACHARY T. HUBERT
Fifth President, 1927-31

A respected chemistry and agriculture professor and former president of the Oklahoma Association of Negro Teachers, Zachary Taylor Hubert came to Langston as the choice of Governor Henry Johnston. His educational background included degrees from Morehouse College, Boston University, and the Massachusetts Agricultural College, as well as further graduate work at the University of Minnesota.

Zachary Taylor Hubert, the fifth president, 1927-31.

The new Home Management House, built in 1930.

During Hubert's administration two dorms were completed, one for men and one for women. Six teachers cottages were built. The new stone home-management house was built in 1930.

Hubert was characterized as "tall, slender, quiet, and unassuming." He was a thorough scholar and lent dignity to the campus. His absorption in intellectual matters prevented him from concerning himself about political matters, and his administration was accompanied by campus unrest, the student strike of 1928, and the general dissatisfaction with the Board of Regents.

After four years at Langston, with a change in state governors he was replaced by I. W. Young.

J. W. SANFORD
Seventh President, 1935-39

After Dr. Young's second administration, the Board of Regents appointed J. W. Sanford to the presidency of Langston. Sanford was a

J. W. Sanford, the seventh president, 1935-39.

Sanford Hall, the girls' dormitory, which also housed the cafeteria.

native of Texas, born at Edna. He graduated from Prairie View College in 1907 and received the bachelor of science degree from Guadalupe College in 1914. He served in the United States Army with the rank of captain. Later he undertook further study at Wiley College, Marshall, Texas, and at the University of Chicago. He earned his master's degree at Kansas State University and was named an honorary doctor of laws by Wiley College. Sanford's wife was Camelia Blackburn, of Hillsboro, Texas.

Before going to Langston, Sanford was principal of Peabody High School, in Hillsboro, Texas, and Douglass High School, in Ardmore, Oklahoma. He helped organize the Southern Teachers Association, was president of the Oklahoma Association of Negro Teachers in 1932, and was vice-president of the Association of

Land Grant College Presidents. After moving to Oklahoma, Sanford became politically active. He was one of the original political supporters of oilman E. W. Marland. When Marland was elected governor in 1935, Sanford was named president of Langston University.

Sanford was a popular president. During his administration, several buildings were completed, including the Administration Building, Sanford Hall, and the annex to the men's dorm.

His administration was closely linked to Marland's political fortunes, and when Marland's term ended, Sanford resigned, leaving the post in 1939. From 1942 to 1946 he was Oklahoma's first black high school inspector. He was a member of Omega Psi Phi and president of the Oklahoma City Negro Chamber of Commerce.

BENJAMIN FRANKLIN LEE
Second Interim President, 1939

Following the administrative turnover after Sanford's resignation, Benjamin Franklin Lee, the dean of Langston's College of Arts and Sciences, was appointed acting president. He had been a mathematics professor at Langston from 1923 to 1934.

After the appointment of a permanent president in January, 1940, Lee returned to his post as dean and held that position until his death in October, 1940.

ALBERT LOUIS TURNER
Eighth President, 1940

Albert Louis Turner was born in New Orleans in 1900. He graduated cum laude from Western Reserve University in 1923 and received a bachelor of laws degree in 1927. He was elected to the honorary legal fraternity the Order of the Coif. At the University of Michigan he received a master's and later a doctoral degree.

Turner went to Langston as both scholar and lawyer, expecting to take complete charge. He found instead a political situation in

Benjamin F. Lee, the second interim president, 1939.

Albert Louis Turner, the eighth president, January 1940. Courtesy of North Carolina Central University Law School.

which most of the appointments had already been made. Salaries, the business office, and key faculty appointments were closely controlled by Fred Holman, chairman of the Board of Regents for Agricultural and Mechanical Colleges. After conferring for two days with Holman, Dean Lee, as well as the editor of the *Black Dispatch,* Roscoe Dunjee, and other faculty members, Turner decided not to step into the muddle of politics. He wrote his resignation and sent it by mail to Holman in Guthrie. Immediately thereafter he left for the University of Michigan to be in time for the opening of classes so that he would not lose a semester from his work on his doctorate.

Turner was nicknamed "President for a Day," and indeed he stayed at Langston only about four days. He later wrote a letter to the university saying that he had been cordially received on campus but that his decision had been prompted by the inability of any educator to run a school under "dual authority." He wrote, "I fear a distorted pattern of control has been created difficult to break."

Rumors circulated that Turner had been "frightened" out of the state. Turner termed such rumors ridiculous and pointed out, accurately, that the presidency of Langston seemed to be controlled by the state senator from Guthrie, Louis Ritzhaupt. In a final comment Turner wrote, "I would not prostitute my professional career at Langston University."

Turner went on to become dean of the North Carolina Central University of Law School and a Carnegie Foundation fellow. He retired in 1965 and died in 1973 in Princeton, New Jersey.

G. LAMAR HARRISON
Ninth President, 1940-60

The shortest Langston administration was followed by the longest, the twenty-year tenure of G. Lamar Harrison. Born in 1900 in

G. Lamar Harrison, the ninth president, 1940-60. Courtesy of Public Relations Office, Langston University.

G. Lamar Harrison Library. Courtesy of Public Relations Office, Langston University.

Seward, Oklahoma, Harrison attended elementary school in Lawton, high school in Kansas City, Missouri, and college in Ohio. He received his bachelor's and his master's degrees at the University of Cincinnati and his Ph.D. from Ohio State University in 1936. He was married to Dorothy Marie Pennman in 1932.

Before going to Langston, Harrison taught at Virginia Union University and West Virginia State College and was dean of education at Prairie View College in Texas. He was a member of the Board of Trustees of Wilberforce University from 1932 to 1937. He was the author of several studies dealing with Negro rural school systems, and the subject of his doctoral dissertation was the training of black teachers to serve in rural school districts.

Harrison went to Langston with sound educational credentials. He brought to a politically disruptive situation a philosophy that

I. W. Young Auditorium, which has a seating capacity of fourteen hundred.

education "must serve the people of the state at the point of their greatest need." He arrived at a time when the Langston Alumni Association was beginning to make progress in removing the presidency from political influence — and when the world situation was about to create dramatic social changes.

The burden of securing accreditation fell on Harrison's new administration. When he began his administration in 1940, Langston had standing only as a "standard four-year college." During his tenure the school was brought up to par in library, physical plant, and faculty. In the very first year he brought to the campus four new faculty members who had earned doctorates.

Changes were made almost at once. The school geared up to participate in the national-defense program. The high school became part of the teacher training unit. And finally, in 1941, the name of the school was officially changed from the Colored Agricultural and Normal University to what it had always popularly been called — Langston University.

Because Harrison stabilized the office of president and remained

The remodeled president's home, now known as the "White House."

for so many years as head of the school, the expansion of the campus under his administration was widespread. A herd of registered beef cattle was started in 1942 with the purchase of a prize bull, T. Royal Rupert 118th, from the Turner Ranch in Sulphur. In 1943-44 the entire campus was provided heat from the central steam plant. Other major improvements included a modern sewage-disposal plant, paved streets, a modern stadium, a new library, and the I.W. Young Auditorium and remodeled gymnasium. Between 1939 and 1954 the value of the physical plant rose from less than $1 million to more than $4 million.

Under Harrison's guidance the school provided for itself what the legislature did not appropriate. Thus the Trade and Industrial Building was reroofed; the home economics labs were remodeled; a radio, shoe, and barber shop was started; and the president's home was completely remodeled — the red brick was covered with white stucco. Jones Hall Science and Agriculture Building was constructed. Langston began printing its own catalogue in the campus printshop.

Jones Hall, named for D. C. Jones, the supervisor of vocational agriculture. Built during Harrison's administration at a cost of $108,000, it ultimately housed the Departments of Agriculture, Home Economics, English, and Mathematics.

    The curriculum underwent drastic revision. Five divisions were established: agriculture, arts and sciences, education, industrial arts, and home economics. Two-year associate programs were added to the home economics and industrial-arts divisions in addition to the four-year degree programs.

    The accrediting came slowly. In 1948, Langston became a member of the Association of American Colleges. The Veterans Administration approved the school for work under the G.I. Bill of Rights. Subsequent accreditation achieved during Harrison's administration included membership in the North Central Association of Colleges and Secondary Schools and the American Association of Colleges for Teacher Education, and affiliation with the State Department for training of foreign students and nationals. Harrison resigned at the end of fiscal 1960.

WILLIAM HENRI HALE
Tenth President, 1960-69

When William Henri Hale was installed as the tenth president of Langston on April 23, 1961, he became the first alumnus to return as head of the school. A full-dress academic procession was held, and delegates from more than seventy colleges and universities attended.

Ironically, one of the most pressing problems Hale had to deal with was integration. Although the Langston and other Oklahoma campuses had been legally desegregated for six years, little change had been noted at Langston, which had continued as a predominantly black school. The big shift was that increasing numbers of black students were going to formerly all-white institutions. Thus

William Henri Hale, the tenth president, 1960-69. Courtesy of Larzette Golden Hale.

Larzette Golden Hale. Courtesy of Larzette Golden Hale.

Langston's goal had to change. In his inaugural address Hale stressed that Langston must function to fill both cultural and educational gaps in the lives of deprived or neglected students.

Both Hale and his wife were native Oklahomans. He was born at Krebs on August 8, 1914. His wife, Larzette Golden, was born in Idabel and lived for a time at the Taft Orphanage. Both attended Langston, were college sweethearts for four years, and married a week after their graduation in 1940. Hale received the master's degree in sociology from University of Wisconsin and the doctorate from the University of Chicago. Mrs. Hale finished her doctorate in finance and accounting at the University of Wisconsin — Langston's first woman graduate to obtain a doctorate of philosophy. She is also a certified public accountant.

Hale went to Langston after seventeen years' teaching experience at Bethune-Cookman College in Florida and Clark College in Atlanta. He proposed an immediate "ten-year plan" to upgrade Langston's physical plant and academic activities. He planned to begin with the entering freshman class, promoting reading and testing programs, cultural projects, and tutoring.

The first phase was completed in 1964 at a cost of almost $2 million. It included the construction of two residence halls, the Student Center and three faculty apartment buildings and remodeling of the dining hall into a dorm.

The second phase, which cost more than $2 million, included construction of three classroom buildings, a library annex, a music building, a science and technology building and more apartments. In an interview held in 1966, Hale described Langston "a greenhouse for the intellectually undernourished." At that time Langston had an enrollment of 1,160, including 9 white students, 250 non-resident students, and 25 foreign students. The 75-member faculty included 20 whites.

The last two phases of the ten-year improvement program called for a new water supply, tennis courts, air conditioning of classroom buildings and the Afro-American Heritage Center. The curriculum revisions were aimed at the general-education requirements mandatory for all students and the special requirements for programs in teacher's education.

Gandy Hall, phase 1, constructed during Hale's administration. It was named for the late Lenouliah E. Gandy, the university home economist. Courtesy of Paul W. Newlin.

Brown Hall, phase 1, constructed during Hale's administration. It was named for Eugene E. Brown, the "father of art" on campus. Courtesy of Paul W. Newlin.

William H. Hale Student Center, phase 1, constructed in the 1960s during Hale's administration. Courtesy of Paul W. Newlin.

Faculty apartments, phase 1, constructed during Hale's administration. Courtesy of Paul W. Newlin.

The wreckage of Old Page Hall, built in 1909 and replaced in 1967.

An article in the April, 1966, issue of the *Southern Education Report* appropriately commented that Langston was passing through an "identity crisis." Desegregation had opened other state institutions to blacks, and the question "what to do with Langston" had been argued in the state legislature. Hale took the attitude that "if it is our destiny to develop people to the extent that they can move on somewhere else, so be it — we've made a contribution."

By the mid-1960s the Langston campus had undergone dramatic growth in physical improvements, and the academic atmosphere had prospered to the point that graduation class size had risen from 72 in 1960 to 160 in 1965. Many sons and daughters of alumni were attending classes. In both growth and student-retention rate Langston ranked near the top of Oklahoma colleges.

New Page Hall, phase 2, also known as the Library Annex. Courtesy of Paul W. Newlin.

Recruitment by industry and government increased dramatically in the 1960s. Representatives from 10 companies visited the campus in 1961; recruiters from more than 150 companies visited Langston in 1966.

A development foundation, aided significantly by Mrs. Hale's acumen in financial affairs, was started to provide scholarships and loans. The fund quickly grew to more than $250,000. Over half the student body used the resources of the fund.

Other improvements during the Hale administration included establishment of a reading clinic and an audiovisual materials lab, an increase in library holdings to 100,000 volumes, and inauguration of an annual high school teachers' conference. The long-standing argument about industrial versus liberal-arts education seemed settled when the tailoring shop gave way to an electronics lab.

The Department of Development and Public Relations undertook follow-up studies of Langston graduates. It showed that in

Hargrove Hall Library Annex, phase 2, built during the Hale administration. It was named for the late Dean S. L. Hargrove. Courtesy of Paul W. Newlin.

Hamilton Hall of Science and Technology, phase 2. It was named for G. C. Hamilton, long-term chairman of the Biology Department. Courtesy of Paul W. Newlin.

The third president's home, built in 1965. Courtesy of Omar Reed.

1968 six alumni received doctoral degrees. On the Langston campus tuition scholarships were awarded to students maintaining a 4.0 (A) average. During the 1968-70 biennium seventy-nine students earned such scholarships. Ten professional honor societies had chapters on campus.

The Head Start Program and Title III funds were used to combat the dropout problem among black youth. Hale's philosophy was that "youngsters must be encouraged and guided to go to college from the time they are old enough to begin their first formal education." When Langston started its "Sixth-Graders Day" on campus, inviting sixth-grade students from across the state to get the feel of college life, the project received national publicity.

The ten-year plan was updated in 1969 to project through 1975. A self-study of the academic program was made, and the divisions were reduced to arts and sciences, education, and technical and vocational education. The National Council for Accreditation of Teacher Education granted provisional accreditation in 1965.

In 1966 a new leave policy encouraged advanced study by faculty members. After two years' experience at the university a faculty member could apply for leave for study (the new policy was in addition to sabbaticals). Faculty study grants were also made from Title III funds. In 1968 ten faculty members were given one-year leaves at full salary to complete Ph.D. degrees.

In October, 1969, Hale was discharged by the Board of Regents after a secret meeting. The meeting, at which seven of the nine regents were present, voted unanimously to discharge Hale because of "lack of confidence." He was given accrued leave until the end of the fiscal year. The academic dean was named acting president.

For several weeks there was talk of legal charges and libel suits, but none were filed. One reason Hale gave for not filing suit against the board of regents was that it would "signal an all-out effort at closing the school." Hale was later given the rest of his annual $22,000 salary. He received popular support from the students, who marched to the State Capitol in his defense, and from the Langston Alumni Council. In December, 1969, after two months of

Breaux Hall of Men, phase 4, constructed during Hale's administration. It was named for Vice-President Breaux. Courtesy of Paul W. Newlin.

Young Hall for Women, phase 4, constructed during Hale's administration. Courtesy of Paul W. Newlin.

discussion, the regents passed a resolution supporting the school and calling for its continued operation.

After dismissal from Langston, Hale finished his juris doctor degree at Oklahoma City University and moved to Utah. He became professor of sociology and special assistant to the vice-president for student affairs at Utah State University in Logan.

Hale died in May, 1974. After services in the auditorium at Langston, he was buried in the McAlester cemetery.

WILLIAM E. SIMS
Third Interim President and Eleventh President, 1969-74

William E. Sims served as acting president of Langston from October, 1969, until January 1970. The Board of Regents then voted to name him president. Several educators from around the nation had been considered for the top post, and Sims had not filed an application for it. He had gone to Langston in 1953 as band director and later served four years as dean of academic affairs.

Sims's early education was in the Chickasha, Oklahoma, public

William E. Sims, third interim president and eleventh president, 1969-74.

schools. He earned a bachelor's degree in music from Lincoln University, at Jefferson City, Missouri, and taught music in Sand Springs and Tulsa, Oklahoma. In 1963 he completed his doctoral studies at Colorado State College in Greeley. Although Sims was not a Langston alumnus, both his wife, Muriel, and his daughter, Dana, were graduates of the school.

After he became president, Sims followed the philosophy that a land-grant school was an equal-opportunity college, open to all who might profit from higher education. His administration noted a continued rise in faculty standing, expansion of the research program, a new concept in cooperative education, a new extension-service program, and the Five College Curriculum Innovative Thrust Program. The library joined the Interlibrary Loan System, by which books and periodicals not available on the Langston campus could be borrowed from other libraries.

After an auditor's report of 1974 showed the school to be overdrawn and in financial straits, Sims resigned. The Board of Regents appointed the director of the Cooperative Extension Service as

The former University Men's Dormitory, now remodeled and converted into the Research Center.

Kerr Plaza, constructed during Sims's administration.

interim president. In explaining his decision to resign, Sims warned the board, "In my opinion, if Langston University does not receive a substantial increase in funding, the college will continue to operate at the brink of financial disaster." He was commended by the board and offered the opportunity to remain on campus in his former position as professor of music. Shortly thereafter, however, he moved to Colorado, where be became a member of the Music Department at Colorado State University at Fort Collins.

JAMES L. MOSLEY
Fourth Interim President, 1974-75

James L. Mosley, born at Tishomingo, Oklahoma, in 1938, grew up in Oklahoma and attended school in Ponca City. He graduated from Attucks Highschool in 1955 as salutatorian, having been a member of the varsity football and basketball teams and the band.

Mosley attended Langston University on a basketball scholarship. He majored in math and minored in physical education. He was basketball team captain in both his junior and his senior years. In 1959 he was All-Oklahoma Collegiate Athletic Conference honoree for basketball. He married Versadell Thompson in 1960.

After graduating from Langston, Mosley earned a master's degree from Central State University, Edmond, Oklahoma, and a doctorate in education in secondary administration from the University of Oklahoma in Norman. Before assuming the acting presidency of Langston, Mosley taught at Wagoner, Oklahoma City, Midwest City, and Langston University. At Langston he was professor of education and director of the Cooperative Extension Service. As program coordinator for the human-awareness-training project, he developed two-day seminars held for municipal employees throughout the state. He served as a member of the Regent's Advisory Committee on Civil Rights.

Mosley assumed the presidency of Langston during a time of financial stress. He predicted that the school would have to engage in "belt-tightening and watching what's being spent very closely." In an audit of July, 1975, a deficit of more than $130,000 in operat-

James L. Mosley, fourth interim president, 1974-75. Courtesy of James L. Mosley.

ing funds was disclosed. The deficits were made up through an extensive fund-raising drive and through contributions from national foundations. Mosley attributed some of the school's problems to the limited job opportunities for students on campus and the need for scholarships by more than three-fourths of the student body.

Mosley's primary concern was to institute a workable management system for the school. To this end his administration restructured the insurance program, developed a filing system, adopted new communications procedures, and revised the payroll system. The summer-school program was continued despite proposals for closing it. At the end of Mosley's year as acting president the college had experienced a turnaround of nearly $1 million; 40 percent of the private debt had been paid off, and the Research Service had been reimbursed $120,000.

Mosley and his family lived in Oklahoma City. He became assistant director of the Cooperative Extension Service maintained by Langston, Oklahoma State University, and the United States Department of Agriculture.

Thomas E. English
Twelfth President, 1975-77

An Oklahoma native and graduate of Langston, Thomas E. English became the twelfth president of the school in July 1, 1975. He was educated in the Cushing public schools. He obtained advanced degrees from Oklahoma State University, where he earned a master's degree in science and a doctorate in educational administration.

When he assumed the leadership of Langston, English stated, "The whole aim of education is to develop that climate of drawing

Thomas E. English, twelfth president, 1975-77. Courtesy of Thomas E. English.

out the better self of every student." Students and faculty members quote his favorite saying: "I am headed due north."

English before assuming his job at Langston, had been active in the Community Action Program in Oklahoma City. He had been executive director of CAP, president of the Biracial School Desegregation Committee, and a member of the Board of Directors of the Oklahoma City Community Council. In addition he had taught in Ada and Cushing and had been a school administrator in the Oklahoma City system.

There was continuing pressure on the administration to put Langston on a firm financial footing. The going was rocky indeed, especially after a special team of financial experts appointed by the Board of Regents worked several months to produce a set of financial records for the school. There was further trouble when the painfully reconstructed records were accidentally thrown out during a

Swimming-pool annex to Gayles Gymnasium, completed in 1976, part of the ten-year plan. Courtesy of Paul W. Newlin.

cleaning operation. The Board of Regents demanded that "financial integrity [must] be established at Langston" and warned that "it must be continued from now on."

In December, 1975, the board publicly warned English that his "continuing employment" hinged on sorting out the school's financial affairs within sixty days. The accounting firm of Hurdman and Cranston was hired to audit the university's records.

In the meantime a general campus cleanup and beautification campaign was being waged. The gymnasium was remodeled, and the swimming pool was constructed.

Financial woes continued to plague the campus. A system of extending credit to students in lieu of tuition caused trouble with the regents, who insisted that the Oklahoma State Constitution forbade the extension of credit to individuals. The chairman of the regents charged in the summer of 1977 that 1,940 credit hours granted to students had not been properly charged for. This deficit, which amounted to approximately $33,000, was not collected.

English was discharged by the Board of Regents at a meeting held in August, 1977. He was given thirty days' severance pay, although he requested a full year's pay.

The regents cited "insufficient" academic, administrative, and management leadership in their 180-page report on Langston's troubles.

Dr. Ernest L. Holloway was named interim president, and a nationwide search for a successor was launched.

ERNEST L. HOLLOWAY
Fifth Interim President, 1977-78, 1978-

Ernest L. Holloway, a widower with three sons, headed Langston from the summer of 1977 through spring, 1978. Born in 1930, Holloway received his early education at Boley, Oklahoma. He is a graduate of Langston University, class of 1952. He received his master's degree from Oklahoma State University in 1955 and did postgraduate work at Ohio State University and the University of

Ernest Holloway, fifth interim president, 1977-78. Courtesy of Ernest Holloway.

California at Berkeley. In 1970 he completed his doctorate in education at the University of Oklahoma.

Before going to Langston, Dr. Holloway taught science at Boley High School and was the principal there. At Langston he held the posts of assistant registrar, registrar, dean of student affairs, professor, and vice-president for administration, as well as interim president. His professional memberships include Phi Delta Kappa, the Oklahoma Education Association, and the Oklahoma Personnel Guidance Association. He belongs to Alpha Phi Alpha fraternity.

Samuel J. Tucker
Thirteenth President, 1978

In March, 1978, Samuel J. Tucker was named president of Langston University by the Board of Regents for Agricultural and Mechanical Colleges. Tucker is a graduate of Morehouse College, Atlanta, Georgia, having received his B.A. degree in 1952. He was awarded the master's degree by Columbia University, New York City, in 1956 and the doctorate in psychology, counseling, and guidance from the University of Atlanta, Atlanta, Georgia, in 1969. In 1976 he undertook postdoctoral work at the Harvard University School of Business Administration.

Before assuming the presidency of Langston, Tucker was academic dean of the University College of Alabama State University, Montgomery. Before that he was president of Edward

Samuel J. Tucker, thirteenth president, 1978. Courtesy of Samuel J. Tucker.

Waters College, Jacksonville, Florida. He has also held positions in higher education at the University of Florida, Atlanta University, Morehouse College.

He assumed his duties at Langston in April, 1978. In his opening address to the university community he voiced support for the role of the predominantly black college in higher education and promised a "new renaissance of excellence" in all areas of the university, including improvement of campus facilities and increased scholarship assistance for students. President Tucker was hopeful that, "working together, we shall fashion a glorious future for Langston University in serving the needs of society."

On December 20, 1978, President Tucker was suddenly dismissed from the presidency by the Oklahoma State Regents for A&M Colleges on grounds of alleged fiscal mismanagement. Tucker denied the charges and said that he would prove in court that they were not true. At the same regents' meeting Ernest Holloway was appointed interim president. This is Holloway's second term as interim president.

CHAPTER FOUR

Vice-Presidents and Academic Deans

LANGSTON University catalogues did not list deans and vice presidents separately until 1920. There were, however, men who functioned in these positions before that date. For example, in 1905-1906, Baxter Whitby held the title Vice-President and Professor of the Natural and Physical Sciences. In the early years there were also deans of the high school. J. D. Elsberry served as the first dean of the Langston University High School in 1922.

The first dean of education was J. Wilson Pettus, and the first dean of agriculture was John Buford. Dean L. G. Moore gave years

W. Bruce Jones, vice-president, 1923-24. Courtesy of Mrs. L. Cudjo, a granddaughter of Jones.

Inman A. Breaux, administrative dean and vice-president. He is the grandson of Langston's first president, Inman page. Courtesy of Public Relations Department, Langston University.

of continuous service to the school, joining the faculty in 1925 and becoming dean of instruction in 1940. A former vice-president, Ernest Holloway, served in 1977-78 as interim president.

One of the early-day Oklahoma educators, W. Bruce Jones, served as vice-president under I. W. Young. Jones, born in Arkansas in 1881, received his bachelor's degree from Arkansas Baptist College. He taught at Black Jack School in Muskogee County, Oklahoma, and in Rentiesville and Lima before moving to Langston. Later, after obtaining a law degree from the University of Chicago, he organized the Seminole County Bar Association. He was the father of four children, all of whom attended Langston University.

A list of Langston's vice-presidents and academic deans and their years of service appears in Appendix D.

CHAPTER FIVE

The Normal (Teacher's) Department

LANGSTON University was established to serve as a training center for future black teachers. At the time of its establishment, teachers' certificates were offered to graduates of "normal schools." The Normal Department of Langston continued until 1932, and in terms of graduates it was by far the largest section of the university.

The formally stated purpose of the Normal Department was to give students "instruction in both the theory and the practice of teaching and also in the laws governing the schools of the Territory."

When the school opened in 1898, most of the prospective education students lacked the prerequisites to begin college study. The candidate was supposed to have completed four years of high school-level work. In the early years no one arrived on the campus ready to start college. Everyone entered either the High School, or College Preparatory Department.

Therefore, when one reads about offerings of the Normal Department in the early catalogues, it should be remembered that few students began at that level.

The High School Department was set up to prepare those wishing to pursue teachers' certificates. Anyone who had completed the eighth grade or was fourteen or older could enter. To graduate from the department, a student must have completed four years of English, two years of mathematics, and one year of American history or civics. No partial credits were allowed in languages, and sixteen credits were required for graduation. Students who arrived late — after helping with the harvest — were allowed to take only reduced schedules. For example, those who enrolled during the fourth week after school opened could take only two courses that term. It took some students many years to get a degree. It is not surprising that the first graduation of a "normal" class did not occur until 1906.

Class offerings in the Normal Department were strongly academic. In the first year of the department's operation the plan of study called for courses in English, algebra, Latin, physiology, and botany. Some of the advanced-course offerings, for third- and fourth-year students were in such esoteric fields as comparative osteology and moral philosophy. In their senior year students were to enroll in astronomy, geology, psychology, pedagogy, nature study, and the history of education.

Graduates from the Normal Department were granted a diploma and the degree "bachelor of scientific didactics." The diploma entitled the holder to teach in the public schools of Oklahoma for five years without reexamination. Normal graduates could also receive a "life" diploma in elementary education. Many student-teachers taught in the schools of the state while working toward their certification. They attended summer schools, took correspondence courses, and later took courses at Langston's Tulsa and Oklahoma City extension branches. When it was apparent that the separate Normal Department would be phased out, the last summer-session enrollment reached over 1,600. In the summer of 1932, when the program was terminated, the last 126 graduated.

The Normal Department curriculum was heavy on theory in the early years, but certain practical aspects were also stressed. Seniors were required to take two periods of "agriculture," which involved field, barn, and lab work. Prospective teachers studied drawing, took field trips in geography, and enrolled in manual training. All women students were required to enroll in one year of home economics, regardless of major.

Over the years the requirements for both admission to and graduation from the Normal Department were strengthened.

The first graduates of the department were issued certificates in 1906. They were J. I. Hazelwood, a Langston merchant, and Ellen Cockrel Strong, a Guthrie schoolteacher. The first summer session was held in 1914 with 200 on the enrollment list.

CHAPTER SIX

The High School Department

LANGSTON University ran its own high school from 1898 until 1946 as a college-preparatory school and center for training prospective teachers in the Education Department. This was an essential program, for few of the prospective college students had high school diplomas. There were two curricula in the prep department — the classical course and the scientific course. A two-year commercial course was begun in 1912. The classical section required three years of study; the scientific, four. It was expected that graduates of the scientific course would be able to pursue science, agricultural, or mechanical majors in college.

In its first year of operation Langston opened the high school doors with class offerings in English, algebra, Latin, and physiology. The academic requirement for Latin remained in force until 1930.

Classical-course students in the high school were required to pursue Latin, Greek, rhetoric, botany, and chemistry, while working up to such subjects as calculus, astronomy, physics, logic, and international law.

Admission requirements to the high school were completion of a regular grammar school course in public school and knowledge of geography, arithmetic, and English. Reports were sent to students and to parents at the end of each term.

The 1912 offerings in commercial courses began a trend that extended through the 1920s. Joseph Bailey began teaching bookkeeping, stenography, and typing. The high school stressed such practical, "breadwinning" courses as trades, commerce, vocational agriculture, and home economics. The high school was accredited in 1923. Under Principal A. M. Salone, who served from 1923 to 1927, the motto for courses was "Quality, Quantity, and Serviceability."

In the early 1920s, Frances M. Hayes was head of "physical culture." She was succeeded by Syble E. Byrd in 1924 and by Cornelia Jones in 1927. During this time all girls wore required "phys-ed" uniforms, consisting of white middy blouses, black bloomers, black ties, black stockings, and white tennis shoes. Some of the required gym activities were calisthenics, exercises on ladder and rings, outdoor games, and folk dancing.

In the academic areas the English Department's philosophy was that "usage is the law of language." Grammar, composition, and classics were required of first- and second-year high school students. Leonelle Young, the daughter of President Young, was the high school English teacher.

The History Department, with the Reverend W. J. Starks as the instructor, offered ancient, medieval, modern European, and American history. The last course emphasized political development. A course in Negro history was offered, a "systematic study of the origin, character, growth and achievements of the Negro race in America and its contributions to American civilization." The regular high school math course consisted of Algebra 1, Algebra 2, and plane and solid geometry.

There was a four-year agricultural course in the 1920s. It was designed for grammar school graduates who intended to farm and wanted to increase their earning capacity. Students who took the "ag" course also took the basic high school courses. The catalogues listed such practical offerings as plant production, shop, animal production, horticulture, poultry and farm mechanics. Course content was specified. For the poultry course included "how to locate a chicken coop, how to construct a suitable chicken house for Oklahoma climate, selection of breeds, feeding, how to select eggs for incubation and treatment of various poultry diseases." One year of agriculture was required.

Manual training included cabinet making, lumbering, shop machines, mechanical drawing, and painting. A full home economics course was given in the high school. Sewing emphasized "making wash dresses, embroidery, and how to set in a pocket on a middy blouse." Patching, darning, and laundering techniques were taught. Advanced seamstress courses included making baby clothes and boy's suits and renovating garments. In the senior year sewing included textile selection, storage of woolens and furs, color combinations and an optional course in millinery, where the girls could frame and trim hats.

The cooking course taught in the ninth grade was in basics, such as how to set the table, sanitation, and care of the kitchen. By the time the girls were seniors, they were taking turns preparing and serving meals in the student kitchen. They also prepared and served meals to the institution's special guests.

In 1923-24, R. N. Pyrtle was director of the scientific course. Instructors were Paul McCree and Ida Wade. The text for the basic course was *General Science,* by Hessler and Smith. Among the science courses, geography focused on lab work and field trips. S. L. Hargrove served as vice-president and dean, 1927-28, principal of the High School Department, 1938-43, and professor of history, 1943-51.

During the early years the function of the prep school was dual: to prepare students for college and to serve those who would leave after high school. Those who graduated from Langston University prep department were said to be able "to enter the best colleges of the country unhindered by any lack of necessary requirements and prerequisites, and, on the other hand, to... enter life's battles more or less prepared to win."

In addition to the high school Langston had a laboratory school, including grades one to eight. In the later years such courses as tailoring, printing, shoemaking, and military science were added to the high school curriculum. The high school was closed in May, 1946.

All elementary and secondary student teaching was done on campus and in the Langston city school until transportation improved. Off-campus student teaching began in the mid-1940s except for agriculture and home economics which had used off-campus centers since 1934 and the early 1940s, respectively. With the closing of the campus prep school, all Langston student teaching was done in the village or at schools throughout the state.

CHAPTER SEVEN

Only Yesterday: Memories of Early Days

ONE of the first students to register at Langston when it opened in September, 1898, was Joseph Roberts. He had moved to Oklahoma from Tennessee the previous year, and became first a student at Langston and later a graduate of the class of 1910. He registered in the village school and attended classes, which were held in the Presbyterian church. Roberts' impression was that the school was born in a political scramble and remained subject to politics with every change of governor, president, and faculty. When Langston was founded, C. M. Barnes, originally from Arkansas, and his friend W. C. Howell, also originally from Arkansas and then the Baptist minister in Langston, suggested Inman E. Page for the presidency. Page was then president of Lincoln University in Jefferson City, Missouri. Encouraged by Howell and Barnes, Page applied for the job. Another slate was proposed by political parties, but Page, being clearly the best-qualified candidate, was duly appointed. For many years after Page's seventeen-year tenure the presidency of Langston changed with each new governor of the state.

During his nine years on campus at Langston, Roberts received both a high school diploma and a college degree. He played football in 1901 and baseball in 1902, belonged to the chorus for eight years, and was a member of Langston's first glee club. He was a member of the student body in 1907, when the first Main Building caught fire and burned to the ground. Many people suspected arson, but no official charges or accusations were ever made. At the time, however, few people doubted that the fire was the result of political agitation concerning the school. The museum was lost in the fire. It had had a value of approximately $15,000 and had contained hard-to-replace specimens of birds and other

Joseph Roberts, one of the first three students to enroll at Langston University, September 14, 1898. This photograph was made after Roberts became a member of Langston University faculty.

scientific specimens, as well as portraits, antiques, and historical documents.

Some equipment and supplies were saved and were used in the new Main Building when it was completed in 1909. Although the new structure had twenty-seven rooms and was handsome, Roberts recalls that it lacked supplies and the fire-damaged equipment from the original building was unsatisfactory.

Another suspicious occurrence was the fire that burned the industrial building. Roberts says that the building that replaced it was not of as good quality or nearly as well equipped as the original. The first industrial building had been rated by instructors from Hampton and Tuskegee institutes as one of the best industrial schools in the country.

The silent accusation about both of the fires was that certain

A. H. Fuhr.
Courtesy of A. H. Fuhr.

black politicians were attempting to oust Inman Page from the presidency.

The memories of A. H. Fuhr go back to his student years, from 1906 to 1913. Certain things stand out in his memory about his arrival on campus. Room and board cost six dollars a month. There were no registration fees. Students had to line up to receive a weekly supply of coal oil for their lamps. There was only one water pump for the entire campus. This meager well had to supply all the drinking, cooking, and bathing water. The students took baths in zinc washtubs. Everyone — students and faculty alike — used outdoor toilets. In the mornings students lined up to march down to the back of the dorms and empty slop jars into the cesspool. The girls were chaperoned everywhere they went and lined up to march to chapel.

One Friday night a month, Fuhr recalls, a social was held. There the students could play "Finch," and the boys could march around with their girl friends, provided "a matron could see daylight between you and your girl." All that was necessary to rate as a big spender was twenty-five cents. Pop or ice cream cost a nickel. Refreshments for two people usually cost twenty cents, for no young lady would dream of accepting a second helping. During those days students could be dismissed and sent home if they were caught dancing, kissing, or holding hands.

Fuhr remembers President Page as "the grand old man of education." He was inspiring to the students despite the primitive conditions of the campus. On the day Fuhr graduated from Langston, June 6, 1913, he helped organize the Langston University Alumni Association.

From its beginning Langston University was the cultural focus of the community and surrounding rural area. The annual commencement, May Day, and Community Free Fair were big events. Families attended these events, exposing their children to campus life from early ages. For a farm family a typical day might begin at 4:00 A.M. so that they could be on the campus in time for a 10:00 A.M. program.

Early transportation was by wagon, buggy, hack, or surrey. The roads leading to the campus were poor and hilly, made of sandstone and rocks. Families heading for a campus event would be attired in their Sunday best. For boys that meant white or blue short pants, matching shirts, and jackets. Girls usually wore embroidered white dresses in the spring and plaid checked or gingham dresses in the fall. Almost all clothing was homemade. Hairstyles for the girls consisted of braids tied with ribbons matching the dresses. Hats sometimes had bows and ribbon streamers or flowers.

Adults were attired in finery for these outings. Men wore dark suits and black bowties. The women wore taffeta dresses, usually all black, or black taffeta skirts and white shirtwaists. Occasionally they wore black satin. Broad-brimmed straw hats trimmed with grosgrain ribbon and net were popular. Shoes were black kid with patent-leather tips. During the long wagon or buggy rides into town the travelers wore "dusters" over their good clothes.

Page Hall at the end of the avenue of locust trees.

On the day before the journey, the horses were curried, fed, and watered. Food for the big luncheon picnic was also prepared the day before. Families not only took plenty of food for themselves and their friends but also carried ample horse fodder in the backs of the wagons. Many families came from seven to fourteen miles away to programs at the university. These journeys required several hours.

The main entrance to the campus was from the south along a coal-cinder road. An avenue of locust trees planted on each side of the road led to the Main Building. The trees were used as hitching posts when the wagons arrived. Ropes were long enough to allow the horses to feed out of the backs of the wagons without bothering the picnic baskets and water jugs that were stored under the front seat.

Programs that drew a good attendance from the community were class plays, baccalaureate, commencement, May Day festival, and band concerts. People also came to hear music recitals, out-of-state artists, oratorical contests, and speeches delivered by prospective university presidents and politicians. Although it was traditional for candidates for university president to make speeches to the public,

The present-day South Entrance to Langston University.

the citizens and students had no part in the selection of the administration.

Among the well-known personalities who appeared at Langston in the early days were educator Mary McLeod Bethune, poet Langston Hughes, contralto Marian Anderson, educator Carter Woodson, Mordecai Wyatt Johnson, and contralto Eta Moten. Langston Hughes appeared in an informal session, read some of his poems, and told stories about how he had almost been born in Guthrie. In his remarks he pointed out to the students, "My feeling is that if you want to be something and want to be it strong enough, you can." He read from *The Weary Blues* and *Jim Crow's Last Stand.*

After the morning programs families had picnics under the locust trees. After the meal the guests watched a baseball game, made a campus tour, or listened to a band concert. Many farm families could not stay for the entire event, for they had to return to their farms to tend stock.

About 1915 students were surprised by the sight of a car. A well-to-do farmer, William Tillman, and his wife owned a new Ford. Tillman would take children for rides around the campus. The only other car around in those days was the president's, which was owned by the state.

For many years the concept of "duty work" remained strong at Langston. Students who attended the school in the period from 1923 to 1930 paid fourteen dollars a month for room and board and performed duties equal to four dollars a month. The only way one could be exempted from duty work was to be able to pay the additional four dollars. Students able to pay the extra fee were allowed to eat together at a long table and were served the better food provided the faculty.

Duty work included keeping the grounds and buildings clean, waiting tables in the dining hall, washing dishes, cleaning restrooms, sweeping and mopping dorms, scrubbing steps, and taking care of the reception and matron's rooms. Some students were assigned the tasks of keeping records, file or act as receptionists. Because the girl students were under many restrictions, it took time to check out each time they left the building to go anywhere other than classes. Men students were assigned the same duty work as the girls except for waiting tables and dishwashing. They also hauled and emptied trash, cut grass, and worked on painting, plumbing, and construction projects.

Though there were no scholarships, students who worked in the kitchen received free room and board. There were a few other jobs for which students could obtain room and board: hauling coal from the railway station in Coyle, working in the boiler plant, working in the president's home, and, later, chauffeuring the president.

Library workers could receive free room and board provided they worked on a continuous basis. One junior woman, usually a home-economics major, was selected as assistant in the dining hall. It was her duty to report at 5:00 A.M. to supervise waitresses and see to the silver, dishes, and linens. She also reported an hour before the other meals of the day. The budget did not permit the purchase of enough knives, forks, and spoons, and waitresses would take each other's tableware to complete their settings.

The dining assistant also rang the gong that signaled the students to line up to march in and out of the hall for meals. The procedure was as follows: The assistant rang the gong. The matron unlocked the doors of the dining hall. Students marched in to piano music, stood behind their chairs, and sang grace ("Thou art great and Thou art good; Lord, we thank Thee for this food...."). Students were allowed twenty-five minutes to eat. No food could be taken from the dining hall. Those who arrived late missed the meal; the doors were locked before grace.

Food for the school was bought at the railroad distribution point in Coyle or grown on the university farm, which produced vegetables from May through October. Eggs were generally served only on Sunday mornings. Milk was available but was often watered down or used for cooking. Raw milk was served until 1941, when the pasteurization plant was built.

Better cuts of meat were usually served only on Wednesday and Sunday. Meals during the rest of the week consisted largely of corned beef, bologna, salmon loaf, pigs' feet, ears and chitterlings, macaroni and cheese, black-eyed peas, and steamed beans. The campus bakery provided bread. One of the students' duty jobs was to pick and wash vegetables. It was a huge task to prepare enough for five hundred servings.

Meals were served family style, at long tables seating eighteen to twenty-one persons. The young men sat on one side of the table, and the girls on the other. Timidity in helping oneself was dangerous and usually led to hunger pangs, for refills from the kitchen were few and far between.

As mentioned earlier, students who could afford to pay the extra four dollars a month were allowed to sit at a separate table. Their meals included meat, biscuits with butter and jelly, fruit, and desserts. Here are some examples of contrasting menus:

The low-income student could expect a supper of peanut butter, syrup, bread, canned fruit, and water about three times a week. The supper menu for the faculty and better-off students might consist of salmon croquettes, mashed potatoes, English preas, a relish plate, sliced peaches, and lemonade. Again, at breakfast, the low-income students were often served prunes, grits, and skim milk, while the separate tables ate bacon, eggs, hot biscuits, coffee, and milk. Sunday dinner was the big meal of the week. The low-income students fared fairly well then. A typical menu called for beef stew, potato salad, green beans, carrots, white bread, and cobbler. Water was served for the beverage. In contrast, the menu for faculty and higher-income students announced steak with brown gravy, baked potato, green beans, combination salad, hot rolls, butter, pie, and coffee.

Sunday-evening supper was combined with the vesper service. No vesper attendance meant no supper. Since most students had no means or money to obtain food elsewhere, vespers usually had full attendance. The vespers service consisted of prayer, hymn singing, a solo, and a speech by the president or a poetry reading by faculty or student leaders. Afterward a light snack of lunch-meat or cheese sandwiches, punch, and cookies was served.

For a student who missed a meal by failing to attend vespers or arriving late at the dining hall, the alternatives were limited. Very little food was available on campus. Sandwiches were sometimes sold in the basement of the president's home. In the bookstore a nickel would buy a soft drink, peppermint or peanut-butter stick candy, chewing gum, oranges, or apples. There were a few places to eat in the town of Langston, but students — and especially women — were not permitted to leave campus without a chaperone. A standby to stave off starvation was a candy bar called Chicken Dinner." The bars were sold along with the other small snacks in the bookstore. The president's wife was usually in charge of the sales. For students with little spending money, it was a hard choice between a Chicken Dinner and the necessary paper, pencils, and pens for schoolwork. Chicken Dinners, larger than the average candy bars and coated with peanuts and chocolate, were easily the most popular snack, and a student with a candy bar was a quick target for his "friends."

Sometimes the food-handling and preparation process came to a halt because of problems with the water supply. At first water was pumped from the Cimarron River and from a well near Coyle. The water was pumped to an elevated storage tank on the campus to provide water for both university and town. The water was hard

Elevated water-storage tank, which supplied water to both the campus and the town.

and salty, causing both health and plumbing problems. Pipes quickly corroded and rusted. In 1970 the problem was resolved when a lake was dug south of the campus.

Along with the water problems the heating and plumbing facilities were inadequate. In the dead of winter the steam power plant was likely to quit, shutting off heat to all the buildings. The power plant also supplied the steam for heating water for cooking, bathing, and cleaning. At times the school would have to close for boiler repairs. Sometimes the water was shut off while plumbers made line repairs.

Living conditions were grim when power-plant breakdowns occurred in the winter. The dorms were cold and humid. Students would huddle in bed crawling out only for meals. When the water supply was off, meals tended to be inadequate and unsanitary, and steam appliances were inoperable. Menus were limited to items that could be cooked on the few coal- or wood-burning stoves — canned foods containing their own liquid and eggs — and cold foods like cheese and peanut butter. Most filling carbohydrate foods were impossible to prepare, and students returned to the dorms cold and hungry.

During bouts of trouble with the steam plant dishwashing was impossible — no steam, no water. Plates caked with syrup and peanut butter. Sometimes, when the water was on but the steam off, dishwashing was attempted in cold water.

Of course, the bakery was handicapped, too. Bread production was limited to what could be baked in the coal-stove ovens. Farm milk was used instead of water in making cornbread and biscuits. Milk for drinking or for cereal was eliminated.

The food situation being what it was, it is no wonder that a student returned from a visit home eagerly besieged with requests for snacks. Often on the weekends students whose families lived within walking or wagon range went home to help on the farms. When they returned, their knapsacks usually contained treats. When the sound of wagon wheels on the gravel roads was heard by those who had remained in the dorms, windows flew open, and the returnees were heartily welcomed.

Food boxes from the country were highly prized. The owner of such a box could expect an overflow crowd of visitors to his room as the aroma of fried chicken, cured ham, butter cake, or mincemeat pie pervaded the corridors. Other favorite foods from home were wild grapes, popcorn, molasses candy, hickory nuts, and black walnuts.

Despite memories of hunger on campus, shortage of food was not the biggest problem — money was. The crops of the late twenties were good-sized, and canning, pickling, and preserving were common. The chief money-making crop was cotton. In good crop years some students were able to pay their whole year's room-and-board bill in advance and thus take advantage of a 20 percent discount.

The amount of money needed to attend Langston in the 1920s

Thomas H. Black, Jr., wearing the required uniform that was in style from 1918 to 1930. These military outfits were worn to class, drill, and meals. Civilian clothes were worn on social occasions, and the boys donned overalls for work.

McKinley Fondren wearing the military-style boys' uniform.

was not out of line with expenses at other institutions. For Oklahoma students tuition was free; for out-of-state students the fee was $4.50. The room-and-board bill was $14.00 a month and the required duty work. In the first month of school the student had to pay athletic, medical, and incidental fees of $13.00, bringing the total needed to enroll to $27.00. There was an additional $5.00 charge for a student enrolled in commercial or instrumental music courses. Laundry was included in the room-and-board fee.

Throughout the 1920s students wore school uniforms and were subject to demerits for improper dress or behavior. When a student had received a certain number of demerits, the student could be sent home.

No boy or girl could appear in the dining hall, a classroom, a church, a Sunday school, a theater, or anywhere else outside his dorm room except in the prescribed uniform. From 1923 to 1934 uniforms were worn year round. Men wore khaki suits, shirts, hats, brown shoes, and spats modeled on World War I uniforms. The young women were required to wear navy-blue pleated skirts, white middy blouses with sailor collars, and silk ties of navy blue or red. A girl who could afford the full monthly fee might have a fancier uniform of blue serge with braid trimming on the middy collar and embroidered stars in the corners. Most of the girls had only two skirts — one for weekdays and a "good" one for Sundays. The pleats were a problem. All laundering and pressing had to be done at the campus laundry; electrical appliances were not allowed in the dorms. One solution was to fold the skirt carefully and put it under the mattress to press the pleats while the owner slept.

Students and faculty alike were required to attend flag-raising ceremonies every Wednesday morning at 5:30. Dormitory students were roused at 4:30. They lined up in the hallway, and everyone joined in a march around the campus that ended at the flagpole. The students marched in pairs, men and women separately. The university band led the procession. Faculty members were not required to march, but assembled at the flagpole. After arriving by the circular campus road, the students watched as the flag was raised. Devotions were held, with prayer, singing, and remarks by the president or dean. Every individual from the president down

The blue-serge middy with braid-trimmed collar, the girls' uniform from 1923 to 1930.

Flora Mae Johnson and Mable Walker wearing the university uniforms.

Hazel Folks wearing the navy-blue-serge suit chosen by girls who could afford them.

One of the weekly reviews at the flag pole each Wednesday from 1923 to 1927.

saluted the flag. The student body then circled the campus again and marched directly into the dining hall for breakfast at 6:30.

Attendance at the flag salute was ensured by dorm matrons, who checked each room. Students who tried to hide and avoid the early-morning procedure were not allowed to have breakfast or dinner that day. Dorm doors were locked to prevent students from returning to their rooms and then appearing for breakfast. They were required to carry their books to the flag salute and breakfast, because no one was permitted to return to the dorm until after the noon meal. Anyone who hid in the dorm was locked in for the whole morning, missing not only breakfast but also morning classes, chapel, and lunch.

Chapel was held every day at 11:45 A.M., and attendance was required. The only excuse was illness. Dorm rooms were checked, and if anyone missed chapel, the penalty was no dinner.

Chapel was held in the auditorium. The seats were numbered and assigned, and the vacancies were checked. On Wednesdays the students marched directly from chapel to the dining hall, following the band.

In the 1920s, chapel programs usually consisted of hymn singing, prayers, speeches, and announcements. The university faculty and students participated; the high school students rarely appeared on the programs. The entire faculty and student body joined in the singing. The chaplain, the Reverend William J. Starks (who also taught social science) led the prayers. When he was president of the school, Dr. I. W. Young sang "Jerusalem' or "I've Done My Work." (Those were his favorite solos). Throughout the year the Music Department presented solo recitals and band and the choral concerts. Faculty members demonstrated their talents as orators, musicians, artists, and poets.

During the football and basketball seasons part of the daily chapel period was given over to pep rallies. The team members were introduced, and the audience practiced school yells.

Sometimes visiting politicians, dignitaries, or members of the Board of Regents appeared. At other times the Art Department class brought easels, and E. J. Brown, the art instructor, and his students sketched or painted to music. Other organizations also presented chapel programs, among them the Philomathean, Spartan, Hyperion, Literati, and glee clubs. Each college class, from freshman to senior, also gave a chapel presentation.

Attendance was also mandatory at church and Sunday school services. Students were assigned the same seats as for weekday chapel, and matrons again checked the dormitory rooms to ensure attendance — and proper dress. Every student had to be out of the dormitories by 9:00 A.M., after signing out on a registration sheet at the matron's desk. Campus church services lasted from 10:00 to 11:00; then, if a chaperone was available, students could go into town to attend church services there. Everyone was expected back on campus for Sunday dinner, served at two in the afternoon.

The chaperone requirement extended beyond churchgoing. No young woman, whether alone or in a group, was allowed to shop, walk to the village, or attend movies or evening social events without a chaperone. A girl could receive a demerit for merely walking in the vicinity of the boys' dorm.

Besides locking the dorm doors to ensure attendance at flag ceremonies and church, faculty members also locked classroom doors upon occasion. Students had ten minutes to go from one classroom to another. Every classroom had a Yale thumb latch. A late student might find himself in the hall with a zero for the day.

Study hours in dorms were 7:00 to 9:00 P.M. No one was permitted out of the dorm room during that time, not even for personal matters. At 9:50 students were to get ready for bed. Lights were turned out at 10:00 P.M. The matron controlled all dorm lights for the dorm through a locked switch box. When the lights went out at ten, there was no more light until 5:30 the next morning.

Time off campus was a rare event and eagerly awaited. Field trips to Dripping Springs of Fitzgerald Creek were popular. Students considered it a treat to explore the campus farm or an old Indian cemetery northwest of the campus. Sewing-class students, accompanied by their instructor or the dorm matron, could go into the village to buy fabric, thread, and class materials. The town's business district was on East Washington Boulevard, about five blocks from campus.

Sometimes the entire class would walk to Coyle, a mile and half away, for a shopping trip. The Coyle Dry-Goods Store, owned by Mr. and Mrs. Goldstein, had a greater variety of dry goods. The students also went to Stockton's Grocery Store, in Coyle for sewing materials and snacks.

Shopping in Guthrie, ten miles from Langston, was out of the question unless parents furnished transportation. The trip took a whole day, even if the student walked to Coyle and then took the train to Guthrie. Of course, students could not go without a chaperone, and the dorm matrons could not be away from the campus for a whole day.

With students largely confined to campus, the social life was limited to weekly movies, dances, the annual spring formal, the yearly junior-senior banquet, hikes, picnics, and club parties. The socials were held in the dining hall after vesper services. At these affairs students could move about and chat with the president, the facuty members, and even members of the opposite sex!

Larger socials were held in the auditorium or gymnasium. A dance was led off with a grand march directed by the physical education instructor. All the students at the dance were required to

Allie B. Jones, R.N., dean of women and campus nurse, 1925-27 and 1935-41.

participate in the grand march, but dancing was optional. The kitchen crew prepared cookies and punch for refreshments. At Christmastime students received nuts, candy, and fruit at a party before dismissal for the holidays.

Movies in the 1920s did not have sound, of course, and a viewer had to read well to understand the plot. There was a ten-cent admission to the movies, which were shown on Wednesday and Friday nights. If a young man wished to escort a girl to the movies (or any other social function), he was required to write a formal note called a "comp." The comp usually took this form:

> Mr. John Jones
> requests the honor of
> the presence of
> Miss Carolyn Smith
> at the movie
> Friday, November 9, 1924
> Page Hall Auditorium
> 7 P.M.

Before the comp was delivered to the girl, it was inspected by the dean of men or women to make sure that it was in good taste — and that the girl was not under restriction. If all was well, then the note was sent to the dorm matron at least a week before the event. The girl who received the invitation had to answer it in writing at least three days before the occasion and deliver her answer to the matron, who would forward it to the sender. If the comp was not returned on time, it was considered rejected. Often girls did not receive comps from their boy friends, because the boys lacked the money for the occasion.

Perhaps the most revealing sign of the social times was an item contained in the 1923-24 student catalogue. It stated that "none of the social extremes of the present day will be tolerated." It permitted only "entertainment commensurate with proper decorum and good breeding" and only allowed "contact between the sexes falling far short of undue familiarity."

Souvenir Program

THE COLORED AGRICULTURAL AND NORMAL UNIVERSITY
LANGSTON, OKLAHOMA

TWENTY-SIXTH ANNUAL COMMENCEMENT
THIRTIETH YEAR OF ORGANIZATION

MAY NINETEENTH
A. D. NINETEEN HUNDRED AND TWENTY-SEVEN

UNIVERSITY AUDITORIUM

The Faculty and Graduating Classes
of the
Colored Agricultural and Normal University
Langston, Oklahoma
Cordially invite you to attend their
Twenty-sixth Commencement Exercises
Beginning Sunday, May 15th
and ending Thursday, May 19th
∼1927∼

Baccalaureate Exercises

Processional—"O Mother Dear Jerusalem" .... *Ward*
Choral Club and Audience No. 46 Assembly Books

Song—"Guide Me O Thou Great Jehovah" .... *Hastings*
No. 90 Assembly Books

Invocation .... Rev. W. J. Starks

Anthem—"Lead Me to the Rock" .... *Scott*
Choral Club

Scripture Reading—

Anthem—"Sanctus" .... *Gounod*

Solo .... Larney Webb, Assisted by Choral Club

Baccalaureate Address .... President I. W. Young

Anthem—"Inflamatus" .... *Rossini*

Solo .... Miss Gladys Tillman, Assisted by Choral Club

Announcements—

Doxology—

Benediction—

SENIOR COLLEGE CLASS

CLASS OFFICERS

NORMAN SHARP .... PRESIDENT
FRANK JONES .... SECRETARY
LEROY TROTTER .... TREASURER

CLASS MOTTO: "Onward"

CLASS FLOWER: White Carnation

CLASS ROLL

BROOKS, FERGUSON
COLLINS, CHARLES
ELLIS, WHIT J.
JONES, FRANK
SCOTT, THOMAS
SHARP, NORMAN
SMITH, MACEO
SPENCER, JOHN
TROTTER, JOHN

Commencement Program

I. Commencement Processional—
   Processional March
II. Song—"Negro National Anthem" .... *Johnson*
   Choral Club and Audience
III. Invocation .... Rev. E. W. McGrew
IV. Spiritual—"Listen to the Lambs" .... *Dett*
   Choral Club
V. Oration (Salutatory)—"Activities of the Subconscious Mind"
   J. H. Spencer
VI. Song—"Oh! Come Fair Maid" .... *Brown*
   Boys' Glee Club
VII. Oration (Agricultural) New Viewpoints In Scientific Agriculture"
   Frank Jones
VIII. Chorus—"Give Me My Native Isle" .... *White*
   Choral Club
IX. Oration (Valedictory) Education the Hope of Civilization
   J. LeRoy Trotter
X. Song—"Creole Love Song" .... *Smith*
   Girls' Glee Club
XI. Commencement Address .... Reverend H. T. S. Johnson, Oklahoma City. Okla.
XII. Spiritual—"He Is The Lilly of the Valley"
   The Choral Club
XIII. Conferring Degrees .... President Young
XIV. Doxology—
XV. Orchestra—
XVI. Honor Announcement—
   Magna Cum Laude—   J. LeRoy Trotter   John Henry Spenser
   Cum Laude—Frank Jones, T. P. Scott, N. R. Sharp, Maceo Smith.
   Distinction in Scholarship and Conduct leading to Certificate in the College of Education.
      Mattye Jackson   Bertha McKeever
      Amberlean Brown   Opaline Carter
   The Degree of Bachelor of Science in Education is conferred upon the following students: J. L. Trotter, Ferguson Brooks, N. R. Sharp, J. H. Spencer.
   The Degree of Bachelor of Arts is conferred upon the following student: T. Phurus Scott.
   The Degree of Bachelor of Science in Agriculture is conferred upon the following students: Charles Collins, Frank Jones, Maceo Smith.
XVII. The Conferring of Degrees .... President Isaac William Young A. M. M. D.
   The Candidates for degrees will be presented by Directors of Departments in the following order.
   Bachelor of Arts—Dean S. L. Hargrove, A. B.
   Bachelor of Science in Education—Prof. W. A. Easter, A. B.
   Bachelor of Science in Agriculture—Prof. Wm. T. Wells, B. S. A.

SENIOR NORMAL CLASS

CLASS OFFICERS

AMBERLEAN BROWN	President
LOTTYE BUSBY	Vice-President
ALCENIA BERNICE HOLMES	Secretary
MATTIE LOU JACKSON	Treasurer
LIZZIE MAE NEAL	Statistician
MARY GLASS	Poetess
Mrs. EMMA M. WELLS	Sponsor

CLASS MOTTO: "Climb Though the Rocks be Rugged"

CLASS COLORS: Old Rose and Gray

CLASS FLOWER: Sweet Pea

NORMAL GRADUATES

MURDAS BRISTER	PICCOLA FOSHEE	MATTIE JACKSON
AMBERLEAN BROWN	CORINNE GILES	HATTIE V. LONG
LOTTIE A. BUSBY	MARY GLASS	LIZZIE M. NEAL
ETHEL CALDWELL	VASSIE HARVEY	EDITH THOMPSON
GENEVA CHATMAN	AKEMIA HOLMES	ANNIE FAYE TRICE
LILLIE MAE COOKSEY	LOLA HUTTON	ORA WYATT
THELMA DICKENS	FAVIE LEE JACKSON	

SENIOR HOME ECONOMICS CLASS

CLASS MOTTO: "Launched but not Anchored"

CLASS FLOWER: Rose Bud (American Beauty)

CLASS COLORS: Tea Rose and White

CLASS OFFICERS

BERTHA MCKEEVER	President
ALMA GRANDBERY	Secretary
LAURA MEAUX	Treasurer

CLASS ROLL

CARTER, OPALINE
MCKEEVER, BERTHA
MEAUX, LAURA
WILLIAMS, ELLA MAE
GRANDBERY, ALMA

CLASS DAY EXERCISES—COLLEGE AND NORMAL CLASSES

Wednesday, May 18, 2:30 o'clock. On the Plaza

I.	"Langston Song"	
II.	Class Essay	Mattie Jackson
III.	Cornet Solo—Selected	Ferguson Brooks
IV.	Class Poem	T. P. Scott
V.	Class Oration	Ferguson Brooks
VI.	Violin Solo—Selected	Anna Fay Trice
VII.	Class History	Norman Sharp
VIII.	Solo Dance	Alsenia Holmes
IX.	Key Oration	Bertha McKeever
X.	Vocal Solo—Selected	Thelma Dickens
XI.	Class Song—Class	*Scott-Trice*
XII.	Appreciation	President I. W. Young

High School Exercises

Wednesday Evening, May VR, VTBG, 7:30 O'clock

—PROGRAM—

Song—"Negro National Anthem" ....*Johnson*
Class and Audience

INvocation ....Rev. W. J. Stark

Spiritual—"Where the work is being done" ....*Linsly*
By the Class

Salutorian ....Harding Jordon

Clarinet Solo—"Romanza" ....W. Wesenborn
Auzzie Garrett

Class Poem ....Bennie E. Toylor

Class History ....Erastus Byrd

Quartette—"Drink to me only with thine eyes" ....*Old English Air*
By members of the Class

Class Will ....Zennie M. Logan

Vocal Solo—"Duna" ....Bennie E. Taylor

Class Prophetess ....Alice Nelson

Valedictorian ....Lillie M. Bufford

Class Song—"Hail to Our Class" ....*Schultz*
The Class

Remarks:

Presentation of Diplomas ....President I. W. Young

The Benediction ....Rev. W. J. Stark

THE HIGH SCHOOL

CLASS MOTTO
"To the stars through bolts and bars"

Class Colors:—Lavender and Gold.

Class Flower:—Pink Carnaation

CLASS ROLL

CALLIE ARMSTRONG	EMMA A. GRIMES	ALICE E. NELSON
LILLIE E. BUFFORD	RUBY R. HOLMES	SAMMIE RUCKER
ZELLA J. BLACK	ANNIE MAY HITHYE	BENNIE ELMO TAYLOR
ERASTUS BAXTER BYRD	HARDING R. JORDON	ROBERT HENRY WILKERSON
CORDELIA E. GLADNEY	ALBERTA E. JOHNSON	JOHN ROBERT WALKER
AUZZIE M. GARRETT	ZENNIE MAY LOGAN	MYRTLE WALTON
		OLA BERTRAND

CLASS OFFICERS

President ....ERASTUS BAXTER BYRD
Vice-Presdent ....BENNIE ELMO TAYLOR
Secretary ....ZENNIE MAY LOGAN
Treasurer ....LILLIE E. BUFFORD
Class Poet ....BENNIE EIMO TAYLOR
Class Prophetess ....ALICE NELSON
Sponsor ....PROFESSOR B. C. EASTER

THE GIRLS' GLEE CLUB LANGSTON UNIVERSITY
will present

"Pan, On a Summer Day"
by Paul Bliss
(The pantomine and Ballet in one Act, nine scenes)
Tuesday evening, May 17, 1927, 7:30.

PERSONNEL

NIGHT .... Margaret Hutchison
BEES —Roy Moore, Jane Frances Moore, Masters Johnson, Eugene Gaines, Vernon Trice, Nolan McNamee, Rueben Hargrove, Lenard Jordan.
RAIN DROPS —Joyce Starks, Geneva McNamee, Olive Mae McDaniels, Flora Bell Benjamin, and Teddy Lovejoy.
COB-WEBBS —Ruth Johnson, Rylva Easter, Joseph Starks, Lorenzo Jordan.
DEW-DROPS —Maria Chapman, Whilahema Starks, Marie McNamee, Margaret Perkins. Rosa Lee Hill.
SUNBEAMS —Viola Miller, Vernice Powell, Francella Sanders, Hattie Gunn, Hattie Starks.
PAN .... Velma Pettus

PROGRAM

Scene I. At Day Break.
Scene II. Pan Awakes the World.
Scene III. Morning Song.
Scene IV A Summer Shower.
Scene V Noontide Rest by the River.
Scene VI Great Storm.
Ecene VII Pan Laments Over a Fallen Oak.
Scene VIII. Pan Pipes a Twilight Serenade.
Scene IX Night.

GLEE CLUB

TILLMAN, GLADYS	GRUMMITT, ESTHER	GREENE, WILLA
DICKENS, THELMA	BROWNLEE, CARRIE	HUSTON, ELWEDA
SHARP, SOLOTTIE	BRYANT, CHARLOTTE LENORE	BROWN, LENA
THOMPSON, ORA	WILLIAMS, MINNIE	PETTUS, GLADYS
JACKSON DOROTHA	HARRIS, LUELLA	BUSHY, LOTTIE
	GARRETT, REBECCA	

PAN, ON A SUMMER DAY
A CANTATA
Text and Music by Paul Bliss

From the first glint of dawn, to the rising of the full moon of summer night.

PAN IS NATURE IN SOUND

The "cheeping" of the birds, the "pit-pat" of the summer showers, the humming of the bees, the roar of the storm, the cracking of thunder, the wail of the wind, the chirp of the crickets, and the mysterious murmurs of the night.

(Synopsis)

On this summer day Pan plays his pipes as the world awakes, now humming softly, now with bird-calls.

The "Sunbeams" steal over the hills to draw up the "Dew-drops," (the "diamonds" which "Night" has dropped) resting on the downy pillows of "Gossamer Webs,' which are "little bits" of Night's trailing garments, torn off as she fled.

A "summer shower" ends abruptly.

At noon, Pan, in the reeds by the river, lulls the world to sleep with the "song of the bees."

In the afternoon, during a "Great Storm" Pan flies from the "Wind" and the "Rain".

After the storm, returning through the forest, Pan flies from the "mighty oak-tree, fallen."

In the twilight, Pan pipes a "serenade" to the myriad of dancing stars; only to hide in terror at the sight of the "slow rising moon."

All sounds of Nature (Pan) hush in breathless adoration to hearken to the music of the spheres in praise of "Night."

THE I. W. YOUNG PRIZE RHETORICALS
Monday Evening, May 16, 1927.

PART I

I. Music—"Dear Langston" .... Sadler-Work
II. Oration—"The New Negro" .... Rebecca Curtis Garrett
III. Oration—"Ideals The Dynamic Forces in American Achievement" .... Willa L. Greene
IV. Piano Solo—"Valse Caprice" .... Newland
    Anne Faye Trice
V. Oration .... Fatrie Jenkins
VI. Oartion .... Gladys Tillman

PART II

I. Oration—"The Renaissance in American Youth-1927'" .... Frank Jones
II. Trombone Sole—"After The Day" .... Anon
    Larney Webb
III. Oration—"The Imperialism of America'" .... Julius Caesar Hill
IV. Oration—"Is War Beneficial?" .... Reuben Maurice Jones Jr.
V. Vocal Solo—"Selected" ....
    Lena Brown
VI. Spiritual—
    School
VII. The Decision of the Judges—
VIII. Felicitations—
    President Isaac William Young

Commencement, 1927

In the early days the graduation activities lasted almost a week. In 1927, Langston held its Twenty-sixth Annual Commencement from Sunday, May 15 to Thursday, May 19. A two-color souvenir program listed the events and showed a picture of the long drive lined with white-washed trees leading to the Main Building.

The baccalaureate exercises began with the processional hymn "O Mother Dear Jerusalem," sung by the audience and the Langston Choral Club. Other music on the program included "Guide Me, O Thou Great Jehovah" and "Lead Me to the Rock." Two special anthems were presented: Gounod's "Sanctus" and Rossini's "Inflammatus." The soloist was Gladys Tillman, assisted by the choral group.

The Reverend W. J. Starks gave the invocation. The president of Langston, I. W. Young, made the baccalaureate address. Scripture reading and announcements, Doxology, and benediction completed the program.

Nine names were listed on the class roll. The senior-class officers for 1927 were Norman Sharp, president; Frank Jones, secretary; and LeRoy Trotter, treasurer. The class motto was the one word "Onward." The white carnation was the class flower.

The degrees were conferred at the commencement exercises, which included a processional march, presentation of candidates by the deans, and orations by the valedictorian and the salutatorian. The musical offerings were the Negro National Anthem, sung by the audience and the Langston Choral Club; "Listen to the Lambs," by the choral group; "O Come, Fair Maid," performed by the Boys' Glee Club; and "Creole Love Song," sung by the Girls' Glee Club. The Reverend H. T. S. Johnson, of Oklahoma City, delivered the commencement address.

Three kinds of degrees were bestowed in 1927: bachelor of arts (one student), bachelor of science in education (four students), and bachelor of science in agriculture (three students). In addition, four students earned certificates from the College of Education.

The degrees were conferred by President Young, with Dean S. L. Hargrove presenting the candidates for bachelor of arts and Professor W. A. Easter and Professor William Wells presenting the remaining candidates.

The class valedictorian was J. LeRoy Trotter, whose oration was entitled "Education, the Hope of Civilization." Trotter also shared with John Henry Spencer the honor of graduating magna cum laude. Spencer, class salutatorian, delivered an address entitled "Activities of the Subconscious Mind."

The senior normal class (the Teacher's College candidates) listed the usual class officers and also a class statistician and class poetess. Their motto for 1927 was "Climb Though the Rocks Be Rugged." In addition to the class flower, the sweet pea, the twenty girls also had class colors, old rose and gray. Finally, the senior home economics class had its own motto, flower, and color, as well as president, secretary, and treasurer for the graduating class of five.

Class-day exercises were held for both college and normal classes on Wednesday, May 18. The exercises, consisting of songs, essays, cornet, and violin solos, and the class history, were conducted on the plaza at 2:30 in the afternoon. The class poem was read by T. P. Scott. Bertha McKeever delivered the key oration. Mattie Jackson gave the class essay, and Norman Sharp read the history. At the end of the program, President Young responded with an "appreciation."

Wednesday evening at 7:30 the high school exercises were held. The class motto was "To the Stars Through Bolts and Bars." The class colors were lavender and gold, and the flower, the pink carnation. Again the program began with the class and audience singing the Negro National Anthem. The Reverend W. J. Starks gave the invocation. The class sang the spiritual "Where the Work Is Being Done." Students among the nineteen graduates participated in the program, giving the class history, the class will, and the class prophecy. A quartet sang "Drink to Me Only With Thine Eyes." Bennie Taylor sang the solo "Duna." The class song, sung in unison, was "Hail to Our Class." Diplomas were presented by President Young.

The president of the 1927 high school graduating class was

Erastus Baxter Byrd, and the valedictorian was Lillie M. Bufford.

On Tuesday evening during commencement week sixteen members of the Girls' Glee Club presented a production of Pan, on a Summer Day, consisting of pantomime and ballet. This was a classic playlet concerning the mythological Pan, who played his pipes as the world awoke. The girls played such roles as "Night," "Bees," "Raindrops," and "Sunbeams." The nine scenes, from daybreak to night, contained such movements as "A Summer Shower," "Pan Laments Over a Fallen Oak," and "Pan Pipes a Twilight Serenade." Music and text were composed by Paul Bliss.

The I. W. Young Prize rhetorical speeches were delivered in a two-part program. The program included piano solos, trombone solos, vocal selections, and the singing of the Langston hymn, "Dear Langston." Rebecca Curtis Garrett delivered an oration entitled "The New Negro." The title of Willa Greene's speech was "Ideals: The Dynamic Forces in American Achievement." Perhaps the most intriguing title was "Is War Beneficial?" The oration was delivered by Reuben Maurice Jones, Jr. Frank Jones spoke on the subject "The Renaissance in American Youth — 1927," and Julius Caesar Hill presented "The Imperialism of America." There is no record of the name of the winner.

CHAPTER EIGHT

Enrollment

WHEN the Colored Agricultural and Normal University opened its doors in Langston on September 3, 1898, the classes held in the Presbyterian church had a total enrollment of 41 students. There were four faculty members and a president, Dr. Page. Both faculty and boarding students had to room and board with citizens living in the town. Within two years the college enrollment had grown to 181 students. Of the total 15 were pursuing college-level work in the Normal Department, and 139 were elementary and high school students. In addition there were 27 students in night school. Of the total student body about 70 percent came from homes in the Langston community.

About 80 students from beyond Logan County had enrolled. The total student body represented twenty-one Oklahoma territorial counties. There was 1 student from Indian Territory, and 4 students came from other states (Texas and Missouri). Most of the students from other territorial counties came from north-central and northern Oklahoma: 9 from Guthrie, 6 from El Reno, 5 from Kingfisher, 3 from Perry, and 3 from Hennessey. Two students from Oklahoma City arrived for classes in 1899-1900.

Most of the students in the early days were enrolled in the elementary division. Statistics for 1900-1901 show that, out of a student body of 187, only 27 were eligible for Teacher's College work. There were 2 in the College Preparatory Department and 2 in the Select Course. The out-of-state students who enrolled at Langston in the formative years appear to have heard of the school through the wide distribution of the *Langston City Herald*. In 1901 students arrived from such faraway points as Cleburne, Texas; Glasco, Missouri; Kentucky, and Colorado. Apparently the students themselves also spread the word about the school during holidays and summers, for the enrollment from Indian Territory jumped from one the first semester to twelve the next.

While the enrollment in the early years continued to climb each semester, the number attending from the Langston community dropped. The first year local children made up approximately 70 percent of the student body; by 1902 it was closer to 40 percent. Thirty-four Oklahoma counties and eight different states were represented in the enrollment for 1902.

In the early years boys outnumbered girls in the College Preparatory Department, while female enrollment at the Teacher's College level was double that of males. In the lower grades (5 to 12) the distribution was more evenly balanced. For 1902-1903 the enrollment in the elementary division was 93 boys and 109 girls. Throughout the early years the largest enrollment was in the lower grades, ranging from 81 fifth-graders to 3 in the College Preparatory Department.

After the turn of the century Langston University began constructing new buildings, dorms, and equipment for labs and library. The improvement in the physical plant was reflected in increased enrollment, 253 in 1903-1904. The campus facilities then included a boy's dorm, the Mechanical Arts Building, the Main Building with an addition, a women's dorm and the president's residence. The acreage of the university had been increased from the original 40 to 160. Plans were under way to install steam heat in the main building and girls' dorm, build a waterworks, and construct a second girls' dorm.

Despite the increase in facilities the local enrollment continued to decline. Only 53 students from the immediate area were enrolled in 1904, while 155 came from Oklahoma Territory and 82 from Indian Territory. There were 16 students from Missouri, Tennessee, Texas, and Arkansas.

The first over-all decline in student enrollment occurred in 1906, a time of political turmoil and an apparent attempt to oust Page from the presidency. The total student body numbered 334, down from the previous year's high of 400. After eight years of operation, the elementary level still had the largest enrollment. The fifth grade was still the biggest class, with 129 children. In contrast, the College

Department had 3 men and 1 woman student. In the Normal Department there were 8 students — including a single male. One explanation for the low ratio of males was that many boys ended their education in the eighth grade in order to help their parents on the farms.

A political atmosphere surfaced periodically at Langston from 1906 onward. Although Dr. Page's administration did not end until 1915, there were attempts to remove him as early as 1906. A hearing by the Board of Regents resulted in a bitter fight, and Page had to make a personal appearance before the board to defend himself. At one point the regents appeared ready to call R. R. Taylor, a professor at Tuskegee Institute, to replace Page. Taylor declined the position after receiving scores of letters from Oklahoma Negroes telling him that he was the cause of political strife. Page went to Oklahoma City to the hearing at the Capitol Building, along with a delegation of fifty blacks. He carried a petition signed by nine hundred supporters.

The Board of Regents, seemingly set on replacing Page, offered him the position of dean of the Academic Department if he would step aside as president. After Taylor refused, several other educators applied for the post, and some of the regents still talked of the possibility of hiring another president by summer. The turmoil finally died down, however, and Page was not removed.

The bitter debate and the resulting publicity had its effect on enrollment. News items reporting the turmoil at the school appeared not only in the Langston paper but throughout the state. These unfavorable reports, together with rumors that the school might be closed, followed by the burning of the Main Building under suspicious circumstances in 1907, took a toll on enrollment.

A see-saw enrollment pattern set in, caused by changes in school administration caused in turn by changes in state governors. In 1908, there was a student body of 356; in 1910, 410. There was a drop to 392 students in 1912 and then an increase to 587 in 1914.

With the advent of World War I, which drained manpower, the election of Robert L. Williams as governor, and the departure of Page, there was a dramatic drop in Langston's enrollment. The number of students in 1915 was half what it had been.

ENROLLMENT

With the ouster of Page an unsettling series of "political" administrations took over at Langston (see Chapter 3). I. B. McCutcheon was president for a brief period, followed by Interim President R. E. Bullitt, who lasted an even shorter time. It was not until January, 1916, that things settled down with the arrival of John M. Marquess as president of Langston. But the rapid changes in administration had left students and prospective students in doubt about the school. Enrollment continued to fluctuate from year to year: the statistics for 1916 list 534 students; those for the next year show only 376. Again in 1918-19 enrollment hovered right at 300, 1920 shows another upswing, with an enrollment of 517.

About the time enrollment settled down and reached a peak of 591, election year 1922 rolled around. A new governor was soon followed by a new president for Langston. Governor John C. Walton began his administration, Dr. I. W. Young became president of Langston, and the roller-coaster enrollment took off again. There was continuing political turmoil during the mid-1920s. Langston students numbered 686 in 1922 when Governor Walton was impeached and removed, the Langston president was deposed, and general unrest again settled in for a siege. Martin Edward Trapp followed Walton as governor; Z. T. Hubert followed Young as president of Langston, and student enrollment dropped in successive years from 686 to a low point in 1928 of 231.

During Hubert's administration at Langston, a slow rebuilding began. About the time 500 students were again on campus the Depression arrived. In 1929 the enrollment was 508; in 1930 it dropped to 367.

Governor William H. Murray was inaugurated in January, 1931, and, as was expected, Langston shortly had a new administration — this time a former president back for a second term, Dr. Young.

During Dr. Young's second term, a leveling off in enrollment began, hovering around the 550 mark for most of the years 1931 to 1935. In Dr. Young's last year as president, 1935, there was a peak enrollment of 682. During those years economic conditions were bad, the dust-bowl era was devastating agriculture, and jobs for students on campus were severely limited.

During the Depression years, the system of student duty work gave way to small-paying jobs. Some students were able to earn a portion of their room and board through the National Youth Administration (NYA). Other government programs that helped Langston students and their families included the Works Progress Administration (WPA), the Federal Emergency Relief Administration (FERA), and federal soil-conservation programs.

Perhaps a sign of the hard times was reflected in the Langston University entrance application for 1934-35. It contained such questions as these: "How many brothers living?" "Has there been any tuberculosis in your family?" "Who will pay your bills with this school?" "Have you had mumps, measles, diphtheria, smallpox, chicken pox, or scarlet fever?"

In addition, prospective students had to sign a pledge promising "strict adherence to the rules and faithful application of... time to the work of the school."

The last years of the 1930s brought stability to the campus through federal relief programs and the administration of President J. W. Sanford, whose term in office coincided with that of Governor Ernest Marland. Enrollment increased by approximately 100 students each year during this time, achieving a total of 1,057 by the end of Sanford's term in 1939.

As related in Chapter 3, in the interim period from late 1939 to early 1940, Dean B. F. Lee served as acting president. Albert Turner was selected as the new president, but when he arrived on campus and found almost all his appointments already made, he left immediately. Finally, on January 5, 1940, G. L. Harrison assumed the presidency, and politics finally dropped out of the picture. Harrison's tenure was twenty years.

In the memories of students and administrators who lived through the topsy-turvy political years, there was never any doubt that the presidency of the school depended on working and voting for the winning gubernatorial candidate. Fuhr, in a Founder's Day address at the college in 1974, recounted how "the Langston University Alumni Association fought 25 years to rid Langston of this curse (politics). Eventually the Langston Alumni Association demanded and won the right to approve any nominee for president of the school. The only requirements the alumni stipulated were that the applicant must be free of Oklahoma political activity, must come from outside Oklahoma, and must hold a doctorate.

With Harrison's arrival, enrollment stabilized at the 900 mark. Then war broke out at the end of 1941, and enrollment fell sharply, to 681 in 1942 and 488 in 1943. In the last year of the war the enrollment was only 314. Of course, most of the students during those years were women. Altogether, 754 graduates and former students served in the armed forces.

With the end of the war and the surge in veterans' enrollment, things began moving again. The year 1945-46 showed a gain of double the previous year's enrollment, to 619 students, and there was a further increase in 1946-47, to 855.

Langston was accredited with the Veterans Administration in 1947, and students could enroll under the G.I. Bill of Rights. Additional improvements in the physical plant were made, and enrollment stabilized in the 700-student range.

Harrison had the distinction of serving as president of Langston under five Oklahoma governors: Leon Philips, Robert S. Kerr, Roy Turner, Johnston Murray, and Raymond Gary. When he resigned in 1960, he left of his own accord.

President William H. Hale began his administration at the beginning of the 1960-61 fiscal year. During his term of office (1960 to 1969), enrollment ranged from 659 to 1,336. The latter figure, reached in 1968, was the all-time high. The leap in enrollment was largely the result of the self-help programs developed by Hale and his wife. Hale's philosophy was that no worthy student, however impoverished, should be denied an education. During his administration the Development Foundation and the work-study and student-loan programs came into being. A huge building program brought facilities and living quarters up to standard. Another factor in Hale's favor was that he was the first Langston alumnus to return to become its president. Hale served under Governors J. Howard Edmondson and Henry Bellmon, a Democrat and a Republican.

A pattern of short-term presidents has been prevalent since the early 1970s. William E. Sims served for five years,, was followed by Interim President James L. Mosley and then by Thomas English, who served from 1955 until August, 1977. Interim President Ernest

Graduation procession, class of 1964. Courtesy of Public Relations Office, Langston University.

Holloway served from 1977 to early 1978. In April, 1978, Samuel J. Tucker became the thirteenth president.

A summary of Oklahoma territorial and state governors and Langston University presidents is given in Appendix B.

Throughout the stormy political seasons that have beset Langston University over the years, charges and countercharges have been leveled. Finances, personnel, and desegregation have been the bases for many investigations. Among the solutions proposed have been a massive building program, abolition of the school, concentration on "disadvantaged" youth, expansion to establish a graduate school, extensive recruitment of white students, and relocation to an urban center. The debate has usually included a cry from some politicians for a separate board of regents for the school.

ENROLLMENT

In 1977 the battle began anew with the resignation under fire of Thomas English. Statements by black political leaders calling for a separate board of regents were opposed by John Montgomery, the black member of the Agricultural and Mechanical Board. Montgomery called the idea of a separate board unworkable and said, "I shudder to think where the university would be without our staff and direction." Others on the board were in favor of shedding their responsibility for the school. Edwin Ketchum, of Duncan, chairman, insisted that Langston's "mismanagement problem has existed for three decades or more" and that Langston lacked a viable location and sufficient variety in course offerings to maintain enrollment.

The enrollment figure for 1975-76 was at 1,155. A graph in the Appendices shows enrollment trends in the years 1898 to 1978. Figures for 1977 show a total of 1,045 students, 722 of whom come from Oklahoma. Less than 10 percent of the student body was non black, despite stepped-up recruiting efforts aimed at whites. With the unsettled atmosphere surrounding the campus following the change of administration in the summer of 1977, Langston's enrollment again declined in the spring of 1978. The school showed 924 full-time students for the spring semester, and 943 students in the fall, 1978 semester. As of this writing the enrollment is 92 percent black.

CHAPTER NINE

Expenses

LANGSTON, being a state funded land-grant college, has never had to rely on student fees to finance the school. Indeed, tuition charges remained modest for many years and below those of other state institutions. From the beginning of classes in 1898 through 1936, tuition was free to Oklahoma residents. Out-of-state tuition began in 1923-24, with a fee of $4.50 per semester. This fee rose to $10.00 a year in 1925-26, payable in advance.

Even without tuition expenses it still cost money to go to school. A member of the first class was charged $6 a month for room and board with a local family. For this fee the student received "board, a furnished room, fuel, and light." Registrants had to bring their own sheets and blankets. The laundry fee was $1 a month, a fee that remained unchanged until the 1950s — and was probably the best bargain in Oklahoma higher education. In addition to room and board a student had to buy his own books.

In the early 1920s a student could reasonably expect to enroll properly for $30. The fees were listed as free tuition, $14 for the first month's room and board, $1 for laundry, $4 for medical service (including doctor's care, nursing, and medicine), and $4 for an athletic deposit. This left $1 for incidentals. At that time twenty-four scholarships were offered in the Agriculture Department, open to boys only. All students were expected to do "duty work" or pay an additional $4 a month. The high school charged a $3 graduation fee.

Various additional fees were instituted in the 1920s: a $5 fee for an instrumental-music course and a $5 fee for a science lab. In 1929 the first general "registration fee" was charged — $3 for each student. Later, student fees included a $5 diploma fee, a $2 "lecture and library" fee, and a $1 lab fee to cover breakage.

During the depression years of the 1930s room, board, and laundry were $15 a month, and athletic, library, and medical fees, grouped together as "student activity fees," totaled $11 a semester. These charges were a reduction of $1 a month in room rent and $2 a semester in activity fees from the years 1930-31. The hard times were reflected both in enrollment statistics and in the fees charged. A late-enrollment surcharge of 50 cents a day was added to the registration fee. The maximum penalty for late enrollment was $2.

With the outbreak of World War II inflation caught up with the university economy. In 1941-42, the registration fee was $17.75, and assorted small fees such as the "regent's fee" of 75 cents and a 25-cent key deposit added to the expenses. The dorms were then charging $21 a month for room and board, except for Sanford Hall (a federally funded dormitory), which cost a dollar more a month.

Fees proliferated during the war years: home economics ($4), commerce ($4), and state property deposit ($5). The registration fee increased to $18 in 1943-44. An additional $25 was charged an out-of-state student. It was suggested in the catalogue that a student could live comfortably at Langston on a budget of $275 a year.

The transition from registration fees to the beginning of the tuition-per-credit-hour system began with the 1948-1950 biennium. The fees were still listed as registration fees but broken down as $3 per semester hour for Oklahoma students and $8 per credit hour for out-of-state enrollees. All fees were payable in advance. Students whose fees were more than five days past due could be sent home. Additional fees were charged for private lessons in the fine arts (speech or applied music at $18 per credit hour), aviation lessons, driving instruction, art, auto mechanics, and carpentry. The proposed "comfortable" budget was estimated at $450 a year. Dorm rooms cost $35, $36, or $37 a month, depending on whether the student selected a "front" room or a federally funded dormitory.

The formal tuition-per-credit-hour system began in 1955-56 and marked the end of the registration-fee system. The tuition structure was $4.50 per credit hour for Oklahoma students. Gradual tuition raises occurred at approximately four-year intervals after the instigation of the credit-hour rates. In 1960-61 the tuition was $5.25 for residents and $13 for out-of-state students. In 1967-69 the estimated budget for a year at Langston was $776 for in-state students and $1,072 for out-of-state students. Room was $15 a month, while board cost $40 a month. The cost of books and supplies was about $75 for the academic year.

The 1970s brought increases in the amounts and numbers of fees paid by students. While tuition rose slowly (from $9 per credit hour in 1970 to $10.50 in 1975-76), the charges in other areas were inflationary. There were "cultural and recreational" fees totaling $12.50 a semester, student-center fees, transcript fees, identification-card fees, and charges for adding or dropping courses. The cost for a semester at Langston at the beginning of the decade was approximately $500, and by the mid-1970s was estimated at closer to $700 a semester for in-state students.

Financially, Langston has always been handicapped by the location of its campus, which prevented many students from securing jobs near the university. In the 1970s a survey of students revealed that fully 80 percent received funds from sources other than parents. These sources included summer savings, part-time campus work, loans, and grants.

Some of the programs providing financial assistance were student loans financed by the federal government, the State Regents Waiver of Tuition, GI benefits, Indian Affairs Bureau grants, and the Basic Educational Opportunity Grants. The last program provided grants of up to $975 for in-state students and $1,238 for out-of-state students. The projected cost of a school year at Langston in 1975-76 was as follows:

Tuition	$ 390
Books and supplies	150
Room and board	960
Personal & Travel	450
	$1,950
Out-of-state, add.	530
	$2,480

All students applying for financial aids are channeled through the College Scholarship Service. Langston offers a variety of aids, all of which can be classified as (1) grants, (2) loans, or (3) work-study programs.

Industrial scholarships increased rapidly in the 1960s. One program, sponsored by Kerr-McGee Oil Corporation of Oklahoma City, provided eight four-year scholarships for students in business administration. In addition, summer jobs were provided at Kerr-McGee facilities. Part of the thrust of the program was to enable graduates to secure employment in Oklahoma. Statistics for the graduating class of 1963 showed that 54 percent had had to move out of state to find jobs.

Commensurate with the low fees charged students in the early years were low faculty salaries. Figures are lacking for faculty salaries of the early years, but the original Board of Regents voted to pay the first president, Inman Page, a salary of $2,500 a year. As late as 1945 a faculty member with a master's degree was receiving only $120 a month. When the university applied for accreditation from the National Council for the Accreditation of Teacher Education, the salary range in the institution ranged from $5,090 a year for instructors to a top salary of $7,440 for full professors. That same year the faculty consisted of forty-six degree-holding members — four with bachelor's degrees, thirty-five with master's degrees, and seven with doctorates.

By 1969 a full professor could expect to receive $12,571 a year. With the stabilizing and raising of salaries, the turnover rate of faculty declined. Langston's self-study report, entitled *Task Forces for the Seventies,* showed that as of 1972 the highest salary range was $25,000 to $31,000 a year for "distinguished professorships" while the base pay for new instructors was $9,500.

In comparison with other state institutions, Langston's faculty salary scale has been below that of the major four-year institutions but above that of the junior colleges. In general, through the mid-1960s, Langston's pay scale was about equal to that of Cameron College, Connors, Panhandle A&M and the college at Chickasha. In 1975 a freeze was put on academic pay increases until a detailed study could be submitted to the State Board of Regents. At a budget meeting, Langston had requested a budget of $1.9 million, an increase from the previous year of $292,000, most of which was earmarked for salary raises. At that time Langston was under the administration of an interim president, James Mosley, and he requested pay increases for 250 of 254 faculty and staff members. Part of the regents' hesitation in the matter was due to the financial problems of the institution, which included a declining enrollment and growing indebtedness. Plans were made to collect student loans that had not been repaid. The regents asked the incoming president, Thomas English to restudy and then resubmit the requests for faculty pay increases.

In 1977 salary increases amounting to 25.5 percent were granted the Langston faculty. The salary of a full professor jumped to an average of $18,861. Instructors' salaries averaged $11,387. Faculty salaries remained in the lower range of the state institution averages, however.

Support personnel employed by the school fared poorly in regard to salaries. For example, in 1943 the proposed annual salaries for the librarian and the business manager were slightly below $3,000. The part-time physician was paid $1,500, and the head nurse, $1,800. At that time department heads and full professors drew $2,900 a year, and the president's salary was $5,700.

The following chart has been constructed from material developed by the Office of Fiscal Affairs for the annual reports of the State Board of Regents:

Average Salaries, Langston University, Selected Years (9-10 Months)

Year	Instructor	Assistant professor	Associate professor	Professor
1961-62	$ 4,820	$ 5,799	$ 6,795	$ 7,215
1964-65	5,215	6,169	7,230	7,654
1968-69	7,608	9,141	10,777	11,666
1974-75	8,553	9,844	11,756	13,178
1977-78	11,579	13,725	16,017	19,000

School Days School Days, 1915

In the early days of the junior and senior high school at Langston University, classes kept histories of their progress through the grades. Here are excerpts from the histories of members of the class that entered the seventh grade in 1915, through their highschool graduation in 1922:

Thirty-five little boys and girls with neatly brushed hair and braided pig tails weighted down with large bows of ribbon, all with shining morning faces — this was the 7th grade in the fall of 1915. At Christmas time a number of our classmates went home and did not return, causing a decrease which left us but twenty strong. The first year we were seen but not heard.

Our next year found among the 16 important 8th graders only three, T. Bannarn, O. Harris and L. Brooks who had belonged to the Old Guard.

These same three, upon entering the freshman class, welcomed a number of new members. Chester Bonam was chosen pilot to guide our little "freshie" plane. Before the school year closed, Louise Brooks had to leave because of illness and at the close of the last term she departed this life.

In our sophomore year we were organized into one family and although our former class president left us before we were organized, only returning a year later, we chose one of the new, yet earnest members of the class for our president. We really spread our wings this year, although we had no basketball team or other organizations.

In the fall of 1920 we entered our Junior year with more pep and determined that if grit and gumption meant crossing any goal, we were on the winning side. Sidney Moore was highly honored by being selected president of the class.

On the faculty we found one of the most prominent scientists among Negro women in the person of Mrs. Meriem Sims Jackson, who was elected as our class sponsor.

In the spring of 1921 we entertained with the annual Junior-Senior banquet which was said by all who attended to be one of the most magnificent affairs ever given by students in old Langston University.

We were fortunate to have the responsibility of placing our basketball team on the floor. The girls' team was led by Bertha Cook. The boys' team was led by Sidney Moore. Everyone was surprised when our boys won the game against the freshman class.

Theresa A. Black and Thomas H. Black, Jr., in 1916, the year Thomas entered Langston Boarding School. (Theresa was still in grade school.)

The fall of 1921 found us entering our senior preparatory class and still nearer our goal. We elected Professor Paul McCree as our sponsor.

We are still fortunate to have Sidney Moore as our president. There were three special vocational courses offered and the senior preparatory class took advantage of these opportunities. Out of the class of 52, there were twelve young ladies who took domestic science and art and four ladies and three young men who took the commercial course. We are not stopping yet but are marching onward to accomplish greater things in the future.

CHAPTER TEN

Student Organizations

THE FIRST GROUP formally organized on the Langston campus was a literary club for girls. Named the Literatae Club, it was started in 1919 under the sponsorship of Bessie Floyd Dungee. The membership consisted of Normal School students, six from the junior class and six from the senior class. The stated goal was the "development of better womanhood." The motto was "Deeds, Not Words," the colors blue and white, and the purpose both literary and social.

Apparently the Literatae was a resounding success, for within two years there were other clubs for both boys and girls. Girls in the Teacher's Department organized the Phyllis Wheatley Club. Boys in the high school could join the Lions Club. The Spartan Club drew its male members from both the College and the Normal Department. For girls in Prep Department, there was the Philomathean Club.

In 1922 the accomplishments of the Literatae Club were listed as furnishing the journal for chapel on Fridays, giving the commencement play and donating thirty-five dollars to the gymnasium fund. They presented two plays, *Engaged by Wednesday* and *The Dust of the Earth*.

The girls' club pin was a circle connecting three triangles. The chairman of the program committee, Wylma Frances Reed, composed a song to build spirit for the group. Sung to the tune of the *Jubilate,* the words were: "Hark! The girls of dear old Langston have organized a club! Lofty ideals, higher standards will our motto ever be."

All the organizations of the early 1920s adopted mottoes and colors. The Philomathean motto was "Knowledge is the Key to Success." The emblem of the club, a golden key, was supposed to open their hearts to learning. Commandments for this girl's club included: "Number One — Preps, thou shalt have no other club before this," and, perhaps more important, "Number Nine — Thou shalt not take another club member's shoelaces, hairpins, beau nor anything that belongs to thy club sister."

Some of the girls who did not join either the Literatae or Philomathean clubs organized the Phyllis Wheatley Club. This organization became known as the Esoteric Club in 1922. In those days junior and senior girls lived in Attucks Hall, a frame dorm, while the freshmen, sophomore and high school girls roomed in Phyllis Wheatley Dorm. The clubs were organized along class and dorm lines because it was against regulations for girls to leave their dorms after seven in the evening.

Two boys' clubs were started in the early 1920s. Mary Smith organized the Lions Club for prep boys. The Spartans were sponsored by William Kelley. The first president of the Spartans was V. N. Ray, and there were fifteen charter members.

The Langston campus YWCA held a membership drive in January, 1922, and enrolled sixteen girls. A continuing drive for members was held every Sunday, and by the time the national secretary, Juliette Derricotte, visited the campus on February 26, there were 76 members. Eventually membership reached 125.

Topics for discussion at YWCA meetings included "Courtesy," "Motherhood," "Everyday Religion," and "The Young Woman of Langston." In 1922 the president of the university, J. M. Marquess, made plans to hire a paid secretary to live on campus and work with the girls in YWCA.

The University Concert Band was open to both men and women. It met twice a week and gave concerts at the Campus Band Stand and in the auditorium and played at ballgames and for campus marches. Also in the music department were the University Choral Club, the Treble Clef Club, Octette, and the Spartan Quartette.

By 1927 clubs took up more than ten pages in the college annual, *The Claw*. The Philomathean was still going strong under the sponsorship of Dean S. L. Hargrove. The Spartan Club proudly told about holding their annual banquet, whitewashing campus trees, building a sidewalk at the east entrance of the Main Building and initiating the college round table. New clubs on the scene were the

Charter members of the Spartan Club, organized in 1922. Front row, seated, left to right: Vernon Ray, president, and William Kelley, sponsor. Second row, left to right: Thomas H. Black, Jr., Roosevelt Hill, Whit Ellis (holding tray), Semond Townsend, Tommy Graves, William Glover, and Floyd King. Top row, left to right: Booker T. Robinson, Thomas Capers, National Hawkins, Herod Ward, and Peter Parrish. Courtesy of Booker T. Robinson.

Hyperion, which seems to have borrowed the Literatae's old motto, "Deeds, Not Words." Literatae now spelled its name Literati. The Lions had a sister club called the Lioness. The Chancelor Club, Utopia, the University Band, the Boys' Glee Club, the Girls' Glee Club, the University Quartette, the Mozart Musical Choral Club, the Mixed Glee Club, the University Orchestra, the Popular Or-

Temporary buildings transported to the campus from Amarillo Air Field at the end of World War II and used as a student recreation hall until 1965. Courtesy of Public Relations Office, Langston University.

chestra, and one Greek-letter fraternity, Delta Gamma Alpha, completed the roster of clubs.

Many of the original clubs lasted through the 1930s and 1940s. Greek-letter fraternities were strong during the 1930s; the 1934-35 catalogue listed chapters of Delta Gamma Alpha, Omega Psi Phi, Alpha Phi Alpha, and Kappa Alpha Psi. Greek sororities on the campus were Alpha Kappa Alpha (Alpha Zeta Chapter), Delta Sigma Theta (Beta Upsilon Chapter), Sigma Gamma Rho (Iota Chapter), and Zeta Phi Beta (Lambda Chapter).

Many clubs existed for several years, changed names and memberships, and then disappeared from the lists in the yearbook, *The Lion*. Some had interesting names, such as the Lampados Club, Zeta Zeta Zeta, L'Etude de Musique, and the Sphinx Club. One of the largest clubs in the 1930s was the Aggie Club, the organization of students in the Agricultural Division. Their achievements for 1934-35 were listed as presentation of a debate in chapel, a fall garden show, an exhibit and a one-act play on Founder's Day, and the organization of a cooperative growing and marketing association.

In the later years of World War II students at Langston formed a traveling entertainment troupe and gave programs for servicemen

Sadie Waterford Jones. Courtesy of Sadie Waterford Jones.

stationed at Fort Sill, the navy bases at Norman, and Camp Gruber, in eastern Oklahoma.

Although details on the early days of student societies are sketchy, apparently some were flourishing shortly after the turn of the century. Sadie Waterford Jones remembers that both the literary society and the YWCA were strong on campus at the time she graduated in 1911. She carried her interest in group organization with her to Muskogee County where she led Red Cross and Liberty Bond drives during World War I. After the war she began a long career of establishing learned and benevolent societies. In Muskogee she organized the War Camp Community Center, which later functioned as the USO. She also began the Social Uplift Club, and this society celebrated its fiftieth anniversary in 1968.

In 1922, Mrs. Jones established the Phyllis Wheatley Community Center in Fort Wayne, Indiana, which is today the Fort Wayne

Urban League. While living in the Chicago area, she founded the Langston University Club of Chicago. In 1940 she returned to the campus as keynote speaker for the Daughters of Langston. In 1954, she spoke at Founder's Day celebration. She also attended Founder's Day and Homecoming activities in 1978. Among her most important projects was the founding of the Halfway House for Dependent Girls, in Chicago. Completed in 1975, it was named Sadie Waterford Manor.

She was married to Gilbert Jones, a former Langston coach (in 1909) and president of Wilberforce University, Wilberforce, Ohio.

In the early 1940s there were seven musical organizations open to students. A collegiate chapter of Kappa Delta Phi, a national educational society, was chartered at Langston in 1953, making the campus the third Negro chapter.

Among Langston's outstanding attractions were the Dust Bowl Players, begun in 1952 under the direction of poet-dramatist Melvin Tolson. Serving as more than a campus drama lab, the Dust Bowl Theatre produced ethnic drama, including original scripts of *Moses of Beale Street, Southern Front,* and an adaptation of George S. Schuyler's novel *Black No More.* The players appeared before the National Baptist Convention in 1952 and performed for the conclave of the NAACP in 1953, presenting *Fire in the Flint.*

The Black Student Union was organized in the early 1970s. In 1975 the name was changed to Black People's Union.

CHAPTER ELEVEN

The Student Strike of 1928 and Other Protests

On the cold autumn morning of November 3, 1928, the entire student body of Langston University assembled in the auditorium of old Page Hall. They met to air their grievances against the university in general and two unpopular deans in particular. The unrest had been growing for some time, particularly over the cases of two girls who had been summarily fired from their campus jobs. A list of demands, termed "resolutions," had been drawn up by a three-man committee and presented to President Zachary T. Hubert. The list of resolutions had called for action no later than 8:00 A.M. on November 2. When the deadline came and went with only a meeting to show for it, the students called their own mass assembly to air their complaints.

The committee that had drafted the resolutions had called their complaints a campaign for human rights. They had called on the president, first, to remedy the actions of instructors that had resulted in the firing of the student employees. They wanted a student-labor wage of twenty cents an hour: the dismissal of the dean of women, whom they accused of having caused "turmoil and a continued aggravation and distemper among the student body since she has been connected with the institution (three years)," and the removal of Thomas as acting dean of the boys' dorm. They asserted that Professor Thomas had threatened students, had drawn a pistol on one, and was in general "ill-tempered, overbearing, unjust and prejudiced" in his disciplinary decisions.

During the Saturday morning assembly, November 3, further complaints were made. The session was called to order by Roosevelt T. Gracey. Among the resolutions were demands that the library stay open in the evenings from seven till nine, that more and better food be served in the dining hall, and that "no student lose his job

J. S. Thomas, acting dean of men.

because of his participation in the campaign for student rights."

There was a general dressing down of President Hubert's administration. Hubert had been on campus nearly two years. He had come from Jackson College in Mississippi with a background in science and chemistry. He was a scholarly man, slender, quiet, and dignified. He did not care about politics — nor, apparently, did he concern himself deeply with the student political situation. He sent word to the assembly that he would like to meet with a committee composed of two members of each class.

At the meeting held at 10 A.M. the same morning, the president received a list of ten issues the students wanted settled. The first item on the demand list was the student wage. President Hubert did not promise the twenty-cent wage for all jobs, but he did compromise and suggest that certain hard manual jobs, such as ditch digging and pipe laying, which had previously been done by off-campus laborers, could be reserved for students, who would be paid thirty-five cents an hour.

Ella P. Baker, dean of women and school nurse.

On the matter of better food Hubert blandly stated there was no reason for anyone to be hungry, especially since board fees had been raised two dollars a month.

The students demanded the removal of Dean Ella P. Baker as dean of women. They had been trying to get her dismissed for nearly two years. Here Hubert displayed his political skills. He implied that the matter was out of his hands, that the Board of Regents had the power to hire and fire, and that perhaps a student council could be organized in two weeks and that *they* could ask the regents to dismiss the dean.

There was complete agreement between Hubert and the student committee that no student lose academic credit for participating in the student protest. On the matter of firing students, Hubert was certain no one would be dismissed who gave "satisfactory results."

On the demand of students that Professor Thomas be replaced as dean of Marquess Hall, Hubert gave in, agreeing to replace the man immediately. The same was true of the request that the library

Moxye Weaver King, chairman of the English Department, presenting an award on Awards Day, 1965. Courtesy of Public Relations Department, Langston University.

be kept open in the evenings. He also thought that the formation of a student council would be a good idea. In his opinion a student council would produce "better results, ... and it would be a relief to the faculty."

One of the basic disagreements concerned the teaching load. Many teachers were wearing two academic hats, teaching in both college and high school departments and carrying large class loads. Many used upper-level students as assistants. For example, a student named Moxye Weaver taught English classes for W. E. Anderson. A few students complained about being taught by one of their peers. The result was her abrupt dismissal. Her summary firing was one of the incidents that triggered the confrontation with Hubert. But Hubert's reply to the charge that the school had insufficient teachers was merely to assure the committee that he was endeavoring to obtain more instructors.

THE STUDENT STRIKE OF 1928 AND OTHER PROTESTS

The tenth and final demand seems incongruous in comparison to the academic tone of the first nine. It concerned setting up a pressing shop where the boys could iron and mend their clothes. Everyone agreed that it was needed and would soon be ready.

Financial records were kept of the costs of financing the strike of 1928. They came to $5.50. The money was raised through student donations, mostly in nickels, the largest contribution being 25 cents. A Mr. McGhee had lent the committee $1.25, and when he was repaid, $4.25 was left in the treasury to meet the expenses of the "Campaign for Student Rights."

By Tuesday, November 6, approximately two-thirds of the students were boycotting classes. For those who did go to class life was not easy. The Committee on Student Rights had met on Monday afternoon at 2:30 to take the nonparticipants to task and "hearing apologies from students who did not cooperate in the movement." Names were taken, and apologies or defenses were heard from each student.

The accusations, countercharges, and apologies ran the gamut from spirited defense of attending class to abject excuses. Most bowed to the committee, saying they felt they had done "an injustice" to the strikers and had not "clearly understood the movement." Some promised that they were "with" the students.

One girl said that she went to class because she feared her grades would drop. Another said that she had a sister on the faculty and felt that she could not oppose her. Some were braver, saying they neither understood nor cared about the strike and would have gone to class under any circumstances. One girl, Minnie Williams, insisted that her conscience was her guide and felt that she had done no injustice to anyone. Savanah Taylor went a step further, saying that she would not cooperate with the strikers under any circumstances. However, most of the students called on the carpet apologized and promised to cooperate.

On the same afternoon the first student council was organized in President Hubert's office. R. T. Gracey was elected president, and the girl whose job had been the cause of much of the commotion, Moxye Weaver, was acting secretary. It was decided that the council should be composed of four seniors, three juniors, two

Roosevelt T. Gracey, leader of the campaign for student rights in the 1928 strike and first president of the Langston Student Council. Gracey was expelled from Langston but later graduated from Lincoln University, Jefferson City, Missouri. Courtesy of R. T. Gracey.

sophomores, and one freshman. The function of the student council was to "solve, judge and pass on problems and matters pertaining to the student body." In fact, all they could do was send their recommendations on to the president. A faculty member appointed by the administration was to serve as an adviser to the student council. Their term on the council was to be one year, and Hubert urged the students not to engage in "too much electioneering," to avoid friction. Candidates were to be nominated by classes and elected by the student body at large. The council members would elect their own officers and draft a constitution and bylaws, which would be ratified by the student body. The first elected officers of the student council were Roosevelt Gracey, president; Joseph Brown, vice-president; Theresa Black, secretary; and Wilnard George, sergeant-at-arms. Professor William Bell was faculty adviser.

The first council meeting was held on November 19, 1928. The members took up the ongoing problem of the firing of Moxye Weaver and also the students' unhappiness with the dean of women. A committee of two boys and one girl was appointed to meet with Dean Baker and see about restoring Miss Weaver's job as well as

THE STUDENT STRIKE OF 1928 AND OTHER PROTESTS

Theresa A. Black, the first secretary of the Langston Student Council.

Miss Marshall's. Concerning discipline, the student council decided to try a demerit system. President Hubert suggested that the council first make up a list of offenses and the penalties to be assessed.

By November 26, the council was back in session, deciding to "investigate" the case of Moxye Weaver, to meet more than once a month, and to ask President Hubert to write out exactly what "power" the council had.

The next day the council met again, establishing Room C upstairs in Page Hall as a permanent meeting place. Again they decided to investigate Moxye Weaver's case and see if they could get her "punishment" lifted in time for her to go to the game on Thursday (she had been restricted to the dorm). Other problems were the conduct of some boys in Marquess Hall and students cutting campus.

By December results were apparent. The library was open from 7:00 until 10:00 P.M. three nights a week. Students of both sexes could go to the library unchaperoned, merely by signing in, though girls and boys still had to study at separate tables.

On December 17 the council summoned its nerve and sent a

letter to the dean of women asking for her resignation. Apparently Dean Baker neither resigned nor mended her ways, for the next communication from the student council read: "Dear Madam: Because of mitigating circumstances, we the student council, recall the letter written to you on 1928 Dec. 17, asking for your resignation. We are filing charges against you with the proper authorities."

Still no action was taken, and with the holidays and promises of investigations, feelings of rebellion subsided. By the middle of January, however, trouble was brewing again. Students felt that no action was going to be taken concerning the dean of women and that, after two years of lobbying against her, they were tired. They presented their case to both alumni and press, to no avail. Finally, on January 24, 1929, one hundred students went out on strike. On the next day, Friday, January 25, 90 percent of the student body stayed away from classes. That left only fifty students in class (out of an enrollment of 533), and the school was closed.

Students printed a long article concerning their grievances entitled "The Other Side of the Question at the C.A.&N.U." In it they accused the dean of women of being uncooperative, unapproachable, unsympathetic in her dual role as school nurse and dean. "Her ideas are old and are those not found in up-to-date institutions." The Board of Regents came to the campus for a meeting on January 11 but tossed the ball back to President Hubert, saying that the matter was in his hands. Hubert refused to take any further action, and the strike ensued.

Several unfortunate incidents occurred during this period, one involving an accident in the chemistry lab. A bottle of sulfuric acid broke, drenching the legs of a girl student who according to reports was not properly cared for by the nurse (who happened to be Dean Baker). Another student, whose mother had died, was refused permission to make telephone calls on campus. Finally, several students were suspended, including the captain of the football team, the president of the literary society, the head of the YMCA, and the presidents of the senior, junior, and sophomore classes.

The faculty met the crisis by recommending the transfer of Dean Baker from the dorm to the Extension Department, the suspension until May 23 of the five leaders of the unrest, and "the suspension

Roosevelt T. Gracey when he graduated from Lincoln University, Jefferson City, Missouri. Courtesy of R. T. Gracey.

from the dining hall and dormitory of all students who did not attend classes."

The strike was still in effect on January 29. By then state newspapers were taking note. The *Black Dispatch* headlined four different stories about the school: "Hubert Clamps Lid on Strike," "Students of Insurrection Find Their Trunks are Labeled for Home," "Faculty and F. D. Moon, Alumni Head, Stand Four Square by President," and "Hargrove Gets Axe." The Oklahoma Association of Negro Teachers passed a resolution "unanimously in favor of government by the President and Faculty."

After the suspension of the five student council members, more than two hundred students signed a petition stating that they were "equally guilty." During this time less than a third of the student body was attending classes.

Of the five students who were suspended, only two returned to the campus. Fourteen students were eventually disciplined for the strike, six more were suspended, and three were temporarily suspended, sentence withheld. The apparent leader of the campaign for student rights, Roosevelt Gracey, was not allowed to reenter the school, but he went on to obtain his B.A. from Lincoln University, in Jefferson City, Missouri, and his master's degree from Columbia University in New York City.

With the transfer of the dean of women to the Extension Department, the removal of the campus leaders, and the reinstatement of Moxye Weaver in her campus job, the turmoil subsided. After she completed her education, Moxye (Weaver) King returned to the Langston campus to teach and later became chairman of the English Department.

There have been other incidents of unrest at Langston during its eighty-year existence. In 1937, during President Sanford's tenure, a food strike was called. Students took their plates and dumped the food, uneaten, into the garbage cans in protest against what they considered "inadequate" nutrition standards.

In the 1960s, following the resignation of popular President William Hale, students marched to the state capitol and kept a vigil. Newsmen were expelled from the Langston campus for a time.

In more moderate times such activists as Dick Gregory have visited the campus without incident. A local disturbance in 1977 concerned the student bookstore. A protest rally was held to complain about book-pricing policy and the conduct of the business manager. Early in 1978 students made several trips to the state capitol to lobby for increased funding for Langston and for promises that the school would remain open. In March students sat in the halls of the governor's office and the legislature, on one occasion blocking exits.

The students unrest stemmed from the university's continuing financial and administrative plight. It was hoped that a pacifying visit to the campus by Governor David Boren and the announcement that Samuel J. Tucker had been selected as the new president of the university would lessen tension.

The adverse publicity and uncertain political stand of the legislature contributed to a drop in enrollment for the spring, 1978, semester, to fewer than one thousand full-time students. The fall, 1978, enrollment showed little if any increase.

CHAPTER TWELVE

The Library

WHEN Langston University opened in 1898, students were asked to bring their own textbooks. Most of the enrollees were in the elementary division, and the approved texts included *McGuffey's Fourth Reader* and *Fifth Reader,* British and American classics, and John Fiske's *History of the United States.* There were forty-one books on the list to be used by the Elementary and Normal departments. Students were told not to buy next texts until they had taken entrance examinations and were properly classified. Textbooks were available in Langston.

The first mention of a "library" occurs in the 1900 edition of the school bulletin. The books available in the library consisted of "carefully selected" reference and general works. The school owned six hundred volumes at that time.

A picture of the library in the 1902-1903 bulletin shows a stark room in the Main Building containing bookshelves reaching all the way to the ceiling. The walls were covered with chalkboard or dark paint halfway to the ceiling. The window and door frames were dark wood. Students sat at two-man desks, facing forward. The seats were either benches or hardback wooden chairs. By that time there were nine hundred books and periodicals in the library. All of them were in this room, part of the Main Building.

When the Main Building burned in 1907, the library holdings were saved. After 1909 the library was housed in an enlarged area in Page Hall. Appropriations for the library were scarce, however, and reference materials were termed only "adequate" for "ordinary" needs through the 1920s. During President Young's tenure in 1923-24, he stated that the $1,000 spent for the library during his term in office was the "first money spent for the library in many years."

During the period from 1923 to 27 the Langston Alumni Association came to the aid of the library. The association had some 500 members, graduates of all departments of the school. It took as its goal the "attainment of a first-class library." As part of the upgrading, the first full-time trained librarian was hired. Mrs. Mayme McDaniel became the first librarian in 1923, followed in 1927 by Henrietta Beasley, who had received her training at Wiley College (Marshall, Texas), and at the Hampton Institute on a library-science scholarship. Her title in 1927 was "librarian and professor of library science," and she began training students as library assistants.

The campaign to improve the library had borne fruit by 1929, when the catalogue boasted an increase in holdings to ten thousand books. Henrietta (Beasley) Wright remained as head librarian until 1935 with a staff of four trained assistants.

In the late 1930s, Langston began its push for college accreditation. A study of the library facilities showed Langston to be far below par. In 1939 the average college expenditure for libraries in the nation was $6.53 per student (or approximately $6,500 per thousand students). At Langston the expenditure averaged $1.40 per student (or $1,650 for 1,249 students). The Langston staff requested a twofold increase to bring the library up to regional standards, recommending an increase in the librarian's salary from $1,650 to $3,300 and increasing the funding for book purchases from $1,000 to $3,000 plus $500 for the purchase of periodicals. Two full-time librarians were recommended as staff.

During the early years of World War II the library occupied the entire north section and half of the south section of the first floor of the original Page Hall. The stack room had a capacity of 11,000 volumes, two reading rooms, and there were a workroom, a reference-book room, and a reserve-book room. The seating capacity was 184. The library included 8,600 books, 7,000 pamphlets, 14 newspaper subscriptions and 205 magazine subscriptions. The staff consisted of a head librarian, an assistant, and circulation and high school librarians, as well as student trainees.

The library received its largest book appropriation in 1942-43: $5,000. At one point new titles were coming in so fast that there was a backlog of 900 books waiting to be catalogued. A binding program was started to organize the periodicals, and one-third of the 296 titles were bound. In a cooperative venture with the A&M campus at Stillwater, many missing back issues were found, purchased, and bound. All the book rebinding and repairing was done on campus, some by the library staff and some by Mrs. E. M. Washington's clothing and crafts classes.

In 1943, for the first time in its history, the library had an accurate shelf list. Until that time the books had been counted and estimated by student inventory takers. Before 1937 there was not enough money for catalogue cards for most of the books; in fact only 10 percent of the books had the cards. A WPA group made author, title, and shelf list cards in 1940.

During the war years, while the number of books at the library increased, the number of students on campus decreased. In 1943-44, the use of the library, despite its upgrading, was down 43 percent. The campus enrollment had dropped 69 percent. The most popular periodical in the library that year was *Life*. There were 134 periodicals that were not checked out once during the whole year.

The expenditure for new books in all departments was less than $1,000. Purchases ranged from $2.30 for a book for the Radio Department to $233 for reference works. Librarians' salaries for this period totaled $6,615. Of the 7,179 books in the library, only 338 dealt with the Negro. There were 13 reference books, 300 nonfiction titles and 25 books of fiction by black authors. A separate high school reading room was maintained, as well as a "War Information Center."

In estimating the improvements that would have to be made in the library before the school could be accredited by the North Central Association, the school administration figured that the number of books would have to be increased by an additional 4,000 titles (to 12,000) with an eventual goal of a library of 25,000 books. A separate library building was recommended, as well as a browsing room, a full-time cataloguer and office space.

The goal of increasing the titles had been met by 1944, when the library contained 13,000 books and 247 periodicals. The new library building was constructed in 1946-47 and was ready for occupancy at the beginning of the 1948 fall term. Named the G. Lamar Harrison Library, it was built on the "modular" plan and

G. Lamar Harrison Library and I. W. Young Auditorium, both opened in 1950.

featured open stacks. By 1950 it had holdings of 35,000 volumes.

The first course in library science was offered at the college in 1952-53 under Elmyra Davis. It was designed to prepare teachers who often had to serve in a dual role as teachers and librarians. The basic curriculum remained unchanged for almost twenty years. From the 1950s onward, the staff of the library remained remarkably stable, many librarians serving more than twenty years. Professor Davis took charge of the reading laboratory in 1963. By the mid-1960s the school had acquired a full-fledged library with holdings of 93,000 volumes and 600 current periodicals. In 1970-71, the Melvin Tolson Black Heritage Center opened as part of the library system, with Virginia Crowell as curator. The holdings of the entire library surpassed the 100,000 mark.

Grants from the federal government under the Higher Education Act of 1965 increased each year through 1977. Title II funds have been used for library materials, audiovisual materials, and tape recordings. Two specific programs that Langston funded with the funds were drug-abuse educational materials and black-ethnic-

Elmyra Richardson Todd Davis.

studies resources. Materials on drug identification, drug legislation, and enforcement techniques were purchased, and books concerning the Negro in the United States since 1933 were acquired.

With the opening of the new G. Lamar Harrison Library in 1950, the library staff prepared a pamphlet giving the history of the library. The first Langston library was in a small basement room of the original Page Hall. During the period when Marquess was president of the school (1916-23), the library moved to a first-floor room even smaller than the one in the basement. Materials consisted mainly of those donated by well wishers. Books became misplaced and lost. In 1926 a section of a study hall was designated the "library," and the books were put under lock and key.

The biggest jump in acquisitions and services came under the leadership of Elmyra Richardson Todd Davis, who supervised the increase of holdings from 8,000 volumes in 1944 to approximately 90,000 volumes in 1961. Periodicals increased from 14 newspapers in 1944 to 459 periodical subscriptions in 1950. When Harrison Library opened, the staff had increased to eight full-time employees. Davis became a full professor in the English department in 1963. The library's holdings continued to grow. In 1965 there were 109,000 volumes, 17 percent of which were on various aspects of education. In 1978 the holdings were 127,257 volumes.

CHAPTER THIRTEEN

The Struggle for Accreditation

LANGSTON University had no accredited standing with state, regional, or national authorities until 1929. In that year the school was approved by the Oklahoma State Board of Regents as "a standard four-year college offering the degrees of Bachelor of Arts and Bachelor of Science."

In 1935, when J. W. Sanford became president of the school, he filed an application for accreditation with the North Central Association of Colleges and Secondary Schools. He filed a second application in the fall of 1938. The response of the association was that Langston still ranked low in crucial areas. For example, Langston ranked in the lowest 6 percent of all colleges in the nation in the number of faculty members holding doctorates. The school ranked in the lowest 14 percent in librarians' salaries and in the lowest 5 percent in student-faculty ratios.

With the North Central Association report in mind, President Sanford prepared a study for the State Board of Education. He noted that in the years 1933 to 1938 the school's enrollment had more than doubled (from 500 to 1,136) while nothing had been done to expand the academic facilities. During the previous ten years dorm space had increased only enough to accommodate 148 more students.

All the administration offices, he reported, were contained in five small rooms. No one but the president had a place for private conferences. Labs for chemistry, physics, biology, and home economics were crammed into the second and third floors of the Administration Building. Classes met from 8:00 A.M. until 6:30 P.M. The auditorium, which had been constructed in 1909, seated only four hundred students, less than one-third of the current student body. Less than 10 percent of the student body could be accommodated in the library reading room. The Music Department was headquartered in one wing of the gym, a situation so bad that the music deans of the University of Oklahoma and Oklahoma A&M College joined in a plea for improvement. The infirmary had a four-bed capacity — two beds for men and two for women.

With all these inadequacies clearly apparent, the budget request for 1938-39 was only $166,000, while the estimated appropriation needed for 1939-40 was set at $1.35 million. The report proposed seven new buildings for the campus. The regents accepted the idea of upgrading the school to meet accreditation requirements but balked at funding all the improvements. The revised budget was $419,000, with emphasis on building a library, a new auditorium, and a new science building.

The Langston University administration changed in January, 1940, with the inauguration of G. Lamar Harrison as president. President Harrison inherited the accrediting problem and fought successfully for Langston's funding during the war years when the budgets of all other state colleges were cut 15 percent. In the biennial report for 1942-44, the State Board of Regents again expressed interest in seeing Langston gain full accreditation. An extra $4,300 from the Governor's Contingency Fund was used for the library, in addition to the budgeted $4,000.

The final, successful drive to meet the requirements for North Central Association accreditation came after the end of World War II. This included raising faculty salaries, hard-surfacing of the streets and sidewalks, and construction of the long-awaited library building.

Some thought was given to establishing a graduate school in education at Langston. In the 1940s black students who wished to pursue advanced degrees were reimbursed by the state for out-of-state tuition and travel costs to avoid integrating Oklahoma institutions. In 1946 the state was paying for 149 black students to pursue degrees out of state: 110 in education, 22 in music, 11 in medicine, 5 in law, and 1 in theology. The cost to the state was $25,000 a year. The regents decided to double that amount (to $50,000) to enable "all eligible students to attend out of state institutions for courses not offered at Langston University."

In 1948 a report by a regents' committee estimated that it would cost $10 to $12 million to establish a gradute school at Langston over a period of four to five years. It was estimated that the graduate school would cost $500,000 a year to operate. The regents also anticipated difficulties in obtaining qualified Negro faculty members, reporting that "in 1947 only 8 Negroes were granted Ph.D. degrees in the United States." Since more than one hundred institutions across the country employed Negro professors, Langston's chances of securing faculty members with doctoral degrees were very slim.

Nevertheless, the regents were under pressure to find graduate educational opportunities for black students. They finally adopted the sensible solution of admitting blacks to the graduate courses at Norman and Stillwater rather than attempting to duplicate courses and facilities at Langston.. (Of course, the extensive legal battles climaxed in the United States Supreme Court decisions moved the regents to this course of action in the McLaurin and Fisher cases.) In the years 1948 to 1950, however, the regents also redoubled their efforts to provide adequate funding to those black students who wished to go out of state for graduate education.

By 1948, Langston had full accreditation from the following groups: the North Central Association of Colleges and Secondary Schools, the Association of American Colleges, the Oklahoma State Board of Education, the United States Department of State (for foreign students), and the Veterans Administration. The next big push for accreditation came in the early 1960s, when the school applied for approval by the National Council for the Accreditation of Teacher Education (NCATE).

In 1963, under President William Hale, the school completed a self-study. At that time Langston was preparing teachers for the following fields: art, bookkeeping, business, home economics, physical education, industrial arts, language arts, mathematics, music, science, and social science. The education faculty included two members with doctorates, ten with master's degrees, and two working toward master's degrees (it should be remembered that in 1940 of the entire Langston faculty only four members held doctorates).

The study also provided some cumulative statistics for the uni-

Erma Walker Ellis, president of the Langston Parents' Organization, presenting a check to President William H. Hale, 1963. Alta Watson (left) and Beulah Tibbs Abraham were also officers.

versity, showing that since its beginning the university had conferred degrees on 3,700 students and had granted trade-course certificates to an additional 2,700.

A ten-year program to expand the physical plant was begun in December, 1963. Financed by a forty-year $1.4 million loan from the Federal Housing and Home Finance Agency, the project included construction of two dorms, a student union and three apartment buildings for faculty.

In 1965, there were 65 faculty members for 1,300 students. A faculty of approximately 80 members was necessary to bring about the "desired" student-faculty ratio. Beginning in 1966, federal grants were made available to faculty members to study full time for one year at full salary.

A team of visitors for NCATE again visited the Langston campus in February, 1965. The first accreditation visit, in 1962-63, had resulted in denial of accreditation for the teacher-education program. After the 1965 visit the school received a three-year provisional accreditation with recommendations for improvements still to be made. In 1968, at the end of the provisional term, Langston received full accreditation status. The teacher-education program was again reviewed by the NCATE Board of Visitors in 1973-74.

Some of the recommended improvements made during the accrediting process included the new Page Hall (the Administration Building), completed in 1968; Hamilton Hall, completed in 1969; the renovation of Moore Hall and Jones Hall in 1969; and the completion of Hargrove Music Building. Two dorms (Breaux Hall for men and Young Hall for women) were finished in 1969. The auditorium, gym, and library were renovated between 1965 and 1969.

Although Langston has not sought further accreditation, it has maintained the standards set by both the North Central Association and the NCATE. In the Oklahoma regents' report entitled *A Plan for the 1970's,* the thrust of education at Langston was revised. The Langston University Task Force report of 1972 concurred in the revision. Subsequent new programs included degrees in broadcast journalism, theatre arts, and accounting.

A proposal in 1977 for a graduate education campus in Tulsa as a branch of Langston University met a cool reception from the Board of Regents. The idea was formally rejected when submitted as part of the Task Force Committee report.

Frederick D. Moon
and the Langston Alumni Association

FREDERICK D. Moon was born on a farm near Fallis, Oklahoma, about 55 miles northeast of Oklahoma City. His family, originally from Arkansas, homesteaded the place in 1892. He and his brother, E. C., went to Langston as ninth- and eighth-graders. The brothers worked for room and board. During their first year on campus they worked in the little hospital and milked cows (Langston then required farm work of every student). Moon tells the story of signing up for carpentry classes, which he disliked, and then playing hooky. When he was finally caught, he claimed that he wanted to enroll in agriculture, which he did not, and again began cutting classes. Later he claimed that it was a mistake not to have some mechanical training.

He graduated from Langston with the summer class of 1929. He married Leosha Harris, a Langston alumna. His master's degree was from the University of Chicago.

Moon's interest in Langston University centered on the Langston Alumni Association, which he served as president from 1926 to 1940. The association was organized in 1922, but did not really function until 1925, when a group of ten or twelve Negro educators met after an Oklahoma City teacher's meeting and decided to activate it. Pennie Kennedy, Joseph Roberts, Nolan and Mary Pyrtle, and Moon were among those present at the Tabernacle Baptist Church that afternoon.

At that first organizational meeting, Moon was elected treasurer (according to his records, he said, he never collected a dollar). Without success the group tried to obtain the old treasurer's record books and account balance of twelve dollars. In those days, little attention was paid to the association. All the members of the board of directors paid their own way to meetings.

Beginning in 1926, with Moon as president, the Langston Alumni Association took a more positive stance. They refused to endorse school administrations automatically. They went on record for a

Frederick D. Moon.
Courtesy of Mrs. F. D. Moon.

strong library system and higher faculty salaries. In 1934 they lobbied for a legislative program to pay out-of-state tuition for Negroes pursuing graduate work.

Other militant ideas expressed by the association included establishing a board of regents for Langston and freeing the office of president from state politics.

The Alumni Association also undertook to develop a public awareness of the school. Under its auspices the first Founder's Day celebration was held in March, 1927. The first president, Inman Page, returned to the campus to deliver a speech and participate in the reception that followed the ceremonies.

In 1934 a group of association officers called on the Democratic candidate for governor, E. W. Marland. They met in the black high school in Ponca City and presented a list of requests: including a black member on the board of regents, accrediting Langston, and *placing the school above politics. Marland then invited the committee to his home and received them graciously. After his election, however, little was done to implement the requests. Marland's appointee to the presidency, Dr. Young, encouraged the formation of a rival to the Alumni Association, the Greater Langston Society.*

There was an attempt to oust Moon from the presidency in 1932, but it failed. Among other early-day supporters of the Alumni Association were A. H. Fuhr, George Tillman, Calvin Johns, William Glover, and C. R. Buford.

Moon served as principal in Crescent and Wewoka and then at Douglass High School in Oklahoma City from 1946 to 1961. F. D. Moon Center, in Oklahoma City, was named for him and dedicated in his honor in May, 1975. He served as the first black member and then as president of the Oklahoma City School Board after his retirement.

CHAPTER FOURTEEN

Agriculture

As mentioned earlier, Langston was set up by statute as an "agricultural and normal university." The emphasis on agriculture was strong from the opening years. In one of its earliest publications the school stressed as its objective "a careful study of the scientific principles underlying the rural institution." Students who majored in agriculture had class work plus nine hours a week of practical field work. The school farm grew cotton, corn, wheat, oats, potatoes, cabbage, beans, and onions.

Courses for agriculture students in 1898 were trigonometry, rhetoric, farm equipment, shopwork, and farm-building plans. In addition to industrial-arts courses for men, beginning in 1900, the school offered sewing, cooking, and other domestic classes for girls.

The school emphasized practical course work. Courses in such projects as "laying out fields and building fences and gates" and "cold frames and hot beds for wintering plants" were offered for many years. In their senior year students took more technical courses, including international law, deeds, business customs, rights and privileges, contracts, notes, mortgages, and farm accounts, and mineralogy. Advanced students could take calculus, landscape gardening, and a course entitled "farm-yard manures."

The school was well situated to teach agriculture. It owned 320 acres of farmland, about 250 acres of which were suitable for cultivation. The university acquired livestock, orchard and garden equipment, a farm library, and farm tools under the supervision of a farming instructor. The buildings owned by the school included a large "Michigan barn" and a piggery. Agriculture students tended the school's herds of cattle, sheep, swine, and farm horses.

All the students in the elementary department were required to take agriculture as part of their regular classwork. Prospective

Practical field work in the early days of the Agriculture Department.

teachers could take a curriculum to certify them as agricultural teachers. Agriculture majors worked at least an hour a day in the barn or garden. A short course was worked out for students who were already engaged in farming. This special one-year plan of study included blacksmithing, carpentry, stock judging, dairying, and insect control.

For dairy farmers a special one-year course was available that offered classes in butter making, cheese production, milk testing, and dairy inspection and laws.

By the 1920s the college curriculum in agriculture had been adjusted to provide a basic liberal-arts educaton along with agricultural training. The four-year program included literature, public speaking, educational psychology, and math in addition to the agriculture subjects. Among the electives offered were pipefitting, rope splicing, farm motors, and soldering.

The first dean of agriculture at Langston was John E. Buford, who served in that position in 1921-22. Others on the agriculture faculty in the early 1920s included J. M. Watlington and D. W. Lee.

The Michigan barn, 1923.

Beginning in 1919 there were twenty-five scholarships for boys studying agriculture. The next year an additional forty scholarships were added, and the boys who received them came from almost every county in the state.

The first Langston student to graduate with a bachelor of science degree in agriculture was Thomas H. Black, Jr., my brother. He was awarded the degree in 1924. The official invitations included the motto, "Not Evening, but Dawn;" the class flower, the American Beauty rose; and the class colors, purple and white. The class roll listed the one name, Thomas J. Black, Jr. As the first Agriculture Department graduate, Thomas was qualified to teach in the public-school system, and he received offers from many institutions. He

The Senior College Class of
Nineteen Hundred Twenty-four
Colored Agricultural and Normal University
requests your presence at its
Commencement Exercises
Wednesday morning, May the Twenty-first
at ten-thirty o'clock   University Auditorium

Class Motto:

"NOT EVENING BUT DAWN"

Class Colors:
Purple and White

Class Flower:
American Beauty Rose

Class Roll:
THOMAS HERBERT BLACK, JR.

Thomas Herbert Black, Jr. B. S.

Announcement and cards of the graduating class of 1924.

taught in Lima, Taft, Chickasha, and Gainesville, Texas. Later he served as county agent for Lincoln and Logan counties.

In a shift in faculty in 1926-27, W. M. T. Wells took over as head of the Agriculture Department. B. M. Mathis and D. W. Lee became associate professors, and a new instructor, D. C. Jones, was added to the faculty. Jones stayed at the school for many years and was given credit for training most of the Negro vocational-agriculture instructors in the state. He was also state supervisor of black vocational-agriculture teachers in the high schools.

Along with the changes in the faculty came revisions in the curriculum. General psychology was added, as well as courses in soils and fertilizers, veterinary field practice, and economics. Students had to complete a minimum of fifty hours of combined supervised practice teaching at Langston or local high schools.

Eugene Moore joined the faculty in 1928 as professor of animal husbandry and became director of the Agriculture Department the following year. Before receiving a degree from the college, a student had to have six months of practical farming experience. The students could major in agricuture education, agronomy, or animal husbandry.

By the early 1930s the campus farm had grown to four hundred acres. The school had Jersey and Holstein cattle; Duroc and Poland China swine; four hundred laying hens, as well as turkeys and geese; Percheron brood mares and colts; and mules. W. E. Simms became dean of agriculture in 1934.

The poultry farm had chickens of five different breeds. The incubator capacity was 2,016 chicks. Approximately 40,000 chickens and 200 turkeys were produced each year. The brooder house was electrically equipped and featured "colony" brooders.

The first director of agriculture to hold the Ph.D. degree was M. F. Spaulding, who became director of the Agriculture Division in 1941. At that time the entire instructional staff held master's degrees except for the farm-shop teacher. The school began granting "certificates" to students who dropped out before finishing the four-year curriculum or to working farmers who enrolled in special subjects. These certificates merely established attendance. No

D. C. Jones, state supervisor of black vocational high school agriculture teachers. Courtesy of Mrs. D. C. Jones.

Jimmie L. White (center) and students with part of the Poland China hog herd kept by the Agriculture Department in the late 1940s. Courtesy of R. E. Kinnard.

credit was given for such courses except by a special vote of the faculty, and the students' grades had to be C or above.

All during the 1940s the school farm operated under D. C. Jones. About 160 acres were kept in cultivation. On the rest of the land was the nine-acre garden, the piggery, the poultry plant, woodland, and pasture.

The Agriculture Department had four brick buildings for classrooms, extension offices, crop and soil labs, and workrooms. The Agricultural and Science Hall was a three-story brick building. The dairy unit included a pasteurizing plant with refrigeration equipment and a Walker-Gordon rotolactor for the production of grade-A milk.

The main barn had two stories and a hay loft, storage rooms for tools and feed, two 159-ton silos, maternity stalls, and calf pens. The slaughter pens and judging arena were adjacent.

The laying house was 80 by 20 feet and accommodated 400 hens. About 1,500 baby chicks could be kept in the gas-heated brooder house.

Farm boys who had begun livestock projects during high school days under the supervision of a county agent could bring their livestock to the Langston campus to help finance their college education.

Various prizes were awarded to students in the Agricuture Department. The State Negro Chamber of Commerce awarded fifty dollars at commencement to a previous year's graduate who had engaged in farming. There was an award to the best "father-son" partnership — that is, a son who went to college, maintained his interest in his father's farm, and returned to rural life after graduation. The Spaulding Award of twenty-five dollars was to help the recipient purchase his own farm. The George Davis Award consisted of a purebred beef animal. By 1942 ten $50 agricultural scholarships were available to entering freshmen.

In addition to classwork and short courses, Langston promoted various agricultural activities. The 4-H Club state exhibit was held on campus in October, 1941. An annual fair occurred in September. There were summer and fall conferences of vocational-agriculture teachers and county home-demonstration agents.

A. B. Prewitt (wearing cap), farm foreman, checking head-feed acreage with an agriculture student, sometime before 1946. Courtesy of R. E. Kinnard.

The livestock-judging arena. Courtesy of R. E. Kinnard.

A student with a grand-champion lamb. Courtesy of R. E. Kinnard.

A faculty-student organization, the New Farmers of America, existed on campus until 1945, after which the Agriculture Club was organized.

AGRICULTURE

The Reverend Richmond E. Kinnard, chairman of the Department of Agriculture.

W. E. Simms retired in March, 1963. The director of agriculture at that time was B. S. Garcha, who held a Ph.D. degree. By that time standards for the bachelor of science degree had been upgraded to include the 57 semester hours of liberal-arts education required of all Langston students plus 38 semester hours of specialization in agriculture, 18 hours in a minor, and 11 elective hours.

In 1967 the division of agriculture was dissolved. Agriculture became a portion of the vocational and technical-education curriculum. Other departments were home economics and technology. Richmond E. Kinnard was chairman of the Agriculture Department. Two degree programs were set up: agricultural economics and animal science. As of this writing Kinnard is chairman of the department. Also in the department are Jimmie L. White, who has been on the staff since 1949 and Benjamin Monroe, farm superintendent, who has served since 1961.

CHAPTER FIFTEEN

Art

WITH the opening of classes at Langston in 1898, students in the fourth to seventh grades were required to take "drawing." Although no students enrolled in the college-level courses, the school stated that it was prepared to offer work in mechanical drawing, architectural perspectives, painting, and decoration. After 1903 art courses began with the fifth grade and continued through the ninth grade. Mechanical drawing was required of agriculture students. The aim of this early-day instruction was "to arouse and develop an appreciation of the beautiful and train students in neatness and accuracy." Texts were *The Eclectic System* and the Webb and Ware *Series of Practical Drawing.*

Girls in the domestic-economy courses of 1905 learned to draft patterns with tape measure and ruler, draw curves freehand, combine colors pleasingly, and trim hats.

Students in the vocational courses took appropriate art courses, such as forge-and-tool design, cabinet design, and blueprint drawing.

Some of the mediums used in art courses during 1912-13 were modeling clay, pencil, charcoal, pen and ink, and watercolor. Students in the mechanical drawing class learned to sketch steam engines, gears, cams, flywheel cylinders, and valve gears.

For students enrolled in the Teacher's College, art was required for six terms. Prospective teachers had to learn to draw geometric forms and sketch from nature, do perspectives, study the history of art, and paint with watercolors. The basic texts for elementary pupils were Louis Prang's *Art Education* and, for penmanship, Eaton's *Writing Book.*

There was no separate art department until 1927-28, when a two-year program was offered for teachers and liberal-arts students. The first formal steps toward establishing an art department had occurred in 1924, when Eugene E. Brown, the new chairman of the department, offered free-hand charcoal drawing. Students could take up to 15 hours of art education and up to 60 hours of art. By 1927-28 the course offerings had tripled. The two-year program expanded to a full four-year, degree-granting curriculum in 1930.

Before 1933 the art department was in the basement of old Page Hall. Sometimes additional classroom space on the first floor was used. In 1933 an art building was built entirely by student labor, as an addition to the mechanical building. The students constructed a gallery area 30 by 20 feet and a 40-by-40-foot art studio with plenty of windows on all sides and skylights in the roof.

The collection in the gallery of the new building included drawings, paintings, wood carvings, pottery, and sculpture. The paintings bore such titles as *Diana from the Hunt, Spring, Fruit Gatherers,* and *Virginia.* There were still lifes, charcoal studies, cast drawings, and antique watercolors.

The new art studio had a private office for the instructor, a storeroom, a tool cabinet, and a blackboard. There were twenty drawing tables, six easels, objects to serve as models for still lifes, and more than fifty prints. The Art Department had a collection of nearly a thousand books and pamphlets on art.

The department scheduled exchange exhibitions with Virginia State College, in Petersburg. Traveling loan exhibits from the University of Oklahoma and Oklahoma A&M College came to Langston. In 1935 an exhibit of Negro prints was held on campus.

During the mid-1930s the class offerings totaled twenty-two art courses, including figure drawing, commercial poster design, sketching from costume models, and landscape drawing in pastels. A course in pottery-making included designing, building, throwing, and turning clay objects. During the years 1941 to 1955 an art major was required to take thirty semester hours of art for a degree.

Sketching and interior decoration were moved from the Art Department to the Home Economics Department in 1941. A course in cosmetology was offered under the National Youth Administration but was dropped two years later.

Eugene E. Brown, chairman of the Art Department, 1924-61. Courtesy of Mrs. Eugene E. Brown.

The development of the Art Department was largely the work of one man, Eugene E. Brown, who was chairman of the department for thirty-seven years, from 1924 until his retirement in 1961. He was born in Pine Bluff, Arkansas, in 1895, attended the University of Kansas, the Carnegie Institute of Technology, Kansas State Teacher's College, the University of Colorado, and Denver University. He was popularly known on campus as Father Brown. In 1964, Brown Hall was named in his honor, and his portrait was unveiled in ceremonies on October 18 of that year.

Succeeding Brown as chairman of the art department was John D. Payne. An opponent of narrow vocational training, Payne was convinced that "all men are biologically equipped to experience space as well as color and can acquire experience which will tend to develop this capacity." He increased requirements for an art major to thirty-six hours. To obtain a degree in art, a student must present a one-man exhibit during the senior year. Payne resigned

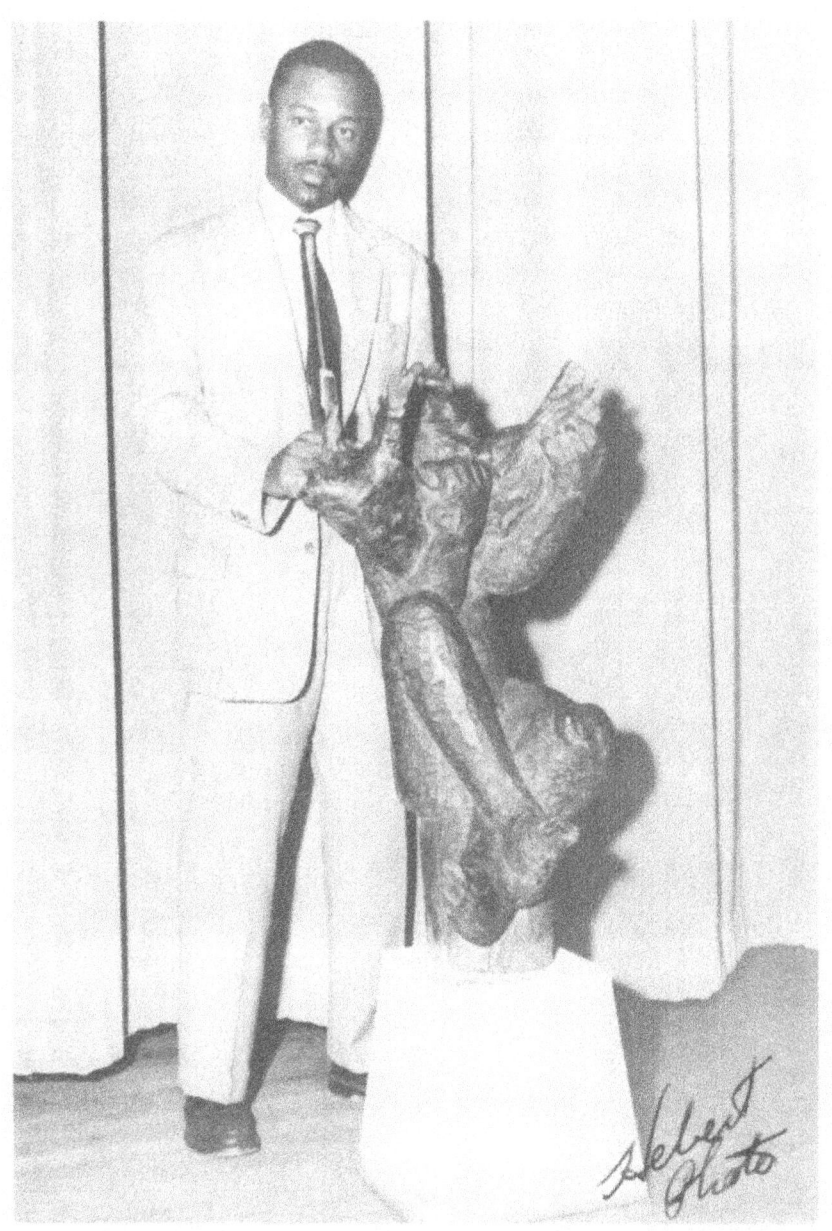

Jackie Jordan, graduate of the Langston Art Department and former faculty member, with one of his sculptures.

Oil painting by Eugene E. Brown.

in 1963, and was succeeded by Mayhugh Sneed as department chairman.

The Art Department found a new home in 1965, when it moved onto the third floor of the new Page Hall. A new program was the teacher-education degree, requiring forty-seven semester hours in art.

Eugene E. Brown's painting hanging in the studio of the Langston Art Department. Courtesy of Art Department.

In the early 1970s two successful artists joined the faculty. Wallace Owens, Jr., a native of Muskogee, Oklahoma, became chairman of the department, and Irabell Juanita Cotton became an instructor.

Owens has produced and exhibited one-man shows at Central State University, Oklahoma State University, and the University of Oklahoma and has participated in group shows at the Oklahoma Art Center, in Oklahoma City, the University of Oklahoma, and the Institute Allende, of Mexico City. He is a graduate of Langston (1959), holds the master's degree in art education, and has undertaken further study at the American Center for Artists, in Paris, France. He was a Fulbright Scholar in art history in Rome, Italy, in the summer of 1970 and was a member of Howard University's study tour to West Africa in 1973.

Mayhugh Sneed, chairman of the Art Department, 1960s.

Irabell Juanita Cotton earned degrees from Langston and the University of Oklahoma and taught at West Virginia State University before returning to Langston. Ms. Cotton, a victim of polio and bone disease at the age of three, did not attend school until she was seventeen years old. At that time, as teacher of the home economics class, I suggested that she attend classes at the Home Economics Department cottage, which was on ground level and would not involve lifting a wheel chair up and down stairs.

In two years she had completed home economics courses for grades 7 through 12. After conferences with the Langston high school principal and superintendent, it was agreed that she could enter high school if she could pass the eighth-grade examination. This she did and began high school at almost the age of twenty. She graduated with honors in 1954, entered Langston University, and received her B.A. in 1959. After that she completed fine-arts and master's degrees at the University of Oklahoma.

Despite her confinement to a wheel chair, Ms. Cotton is an accomplished seamstress and the mother of two adopted daughters. She has exhibited three one-woman shows, entered exhibitions in West Virginia and Oklahoma, and contributed to the national permanent collection in Atlanta, Georgia. Most of her work has been in sculpture, in stone, clay, and bronze.

Wallace Owens, chairman of the Art Department, 1970s.

Juanita Cotton with bronze sculpture. Courtesy of Juanita Cotton.

CHAPTER SIXTEEN

Athletics

THE FIRST official indication of an athletic program at Langston is a picture of a baseball team in the 1902-1903 catalogue. In the next issue of the catalogue the *same* picture appears. Apparently other sports were played unofficially. In October, 1905, the newspaper *Western Age* reported on a big football rally in Langston and the first game of the season against an Oklahoma City high school. No team members or coaches were identified — perhaps because the event ended in Langston's defeat.

The early days of football were recorded by A. H. Fuhr, who was a member of the team for three years and stayed around until 1913 as a "semiofficial player." When he first went out for football in 1907, the game was a highly informal affair. There were no faculty coaches; players practiced on their own. Professor Shields, an agriculture teacher from Cornell University, knew something about the game and donated some of his spare time and served as chaperone to the team. The team was organized by word of mouth. Fuhr says:

> I was introduced to football in 1907 on the same field where it is played now. I had never seen a ball game, and I knew nothing about it except what I had heard. School was opening, and the word spread that anyone who wanted to play football was to show up on the football field on a certain afternoon.

The boys who arrived for the game proceeded to elect a captain, who then served as coach. Each player brought his own uniform. Fuhr (who at the time weighed only 135 pounds), picked cotton in the fall to earn money to buy khaki football pants and a red jersey, which he ordered from Sears and Roebuck in Kansas City. Most of the team members nailed small squares of old leather to the bottom of their regular shoes. A few affluent players had shin guards, nose guards, or mouthpieces.

ATHLETICS

The team proceeded to invent a play called the "flying wedge." After a player had received the ball, all the players locked arms and took off down the field like a wedge, fending off the opposing defense with devastating force. Owing to the number of injuries this formation produced, it was outlawed in 1908. Another inspired formation, which was also subsequently outlawed, was the "locked-arm interference." During the time these formations were used, Fuhr worked his way up from scrub-team tackle to first-string halfback and then to quarterback.

The first semblance of a coaching staff was set up about 1909, when Gilbert Jones (who later became president of Wilberforce University) joined Professor Shields in showing the players a few formations. The team still furnished its own uniforms and equipment. There were no such things as "football scholarships" or "training-table" meals. Football was strictly a game played for fun. During the early years anyone who showed up on the field was eligible to play. Some members of the team did not even attend school regularly. Several young farmers from the surrounding area would come into town on Saturdays and play with the team. Also student players could play for as many seasons as they wished, there being no eligibility requirements. Some players stayed on the team as long as eight years.

The early schedule of opponents included mostly Tulsa and Oklahoma City high schools. Occasionally Langston played small colleges from Kansas and Texas. When the team played out of state, they had to raise their own train fare.

One particularly memorable game was in Quinter, Kansas, in 1909. The Langston team had never heard of either the huddle or the forward pass. Their quarterback called all plays by signal. The Kansas team was able to score at will because the Oklahoma players "had never seen or heard of the forward pass and therefore had no defense against it."

Organized athletics were introduced sometime before 1919, but the Langston catalogues are vague about details. In 1913 there was mention of a "four-acre field arranged for football, baseball, and general athletics." Young women were given "suitable athletic training." An athletic association composed of the student body and faculty representatives was supposedly in charge of the athletic program.

Until the early 1920s the players on the football team were still mainly high school students, with some boys from the Normal Department. Playing conditions were still spartan — only a few team members could afford hip and shoulder pads. A "football scholarship" meant a job on campus for room and board. Booker Robinson, a member of the team from 1919 to 1924 remembered taking cold baths after practice sessions because the school was economizing on the use of coal to fire the boilers. Head gear was thin, light, or nonexistent. Players were still providing their own "shoes," taking their school shoes down to the leather shop to have cleats built on.

The coach at the time was William V. Kelley, who had had an outstanding record as an athlete at Fisk University, in Nashville, Tennessee. The president of Langston at the time was John Marquess, who was a dedicated football fan. He would come to the practice sessions and assist Coach Kelley. The basic formations were the right and left half square, the box, the T, and the spread.

Opponents were still Oklahoma high schools. The schedule called for games against Tulsa Washington, Muskogee Manual, Oklahoma City Douglass, Guthrie Faver, Okmulgee Dunbar, and the black high school at Nowata. A high school coach was allowed to play along with his team, and the Nowata and Tulsa coaches did so.

Langston also found opponents in teams composed of former students who had attended out-of-state schools or dropped out of either high school or college. These teams, tougher and older, gave Langston plenty of trouble and practice.

An archrival in the early twenties was Topeka Institute in Kansas. The school had an excellent team coached by Steve Abbott with All-American Ben Stevens as a player. For two years Langston tried and failed to defeat Topeka. President Marquess was so determined to overcome this team that he took the unprecedented step of hiring a white coach for Langston, a student coach named McClure from Oklahoma University. Despite Coach McClure's efforts, Topeka again defeated Langston the next year.

In 1922 the coaching staff changed again with Harry Long from Texas taking the position as head coach. He too lasted only a year. It should be remembered that in this era politics ruled Langston both at the state level and internally. With each new state governor the school changed presidents, and with each new president there was a turnover in the faculty and coaching staffs.

By 1923 the players and staff at Langston had matured to the point that other high schools no longer wanted to play them. After a particularly punishing game with Tulsa Washington, the coach of the Tulsa team insisted that Langston should compete on the college level from then on.

With I. W. Young as president and W. E. Anderson as football coach, Langston expanded its athletic program. In 1923 crowds and interest were sufficient to play a match in Oklahoma City against Bishop College in Dallas. That game was the real beginning of intercollegiate games for Langston. Most of the crowd was for the Texas school, which drew many students from the Oklahoma City area. Some of its players had attended Douglass. Despite all the Bishop rooters, flags, and pennants, Langston won 7 to 0. That game also marked the beginning of championship seasons. No opponent scored on Langston for the next two years. It is no accident that the football field is named in honor of W. E. Anderson.

The average weight of the players was about 160 pounds. Their motto was "Be a Good Loser and a Fair Winner." In the early 1920s the dining hall set aside two special tables where the players could eat together. In the 1921 season Langston scored 97 points. In 1922, under the white coach from OU, Langston was state champion.

Under the brief reign of Coach H. J. ("Little") Long, Langston offered football, baseball, and track, as well as gymnastics, calisthenics, and swimming theory.

Girls in "physical culture" in the early twenties played basketball and volleyball and practiced calisthenics. Cornelia Jones was the women's physical education instructor.

The members of the male coaching staff were wearing several academic hats. In 1924, W. E. Anderson was appointed director of athletics. He retained that position when, in 1930, he was appointed acting dean. He was also an English professor. Similarly,

LeRoy G. Moore served one year as football coach (1928-29), was a member of the science faculty, became acting administrative dean in 1939, and was dean from 1940 to 1962. During this long period — thirty-seven years — he assisted with the coaching.

Stability in the Athletic Department came with the appointment of C. Felton ("Zip") Gayles in 1930. He remained as football coach until 1958. Gayles, a graduate of Morehouse College in Atlanta, Georgia, and a graduate student at Northwestern in Chicago, came to Langston at the same time some exceptionally talented players arrived: John T. Williams was considered the nation's best punter. Moses Miller, captain of the team, was elected All-American in 1935. T. M. Crisp, "the player with the educated toe," would eventually return to coach at Langston.

The high point of the 1941 season was the period when the Langston Lions reigned as national black champions. They defeated Brown College, of Atlanta, Georgia, 13 to 0 in the Vulcan Bowl.

By 1943, Langston had upgraded all its athletic programs to the point that intercollegiate competition was offered in football, basketball, track, and tennis. The university was a member of the Southwestern Athletic Conference. Under the rules of that association student athletes had to be bona fide resident-student amateurs and maintain satisfactory grades. An athletic council, made up of three faculty members, one student, and one alumnus, supervised the sports program. All students, men and women, were required to take physical education. The only exemptions were married or handicapped students.

Despite the decline in male enrollment in the World War II years, Langston fielded championship teams in both football and basketball in 1944-45. In football the team was conference champion. Clarence Harkins, end and pass receiver, was nominated for All-American as a sophomore. Fifteen players earned membership in the Langston Lions Lettermen's Club.

The basketball team won fifty-one games in a row, taking the Southwestern Conference championship three years out of four. Marques Haynes was selected as all-tournament forward in 1945. He was a member of the Langston basketball team that played an exhibition game with the Harlem Globetrotters. The clowning

Moses F. Miller, inducted into the Oklahoma Football Hall of Fame. Courtesy of Mrs. Moses F. Miller.

quickly ceased, and the "exhibition" turned into a full-fledged athletic competition. It ended with Langston defeating the Globetrotters. Haynes later played with the Globetrotters and then formed his own touring professional team, the Harlem Magicians.

The postwar years brought a boom in enrollment and building construction. In 1947 the football program issued an apology for the poor conditions of the bleachers and athletic field but promised that, "when you next attend a football game on Langston's campus in the fall of 1948, a modern stadium will be completed seating 4,000 fans and... providing all the accommodations necessary for the football public to enjoy a football game." The promise was kept.

Beginning in the 1948-50 biennium, the physical-education curriculum was revised to include health courses. Two years of physical education were required of both men and women. All activities were conducted in uniform. Women wore gym suits, socks, and rubber-soled shoes. Men wore white athletic shirts, athletic supporters, shorts, gym shoes, and socks.

Langston coaches who served through most of the period from 1950 to 1960. Left to right: Tim Crisp, Ray Johnson, and Bernard Crowell. Crisp was inducted into the Oklahoma Football Hall of Fame. Courtesy of Public Relations Department, Langston University.

Excuses from "phys ed" were hard to obtain and were granted only by the university physician. In the 1950s the only women exempt from classes were married students or those over twenty-five. Students who majored in health or physical education had to complete thirty-five semester hours, not counting the two years required of freshmen and sophomores.

In 1954, Bernard Crowell became track coach, and Langston began participating in intercollegiate track events. In 1957, Langston became a member of the Oklahoma Collegiate Athletic Conference. In 1958, "Zip" Gayles gave up the post of head football coach and was succeeded by former Langston player T. M. Crisp, of Ardmore. Gayles remained as athletic director. In 1960, under Crisp's coaching, Langston defeated Florida A&M in the Orange

Edison ("Hercules") Harrington, deadlift-weight champion, "Mr. Oklahoma" of 1960. He set the state record for deadlift on June 18, 1960, entered three AAU contests, and won all three.

Blossom Classic. Crisp retired from teaching in 1971 and became a youth-development specialist with the Cooperative Extension Service. He retired from that career in 1973.

Gayles's student and professional career record at Langston included All-American honors in football and basketball. His football teams won seven conference and two national championships. The over-all record in football from 1930 to 1957 was 146 games won, 78 lost, and 18 tied. In addition he coached two all-conference basketball teams and a national-champion team. The C. Felton Gayles Gymnasium is named in his honor.

Athletic programs were gradually broadened in the late 1950s and 1960s. A gymnastic team was organized, a dance group was formed and more attention was given to excellence in track and field events. For three consecutive years the Oklahoma collegiate discus championship was held by Willie Dixon. Dixon, a chemistry major, also won the national championship with a throw of 173.1½ feet in 1964.

In the spring of 1965 the Langston track-and-field team won the Oklahoma collegiate championship. Ed Brazile set a new conference mark in the shot put, L. Parker established a new record for 440 low hurdles, and the mile relay team set a new conference record. In addition, team members set new Langston school records in shot put, the mile run, the discus throw, and low hurdles. Langston outscored Oklahoma Baptist University and Central State University to take the title.

Throughout the 1960s Langston faced recruiting competition from the other Oklahoma four-year institutions. The athletic scholarship program remained limited. Most of the recruiting was done in state, although the basketball roster for 1969-70 showed players from six other states. The football team of 1969 had only sixteen returning lettermen, five of them on the offensive team. In addition, Coach Crisp was facing the double problems of having no center and no quarterback. He said, correctly, "We have a lot of holes to fill."

The year was saved in part by a player who had not played football in six years — Langston's first white player to win a football letter: Carl Vinci. A twenty-two-year-old former Marine, Vinci was a native of Rome, New York. He came west for the first time in his life to attend Saint Gregory's College, Shawnee. Later he transferred to Langston, earned a starting berth on the 1968 team, and was then sidelined with injuries during the first game of the season. When he began playing football at Langston, he was on a baseball scholarship. After he got in top condition, the five-foot, eight-inch, 220-pound guard majored in physical education. He and his wife lived in Guthrie, where he operated a pizza parlor. After graduation Vinci returned to coach at Guthrie.

Also helping the situation in 1969 was the return of former Langston All-American Donald Lee Smith as assistant football coach. Smith had had a long association with Head Coach Crisp. At Ardmore Douglass, he had quarterbacked under Crisp, winning the state high school football title for Ardmore in 1957. Later he played at Langston under Crisp, helping the Lions win back-to-back league championships in 1959 and 1960. Before returning to Langston, he coached at Okmulgee.

Beginning with the 1970 season, Langston had six instructors in the Physical Education Department, Albert Schoats was director of athletics and head football coach. Smith remained as assistant football coach. Instructors in physical education were Joe Hornbeak, Erma Hodge, and Anna Corrado. Chairman of the department was B. G. Crowell.

During the early 1970s Langston's seasonal football schedule contained twelve games, four of which were played out of state. In 1973 the team was undefeated, largely because of Thomas ("Wild Man") Henderson. Henderson was a six-foot, 3-inch, 225-pound lineman. Twice selected by the National Association of Intercollegiate Athletics as lineman of the week in 1973, Henderson finished the season as the Oklahoma collegiate conference defensive player of the year. He was credited with 60 defensive tackles, 42 assists, 1 interception, and 3 fumble recoveries. He was named to the first team on AP, UPI, and NAIA All-America teams. After graduating from Langston in 1975, Henderson was the number-one draft choice of the Dallas Cowboys. In 1977 he played strong-side linebacker on the starting team.

Other Langston graduates who played professional football after

Former Coach W. E. Anderson visiting the campus and President William Hale in 1961.

graduation included Kenneth Payne, who joined the Green Bay Packers; and Larry Cunningham who joined the New York Giants after a stint with the Atlanta Falcons. John Goodie, a running back, and James Thatcher, a wide receiver, were both picked up in the 1975 player draft. Goodie was taken by the Baltimore Colts, and Thatcher by the Pittsburgh Steelers.

Track continued to be strong in the Langston athletic program during the mid-1970s. Langston took first-place ribbons for discus, triple jump, 440 dash, and 880 run at the 1974 Eastern Invitational Track and Field Meet. Langston fielded a team that took second place over all and participated in such diverse events as the mile run, javelin throw, pole vault, high hurdles, and shot put.

An outstanding addition to the 1975 coaching staff was Benjamin F. Hart, Jr. He was signed as coach of the special teams and the defensive secondary. Hart had played college ball at the University

Basketball coach Lawrence Cudjo.

Coach Albert Schoats. Courtesy of Mrs. Albert Schoats.

of Oklahoma, where he was the first black high school player to earn All-America as quarterback after integration of the university.

Of the 57 players on the 1975 football roster, 38 came from out of state, including 8 from Washington, D.C. They averaged six feet in height with an average weight of 190 pounds.

In basketball the same pattern held true, with only four of the eleven players coming from Oklahoma. All the four were from Oklahoma City. The rest of the team members were from Missouri, Tennessee, and California.

Langston continued to require four semester hours of physical education of all students. Teacher-education programs were offered in health, physical education, and recreation.

Under Head Coach Albert Schoats, football became a more relaxed concern. The team appeared for practices in such attire as cutoff blue jeans, floppy hats, and tee shirts. Exercises were performed to various jiving rhythms. Schoats attributed the easygoing regimen to two ongoing problems: lack of money for equipment and lack of interference from alumni. He said: "I'd like to have a new addition onto the dressing room area. I'd just like to have new sod for the football field. But I don't worry about it..." He apparently took in stride the necessity for making do.

On the other hand, Schoats set high scholastic standards, demanding that student athletes maintain a 2.0 average, while the NAIA requirement was only 1.5 Seventy-eight players came out for football in 1977, including six returning starters and two senior quarterbacks.

Football Fever: The Wonder Team of 1924

A bad case of football fever struck the Langston campus in 1924, when the celebrated Wonder Team had an undefeated and unscored-upon season. Langston's goal line had not been crossed all season as the final home game opened during Thanksgiving week.

The opponent was Wiley College in Marshall, Texas. "Big" Long arrived in town with his talented Chargers, hoping to hand Langston its first defeat in two years. Nevertheless, Langston's Lions were favored to win. Among the seniors playing their last home game were quarterback Clarence Alwell, right end William Glover, tackle Tommie Norris Graves, and right halfback and captain Booker T. Robinson. All four men were vocational-agriculture majors. Alwell was from Nowata and was small for a football player. But despite his size, he was fast, tough, and a good runner.

Glover was from Chandler. He did not play with the Lions during his freshman year, but was discovered by Coach Kelley during the spring track season. He had great speed and good hands and was an outstanding pass receiver. He also played second base on the university baseball team.

Tommie Graves served in World War I before enrolling at Langston as a third-year high school student in 1919. He played tackle, first for two years on the high school team and then for four years in college. The coaches nicknamed him "the biggest little man" on the squad. In the era in which he played, there was no such thing as the platoon system. Players good enough to make the team played both offense and defense.

Booker Robinson came to Langston from Rentiesville High School in his junior year. He and Graves were roommates. The first year he played fullback, but because of his speed was moved to right halfback the next year. During his career his longest touchdown run was 90 yards. His strong suit was passing, and he was captain of the 1924 championship team. In addition to football he played third-baseman on the baseball team, center on the basketball team, and ran on the track team. In a 1920 track meet he was

The Wonder Football Team of 1923-24. Coach Anderson is in the second row, left. President Young is standing, far right. Courtesy of the late Booker T. Robinson.

timed at 10 seconds for the 100-yard dash — wearing tennis shoes, for track shoes were not in style in those days. He also competed in the broad jump.

The big game with Wiley got under way with partisan Wiley College fans yelling, "We'll cross your goal line today!" The first score was made on a pass from Robinson to Glover. John Williams, a freshman, kicked the extra point. Williams, a six-foot, six-inch right end, could send punts sixty and seventy yards (later he was named to the All Sports Writers All-American Team). During the third quarter he also caught a touchdown pass and then converted the extra point. Langston 14, Wiley, 0. The final score of the game came when Captain Robinson dropped back, faked a pass, ran downfield, picking up good blocking along the way, and scored a touchdown. Langston's goal line remained uncrossed. The final score: 21 to 0.

After this victory all Langston eyes were on Tuskegee Institute and Paul Quinn College (Waco, Texas), which were battling for the national championship. Langston was certain that it would receive an invitation to a postseason game from the national winner. In fact, Langston was so sure that it decided to send Coach Anderson to scout the Tuskegee-Paul Quinn match. To everyone's amazement the big game for the national championship ended in a scoreless tie: 0 to 0. Coach Anderson, reporting home from his trip, called his squad together and announced, "Fellows, if you-all could not defeat Paul Quinn or Tuskegee, I would not own you."

Paul Quinn sent an invitation to Langston to play a "classic" on Christmas Day. Langston accepted with delight. The Paul Quinn team was coached that year by Harry Long, who had earlier served one year at Langston. Paul Quinn's team included All-American center Tom Sanders, tackle "Big" Morgan, and drop kicker Ray Shepard.

But Langston was confident — until a big snowstorm arrived, and the football practice field disappeared for the rest of December. It began snowing shortly after Thanksgiving and continued until the Christmas holidays. The team could not hold any outdoor practice sessions. Booker Robinson remembers: "We would meet in the gym and use the basketball court to practice our old plays and run a few new plays."

The lack of practice was bad for the players physically as well as psychologically. Some of the players had been injured during the last regular game, and the extent of the injuries did not become apparent until the Christmas Day game, when several players had to be taken from the game.

On the night before the game the Langston players were housed in a dorm on the Paul Quinn campus. Coach Anderson was not staying in the same building — in fact, there was no adult supervision at all. As a result a lot of horseplay and betting went on far into the night. The Langston boys were confident. When approached for bets by Paul Quinn students and players, they did not hesitate. Most of them had their Christmas money along, and they were not adverse to the idea of adding to it. Some of the players talked over the situation and decided that it would be best if Coach Anderson and President Young remained uninformed about what was happening. After all, the team had been undefeated for two years and unscored on for a whole season — why wouldn't they win easily on Christmas Day? As one team member remembers, "Christmas Day could not come too soon as far as we were concerned, for we looked forward to a great football victory in addition to winning the Texas boys' money." The team members pooled their money and bet on themselves to show "how rich and brave we Oklahomans were!"

The Christmas Day game of 1924 brought out a huge crowd of spectators, both black and white. The local newspaper headlined: "The Langston Wonder Team Is in Town," reporting that Booker Robinson "has a perfect stiff arm" and punter John Williams "is known to kick the ball from goalpost to goalpost."

At game time the stadium was packed. Fans stood all around the field so tightly that they could not be kept off the playing area. Everyone agreed that it was to be "the game of the year." And it was — a defensive battle from beginning to end.

The first three points came early in the first quarter. Langston received the kickoff and was stopped on the 10-yard line. After two plays only 1 yard was needed for a first down. Then the ball was

FOOTBALL FEVER: THE WONDER TEAM OF 1924

Booker T. Robinson, right halfback and captain of the 1924 football team. Courtesy of the late Booker T. Robinson.

John ("Big John") Williams, noted for his punts and drop kicks, who played for the Lions from 1924 to 1927. Courtesy of the late Booker T. Robinson.

fumbled, ending up in Paul Quinn's hands. Quinn's kicker, Ray Shepard, made the easy field goal, giving the team a 3 to 0 lead over Langston.

Late in the first half kicker Shepard repeated his performance with another field goal. The half ended Paul Quinn 6, Langston 0.

The second half of the game was scoreless. John Williams did try one field goal, but it went wide.

So the game of the year was lost 0 to 6. The loss was a bitter one for Langston players, staff, and fans — lost was all the players' Christmas money. The next day the Langston team members were given train fare to their homes in Oklahoma, for they would not go back to school until after the holidays. When they got home, they found more snow on the ground.

Why did Langston let its first national championship get away? First, undoubtedly the scout underestimated the Paul Quinn team. Some people believed that the overcrowded and sometimes violent conditions on the playing field were to blame. The game had to be stopped many times to eject fans from the playing area. Certainly the lack of practice after Thanksgiving hurt the team. Above all, Langston did not prepare for a defensive game and failed to use kicker John Williams. Many times they ran and passed from deep in their own territory. Langston punted only once during the game. As team captain Robinson put it, "Punting was not in our game plan at all — a big mistake." The critics concurred. The newspaper on the morning after the game said, "Langston failed to use their advantage in the kicking game."

Through the years Langston went on to win seven conference championships and two national titles — but football fever never reached the pitch it had in 1924.

The captain of the Wonder Team, Booker Robinson, maintained a lifelong interest in athletics and Langston. He died in March, 1978.

Caesar Felton ("Zip") Gayles:
A Man for All Sports Seasons

During his thirty-five years at Langston, "Zip" Gayles coached football and basketball teams to national prominence. But on the home front he remained a coach surrounded by controversy, stirring both intense loyalty and overt hostility. During the twenty-seven years he coached football, from 1930 to 1957, his teams won 146 games, lost 78, and tied 18. They won seven conference titles and two national championships. In basketball two of his players were all-conference choices, and one was a national champion.

During his playing career Gayles had won All-American honors in football and basketball. He was featured in a writeup about the Oklahoma Athletic Hall of Fame in the spring, 1972, issue of Oklahoma Today. He was inducted into the Oklahoma Hall of Fame in 1974. Earlier, in 1949, at th height of his glory at Langston, grateful alumni had presented him with an expensive car. The C. Felton Gayles Gymnasium on Langston's campus is named in his honor.

Former Athletic Director C. Felton ("Zip") Gayles. Courtesy of Mrs. C. Felton Gayles.

One of "Zip" Gayles's winning basketball teams.

Gayles Gymnasium.

CAESAR FELTON ("ZIP") GAYLES

The history of Caesar Felton Gayles begins with the new century. He was born on May 22, 1900, in Macon County, Mississippi. He was educated at Morehouse College, from which he received his B.A. degree in 1924. Before moving to Langston in 1930, he taught social science and coached at Tennessee A&I State University, in Nashville, and at Arkansas A&M, in Pine Bluff.

In his most successful coaching days at Langston, Gayles was fielding championship teams in both basketball and football. The years 1944-45 were especially good ones. Although manpower was short, Langston managed to achieve fifty-one straight basketball victories. His teams played YMCA teams, armed-services teams, all-star professionals, and colleges of the Southwestern Conference. In 1945 they won the conference title at Baton Rouge for the second consecutive year and for the third time in four years.

In football the 1944-45 record was six victories, one tie (with Tennessee State, and two losses (to Texas College and Tennessee State). They were tied with Texas College and Wiley College for the Southwestern Athletic Conference title. In 1956, when the Atlanta (Georgia) Daily World picked its all-time football team spanning the years 1900 to 1950, Gayles was named one of the all-time star ends on the team. He attended the awards banquet in Atlanta.

He was a strict and demanding coach. Marquis Haynes, a former student and basketball star, tells the story of how Coach Gayles nearly took him off the team for fancy dribbling. Gayles disliked such tricks. When he retired in 1965, Gayles was honored at a banquet along with Frances Anderson and Melvin Tolson, who also retired that year. William Sims was toastmaster, and awards were presented by President Hale.

Among his civic and professional services Gayles was a member of the United States Civil Rights Commission from 1958 to 1960. He was named an honorary life member of the Oklahoma 4-H clubs. He belonged to the Guthrie Library Board and the Guthrie Chamber of Commerce, served as a trustee of the First Baptist Church of Guthrie, and was a member of the NAACP. In 1977 he was appointed appointed to a two-year term on the Oklahoma Governor's Commission on Employment of the Handicapped.

A lifetime interest of Gayles has been his fraternity, Kappa Alpha

Psi. The Langston chapter of the fraternity was founded by Gayles, Walter Kennedy, and others on October 28, 1933. He also helped establish a chapter at Morehouse College and an alumni group in Tulsa. He holds a life membership in the fraternity and is currently active in the Muskogee unit. In January, 1978, he was honored at the Sixty-first Grand Conclave in Denver, where he was presented the Laurel Wreath, the fraternity's highest decoration. The award had been presented only twenty-six times in the fraternity's history.

CHAPTER SEVENTEEN

Community Service

THE HISTORY of relations between the town of Langston and the university begins with the establishment of the university. The institution was founded at Langston as a result of persistent efforts by the townspeople. The citizens worked together to raise the money to buy the forty-acre site for the school. When the elementary division opened in 1898 with four teachers and forty-one students, most of the children came from within the community.

In the early years there was strong rapport between university and community. As early as 1902 members of the college staff were helping farmers select and purchase farms. Early efforts were made to bring more business and industry to the town. Under the first president, Inman Page, a program was set up through the United States Department of Agriculture to help local citizens construct farm buildings, lay out fields, and build gates and fences. Page's administration also contributed to community-college involvement by ruling that all students were required to attend church in town at least once on the Sabbath.

In general, in the pioneer days the residents of the community had a feeling of pride and paternalism about "their" school. After all, many of them had helped found it. Similarly, the early-day presidents and faculty were sympathetic about the problems of the farming community.

Programs at the college were open to town residents and those from the surrounding countryside. The university museum was free, as were the farmers' conferences that were held on the second Saturday of each month. The conferences were open to all state farmers.

The Community Fair was begun by President Marquess, who also sought to improve relations with the town by visiting its school and churches. In addition he is credited with helping bring electricity and running water to the town.

As the college expanded and the population of the town decreased, feelings of lack of cooperation set in. The community did not grow as large or as fast as had been expected by early-day settlers. Both Indian and white pioneer families moved away from the community. The railroad acquired right of way at Coyle; two miles away. Many areas newly opened for settlement lured families to them. The economic base for all of Logan County remained farming. The soil is the "red plains" type, which is highly erodible. Farmers trying to grow cotton had periods of bad weather and insect invasion. The town's economic base declined to the point that the population of the village was listed in the 1940 census as 514. Between 1935 and 1940 almost two hundred Negro families had sold their farms.

With the decline in the black population of the country and the influx of students from other parts of the state and other regions of the United States, disharmony and the classic town-gown rivalry set in. In their study "Culture of a Contemporary All Negro Community," Mozell Hill and Thelma Ackiss attributed the bad feeling to "indifference on the part of new teachers to the community people and bitter resentment by the old settlers at being 'left out' of college activities and affairs."

Both town and college suffered hardships during the depression and dust-bowl years. In that era the school made an important contribution to the community through the Vocational Agriculture, Extension and Home Economics departments. The instructors worked with nearby residents, helping with farm and family problems. The Agriculture Department consulted with individual farmers on such matters as terracing, construction of poultry houses, and crop production and explained the new idea of "farm parity."

In house-to-house visits the teachers of vocational home economics taught canning, sewing, and home improvement. Such assistance was badly needed. The economic status of the Logan County Negro farmer was extremely low. About 44,000 acres were farmed by blacks, but only 10,000 acres were cultivated by the owners, meaning that nearly 34,000 acres were farmed by tenants

The oldest house in the city of Langston. Courtesy of Mrs. Viola Jones, Cooperative Extension Service.

or sharecroppers. The total value of farm implements owned by sharecroppers in 1940 was $2,090. Farmowners had $25,000 worth of equipment to work with.

Those who left the farms and moved to Langston had trouble finding jobs. In 1940 there were 3,799 Negroes over fourteen years of age in Logan County. Only 1,084 were employed. The low income level brought additional problems of housing and living conditions. Over half the blacks in the county lived in rent houses. Of nearly 1,500 houses occupied by Negroes, 1,178 were in need of major repairs. There was no running water in 949 houses and no electricity in 1,153, and only 83 housing units in the entire county had private baths and flush toilets. The median monthly rent for these units was $3.70. Two families paid over $100.00 a month.

At the time most of the best homes in Langston were valued at less than $500. There were many houses with a reported valuation of about $15. In 1942, M. F. Spaulding surveyed housing con-

Old Meeks Store on Washington Boulevard. Courtesy of Mrs. Viola Jones.

ditions in Langston and found that 91 percent had outdoor toilets, 5 percent had telephones, 13 percent had refrigerators, and 44 percent had radios. In the same year the Langston Board of Trustees (the city council) operated the town on a yearly revenue of $234. Its estimated needs were around $800. It was virtually impossible to tax a population in which the average wage was 66 cents a day. The average monthly income was $44.81 among the families who had any income at all.

With this economic base it is clear that the businesses of Langston were almost entirely dependent on college students and faculty members. There were, however, a number of teachers who deliberately avoided contact with the community. The Ackiss and Hill report found that this group "deliberately" did their shopping in Guthrie or elsewhere. Further, this segment of the academic community refrained from "even friendly relations with community residents and in general regard themselves as untouched and untouchable by anything in Langston which did not directly affect the university." The college staff complained constantly about the dirt streets and lack of firefighting equipment.

In 1940 the Campus Grocery, the largest business in Langston, was eight years old and employed three persons. It had two full-time clerks and electricity but lacked adequate ventilation. The most popular — and modern — business in town was the Collegian Club, which specialized in barbecue, hamburgers, soft drinks, and beer. Apparently it was well patronized by townspeople, students, and faculty.

Other than teachers and ministers there were no professionals in Langston. Only four of the seven local churches remained active. The town population and the business district continued to decline throughout the postwar years.

Attempts at college and community cohesiveness were few and far between. A federal credit union was organized in the town, which included some faculty members among its eighty enrollees. Both the home-economics and the vocational-agriculture teachers of the college prep school taught adult-education classes in Langston and in the surrounding area from 1937 to 1946. In earlier years, under President Young, a correspondence and extension department had been organized for those unable to come to campus for study. In early years Langston offered a six-week short course for teachers during the months that many Oklahoma elementary schools were closed for harvest. Most of the schools operated in July and August and then closed during September and October. Langston did not follow this practice, though until 1925 students could enter late — after harvest.

The city of Langston had its own high school from 1946 to 1960. During that period one of the college sororities, Alpha Kappa Alpha, sponsored guidance clinics. The college women met with high school students one afternoon a month and brought in speakers from various occupations. There was good attendance at the group discussion, which included question-and-answer sessions and refreshments.

Alpha Kappa Alpha also matched the funds that underwrote

Langston's first work-study program in the 1960s. Instead of working on campus, eligible students conducted a night school for adults and children at the Langston Elementary School.

Under President Hale several self-studies were completed within the university. One such survey, entitled "Teacher Education Program," stressed the community service provided through alumni conferences, speaking appearances by faculty members, in-service teachers' conferences, and consultant services, provided by faculty members. All evening classes, correspondence courses, and extension courses were handled by full-time employees of the university.

Hale apparently made an effort to reestablish rapport with the town. It was during his tenure that the university began hiring townspeople in various capacities. The campus infirmary provided medical care and emergency treatment for Langston residents.

A remarkable innovation came in 1963, when Langston University launched a program to counter the "dropout syndrome," holding "Langston University Day for Sixth-Graders." Twelve hundred sixth-grade students from across the state visited the campus for a full day of activities designed to interest them in higher education and introduce them to campus life. The program was a marked success. The next year fifteen hundred sixth-graders attended, and the event received national attention.

Also in 1963 the university observed the centennial of the Emancipation Proclamation by preparing an exhibit on "The Negro in American Life." The exhibit, as well as a study-discussion program series, was presented across the state.

University-sponsored conferences for high school teachers and their counterparts at the college level were held in the areas of language arts, science, social studies, mathematics and physical education. These conferences were well attended and brought closer cooperation between the secondary schools and the university.

Two far-reaching federal programs were launched at Langston during Hale's administration. The Upward Bound program gave high school students the opportunity to live on campus during the summer months and receive tutoring to prepare them for college work. The Head Start program initiated educational opportunities for young children of low-income families. Preschool youngsters from Langston, Guthrie, and nearby rural Logan County took part. In the 1970s the Upward Bound program expanded to include both on-campus and off-campus tutoring. After eight years of operation at Langston more than six hundred students in grades 9 to 12 in eight area high schools had participated.

Langston launched programs in human awareness in 1970. Three university faculty members conducted seminars in selected cities of the state, emphasizing human and group sensitivity. The seminars lasted two days and offered sessions on minority history, contemporary sociological problems, and psychology. The seminars were held in Tulsa, Oklahoma City, McAlester, Ponca City, Lawton, Ardmore, Altus, Chickasha, Bartlesville, Muskogee, Enid, Okmulgee, and Sand Springs.

A similar program grew out of the Higher Education Act of 1965, which provided Title I funds for further education of municipal employees. Designed to improve the quality of public administration and city services, the courses were administered by Langston faculty members but held off campus, most of them in Oklahoma City.

In May, 1972, a full-scale self-study report was issued by the Committee on Community Service of Langston University. In their research the members of the committee explored the extent of university services within the town. Some members of the committee felt that the university's service should be statewide. Others believed that it should extend even beyond the state — to other states and foreign countries from which Langston's students were drawn and to which they would return as graduates. All agreed, however, that "charity begins at home" and that the university and the community must work together, not only to avoid "alienation" but also to "revitalize the old spirit."

The committee summarized the services the university had rendered to the town, including helping landscape the city park, helping provide facilities for rodeos, teaching arts and crafts in the city school, spearheading a Langston clean-up campaign, and helping with home-beautification projects. (Later, as an outgrowth of the study, the University fire truck was placed at the service of the community.)

The self-study indicated that twenty-eight faculty members provided community services of one kind or another, mainly in counseling or consulting roles, although the university lacked a directed community-service program.

The study recommended a permanent high-level administrative officer for community service. It reaffirmed the policy under which Langston had traditionally operated: "educating capable individuals irrespective of their disadvantaged status in society." The report also recommended that the college should concern itself with the best means of providing its services to the poor: "Broadly put, the university should assume a posture which commits itself to both the rural and the urban poor."

Under the Agricultural Appropriations Act of 1972, funding was provided to institutions founded under the 1890 Land Grant Act to set up cooperative extension programs that would concentrate on the social, cultural, and economic problems of rural families. Langston set up its program in coordination with Oklahoma State University.

The committee's comments about the city of Langston remain true today. Since the Hill-Ackiss study in 1940, the size of the town has changed very little. The current population is approximately five hundred.

Washington Boulevard, the town's main street, is a hard-surface street. The other inner streets are chat (and suffered damage during the construction of a sewage system in 1977). Meridian Line, leading to State Highway 33 north, is a hard-surface road along the east edge of town.

The townspeople go to Guthrie, Coyle, and Oklahoma City to shop. For three years in the 1970s Langston did not have a grocery store. In 1977 a convenience store opened on Highway 33 north of town. In 1978, Langston had three cafes, one gas station, and a liquor store. The town's only cleaning establishment closed in 1977 with the retirement of the owners.

The Federal Credit Union has continued in operation, serving both town and university. An office is maintained on campus, staffed by two retired Langston employees, Ella Clement, former professor of mathematics, and Mizura Allen, C.P.A, former professor and head of the Business Administration Department.

Home construction in recent decades has included modern brick houses, mobile homes, remodeling projects, and construction of thirty low-income housing units and a community center, known as the M&M Building. The executive director of the center, Jimmie White, was a member of Langston University's Agriculture Department. The project was financed by a fifty-year $500,000 appropriation from the United States Department of Housing and Urban Development (HUD). The homes were spread through the existing community to avoid "grouping." Thirteen different sites, each with one to six houses, were developed.

Home valuations now range from $2,500 to $35,000. Virtually all homes are equipped with modern plumbing and heating.

Another major improvement was the construction in 1975-77 of an adequate sewage system for both town and university. Before the installation of the new system many homes had to rely on cesspools. The city is served with natural gas, electricity, and a waterworks. Langston Lake, developed jointly with the university, provides both water and recreational facilities.

Since the 1940 study seven new churches have been built, three of which were replacements of older buildings. The active congregations include Salter's Chapel AME, the New Hope Baptist Church, the Church of the Living God, the Church of Christ, the Catholic Church, the Seventh-Day Adventist Church, the Church of God in Christ, the ME United Methodist Church, and Mount Bethel Baptist Church. Members of the Episcopal Church worship in the Catholic Church building. There are three inactive congregations.

Despite the 1972 study, the persistent pattern of campus-town dissociation has remained through the years. Many university employees commute daily from homes in Stillwater, Guthrie, and Oklahoma City. In 1978, thirty-four Langston University employees lived in the city of Langston. Their positions ranged from professor to snack-bar supervisor and included librarians, accountants, maintenance men, and counselors. Nineteen retired university

The Ulysses Cumby home. Courtesy of Omar Reed.

The home of Mr. and Mrs. Billy Ray Owens, Langston. Courtesy of Mrs. Hortense Owens.

Low-rent houses in Langston. Courtesy of George R. Milsap.

The old Morten home in Langston, owned and remodeled by Mrs. Letha Benson. Courtesy of Mrs. Viola Jones.

employees were also living in the town. Many of those who live in the Langston community seem to gather in an area on Highway 33 between Langston and Guthrie. There are about nine faculty homes along this stretch of road, which is commonly considered part of Guthrie rather than Langston.

Since 1940 marked changes have occurred in the countryside around Langston. Small-scale farming has given way to ranching on relatively large acreages. Sharecropping has disappeared entirely. Many of the townspeople work at the university, at a furniture factory in Guthrie, and as far away as Tinker Field, in Midwest City.

CHAPTER EIGHTEEN

The Cooperative Extension Service

COOPERATIVE extension work is essentially teaching. Agriculture and home economics teachers provide practical demonstrations for farm families, either in the rural setting or on campus, of ways to apply the latest results of studies by the United States Department of Agriculture, the state agriculture department, and state colleges. Teaching is not primarily from books or theory but is concerned with orchards, barns, gardens, and the farm home. The primary emphasis is on practical demonstration.

Farm demonstration work began in the United States in 1903. All the first agents were white. Negro involvement came through the Department of Agriculture to Tuskegee Institute. Oklahoma came into the program in 1910.

The extension program was of enormous benefit to the blacks who lived in the sixteen southern states. The 1920 census showed more than 920,000 Negro farmers in those states working on 27 million acres of improved land. To reach this population, programs were set up with black auxiliary extension agents through the 1862 and 1890 land-grant colleges.

Extension work really began with Booker T. Washington and his Tuskegee Institute in Alabama. The school held farm conferences, issued bulletins, and offered agricultural demonstrations through its faculty. Washington used a "Jesup wagon" to go out into the rural areas and show farmers practical new methods of farming. He had great hopes for the farm-demonstration method, praising it as "taking education to the man on the job." He believed that through the cooperation of the Department of Agriculture with the institute, farmers would be taught newer and better methods. He said, "No other single agency, I am sure, is destined to do more in the task of creating a New South."

In 1906 the first Negro demonstration agent was appointed — T. M. Campbell, of Tuskegee. Alabama and Virginia (through Hampton Institute) set up programs for blacks that year. Mississippi followed in 1909, and in 1910, Oklahoma became the fourth state to provide demonstrations.

Oklahoma also had the honor of appointing the first Negro woman home-demonstration agent — Annie Peters, of Boley, in 1912. The cost of keeping her in the field for a year was recorded as $180.

Until World War I there were never more than one black man and one black woman agent at work in Oklahoma. The big push began in 1919, when six men and four women began working among the state's black farmers. In 1921 there were fourteen Negro agents in the field at an annual cost of $26,000. The men's district director was W. A. Hill, of Langston University. In that year the program extended to Kingfisher, Logan, Oklahoma, Lincoln, Okfuskee, Seminole, Creek, Wagoner, McIntosh and McCurtain counties. The budget at Langston University was so tight that year that the college did not contribute any funds to the program.

All the agents met at Langston for a conference in July, 1921. A summary of the previous year's work of the male agents showed that forty-three community farmers' clubs had been organized, ninety-two adult Negroes had been taught to give corn demonstrations, and eighty-four had been trained in cotton demonstrations. Demonstrators were instructing farmers in the newest methods of raising corn, kafir, cotton, tomatoes, oats, alfalfa, Sudan grass, cowpeas, peanuts, and potatoes. In orchard dmonstrations agents had taught gardeners to inspect, set out, spray, and prune fruit trees.

At an annual salary of $2,000 each, the agents had attended 915 meetings during the year, traveled 40,000 miles and met with more than 44,000 people. They listed among the main accomplishments installing eleven telephone systems, screening 160 homes, putting in three lighting systems, and building 42 sanitary privies.

In the early days of farm-demonstration work, boys' clubs were formed in several areas of crop or breeding specialty. In 1921, Oklahoma had 148 boys' clubs, enrolling members in corn clubs (with membership of 639), pig clubs (with 53 enrolled in breeding) and peanut-hay demonstration clubs. Through the influence of these clubs twenty-five boys entered college. They were also encouraged to enter club competitions and fairs. Twenty-one entered the State Fair of Oklahoma that year and won more than $1,300 in prizes. It was duly reported that seventy-three boys had opened their own bank accounts.

The four black women agents worked under the supervision of a white district agent. They attended the conferences for white agents, as well as the black conference at Langston in July. Girls, too, had been organized into clubs. There were 658 girls enrolled in canning clubs and 197 in poultry clubs (one requirement of the poultry clubs was to "set a hen"). The canning-club members were required to make jelly and vinegar. All the girls had to learn to sew; the report showed that they had made aprons, caps, dresses, towels, and curtains.

Several Negro community fairs were held in Lincoln, Muskogee, and McIntosh counties. Some of the highest-scoring exhibits were sent to the Langston Fair, and the girls were allowed to go to the campus for instruction in sewing, games, and club work.

The women agents, whose salaries were $1,200 a year, reported achievements for 1921 including repairing ten septic tanks, constructing 230 flower boxes, screening three houses, and purchasing barrel churns, milk separators, milk pails, butter molds, and kitchen cabinets. The women agents had also visited 202 schools, had met with 817 girls' club members, and had given 732 adult home demonstrations.

The early years of Negro home-demonstration work was led by the guiding spirit of Booker T. Washington. He saw the South as the permanent home of the black family and urged full development of the soil, forest, and the human potential. With this philosophy strong among his many followers, the field was promising for black extension work. Later many blacks grew to resent the farming emphasis and urged a shift away from concentration on agricultural and vocational training. Langston was involved in the often bitter dispute between "academic" and "agricultural" forces.

The first 4-H Club for Negro boys and girls was organized at Langston in 1918. Through the years the university served as a statewide center for the 4-H Club roundups, short courses, and state junior livestock shows, adult short courses; and conferences of county extension agents. 4-H Club members who were at least twelve years old could become candidates for attendance at 4-H camps held during the annual state fair and the Oklahoma free state fair. From 1916 to 1923 Langston also held an annual on-campus community free fair in the early fall.

The area field agent of demonstration work at Langston was T. M. Campbell, of Tuskegee. His district included eight southern states. He visited the campus every year and gave inspiring speeches in chapel. He had a fine singing voice and would often give concerts as well.

A good example of the involvement of Langston in the agricultural and home economics extension work was the program planned for 1924. The school issued a special *Agricultural and Home Economics* bulletin announcing the Second Annual Oklahoma Farm and Home Congress to be held on campus July 23 to 25. It promised demonstrations, a junior congress, free lodging, and three meals a day for seventy-five cents. The practical demonstrations included dairying, clothing, farm shop work and terracing. In

J. E. Taylor, Sr., Cooperative Extension Service agent. Courtesy of Mrs. A. R. Taylor.

the evening there were motion pictures. Speakers included Langston's President Young; Bradford Knapp, the president of Oklahoma A&M; and George Washington Carver, of Tuskegee.

Most of the extension work was funded by the United States Department of Agriculture or through Smith-Lever Act funds. Sometimes, however, Negro county councils raised funds from among black members. White citizens of some counties appeared before courts or chambers of commerce to urge appointment of Negro agents.

It was estimated that by 1923 the work in Oklahoma was reaching about 40 percent of the rural Negro population. Langston extension work was led by State Agent J. E. Taylor, Sr. In the early 1930s Julia Miller joined the Langston extension staff. The two supervised field agents and coordinated local programs in various counties. Nine men and five women worked under their supervision in their district.

All through the dust bowl and depression years the county demonstration work followed the "Ten Commandments" for Negro agriculture devised by Seamon Knapp, of the United States Department of Agriculture. The commandments were eminently practical maxims, including: "Produce all the food required for the men and animals on the farm;" "Keep an account of each farm product in order to know from which the gain or loss arises;" and "Accomplish more work in a day by using more horsepower and better implements."

In general, the goal of Negro vocational agriculture had not changed since the first Farmer's Conference held at Tuskegee in 1892. At that conference a resolution was passed setting forth the goals: aiming to "raise at home our own meat and bread," attempting to "buy land, even though a very few acres at a time," and seeing that young people were "taught trades."

The first shift in goals occurred in World War II, when the aim became Victory Gardens. "Victory Food" became the slogan for 4-H clubs and farm families. The extension leaders agreed that, while the essential goal was to assure that black farm families were reasonably well fed and housed, the Victory Food goals must include putting in gardens, canning produce, drying fruits, curing

4-H Club girls, accompanied by Helen Hewlett, district home demonstration agent, welcomed to the Langston campus by President Harrison, 1948.

meats, and increasing egg production. During the war every farm family was encouraged to maintain a garden that would supply its needs, and city families were encouraged to maintain gardens too. The district supervisors in 1944 were Paul Brooks and Helen Fowler Hewlett.

After the war the extension work was broadened to include Choctaw and McCurtain counties. Until that time only short-term depression-era projects had operated in those counties. It was also recognized that times had changed and that extension work must allow for the fact that not all rural children would become farmers when they grew up.

Langston University continued to furnish many of the extension field workers. In the mid-1950s the roster of agents in agriculture and home-demonstration work showed that the director of women agents, five of the men agents, and eight of the women agents had studied at Langston.

The Langston University Cooperative Extension Service Office was discontinued in 1965, and the program merged with the Oklahoma State University unit. Hazel King, the director at Langston, transferred to the Stillwater campus to work with the human-resources program.

In 1972 approximately $4 million in federal funds were available for extension programs administered by the 1890 land-grant institutions. Langston-OSU objectives under this program included community development of poor rural townships, family-living training in home and money management, and educational programs for youth of low-income families. The Langston staff consisted of four full-time specialists, six paraprofessionals, a fiscal officer, and support personnel under the director, James Mosley.

Langston tried to reach the target families through such groups as the Oklahoma Association of Colored Women's Federated Clubs, the Black Minister's Alliance, and the Prince Hall Grand Lodge. In 1972 work was begun in twelve counties with large black or Indian populations living in primarily rural farming communities. A home economist was assigned to each three-county area and a youth specialist to each four-county unit. The family-living program emphasized nutrition, consumer education, and home improvement.

In April, 1974, a team of inspectors from the United States Department of Agriculture visited the state to observe the workings of the extension program. Their report indicated that the extension service was pinpointing the target families well but also noted that, instead of "one cooperative program," there were still two extension services operating, Langston for blacks and OSU for whites. Since 1974 an adjustment has been made. Langston works in cooperation with OSU and the U.S. Department of Agriculture to a greater extent.

CHAPTER NINETEEN

English, Ancient Languages, and Modern Languages

ENGLISH GRAMMAR, literature, and ancient and modern foreign languages have been a part of the Langston curriculum since its founding. Many of the courses continue to the present day. With the opening of the school the bulletin promised courses "available" in English, Latin, Greek, German, and French. The first instructor was Moses J. Johnson, who from 1898 until 1905 taught all the English, language, and literature courses. Since few students enrolled in the upper-level curricula in those years, it is doubtful that all the courses listed were actually taught.

The early-day elementary and high school students spent a lot of time doing "rhetorical exercises," which consisted of writing proper letters and "interpreting and rendering masterpieces in prose and poetry."

Elementary students (who comprised most of the student body from 1898 to 1901) studied *McGuffey's* fourth and fifth readers and used Maxwell's *Introductory Lessons* as the grammar text. As an example of the course of study, the bulletin announced that seventh-grade grammar students learned "parts of speech, classification of sentences, principles of orthography, analysis and parsing, ... spelling and composition," as well as etymology and clauses.

For students who might enroll in the upper-division classical course, a rigorous language program was planned. Freshmen were to study Latin, Greek, and rhetoric, while sophomores were to undertake courses in Latin, Greek, and French. The junior student was to begin German, as well as keep up the study of both English and American literature. It was proposed that students in the scientific course take French, Spanish, and German.

In 1905 a second instructor in reading and Latin, William E. Guy, joined the faculty. Students who completed the high school years were well versed in Latin. Study began in the ninth grade, and Cellar and Daniell's *First Year Latin* was used as the text. This was followed by a second-year text and a book on composition. Students would translate the *Aeneid* and pursue Latin grammar. The text for the study of Latin meter was that by Greenough and Kittredge. Third-year students in the Normal Department curriculum studied Cicero, translating four of the Cataline Orations.

Study of literature in the early years was centered on English works. There were courses in Elizabethan, Commonwealth, Restoration, and eighteenth-century English writings. In the last half of the freshman year some colonial and national American literature was covered. Students studied the works of John Lyly, William Tyndale, Thomas Gray, T. H. Huxley, Thomas Maccaulay, James Russell Lowell, Richard Henry Dana, and others.

In 1906, Gilbert Jones joined the faculty as professor of ancient languages, and the catalogue began offering courses in Greek and advanced Latin. The college-level work in Greek began with White's *First Greek* as the text and continued until students were proficient enough to translate the *Anabasis*. An ambious program of Greek translation included New Testament Greek, *Oedipus Tyrannus*, and Plato's *Apology.*

Similarly, Latin students did library work in Roman history and in the four-year course translated Cicero's *De Amicitia* and *De Senectute,* and works of Tacitus, Horace, Plautus, and Juvenal.

Until World War I science, agricultural, and mechanical students were required to take German for two years. The basic text was *German Method,* by Lange. Students translated Baumbach's *Der Schwiegersohn* (The Son-in-Law) and Johnn Schiller's *Wilhelm Tell.* After the two German courses, students could study French in the junior year. The basic French text was Edgren's *Grammar.* It was noted that as much French was read as "the ability and energy of the class made possible."

Spanish was listed as a course offering in 1905, but no text was mentioned. The course work consisted of "vocabulary, translating and writing sentences." In the spring semester students read stories by Spanish authors.

An interesting course required of third-year education students was elocution. It was a practical course in public speaking. The instructors promised to give "special attention . . . to correcting mistakes in pronunciation, proper utterance of English sounds, articulation, syllabication, and accentuation." The text was *Practical Elocution,* by Fulton and Trueblood.

In 1905 the English faculty consisted of three instructors. George Carry was professor of English and literature, Paralee V. Lucas was instructor in English and mathematics, and William Guy was professor of Latin and Elocution. Both Carry and Guy resigned the following year. In 1907, Ada Hawes became English instructor, and Gilbert Jones took over ancient languages.

By 1912-13, the entrance standards for the school were becoming stricter. Entering freshmen were "required to be able to write a composition that was very nearly correct in respect to spelling, grammar, idiom, punctuation, and division into paragraphs." The literature course, which presupposed some familiarity with the classics, promised instruction in English literature from the Anglo-Saxon period to modern times.

After another turnover in faculty Samuel Levi Sadler became instructor in English. Sadler, who had earned his B.S. from Langston, is remembered as the composer of the school song, "Dear Langston" (see appendices).

During this period required readings in the English department included two Shakespearean plays, *As You Like It* and *Macbeth,* Daniel Webster's *Bunker Hill Oration,* and Cairn's *Forms of Discourse.* Seniors were offered courses in Chaucer, Milton, and Spenser. From the catalogues the most difficult language course was advanced Greek, which proposed that students would read selections from books I to IV of the *Hellenica:* study Greek history from the Persian to the Pelopennesian wars, particularly Athenian history in the Age of Pericles; and read selections from Plato's *Phaedo.*

In Latin the requirements for admittance to the freshmen year included the ability to translate Cicero's orations, knowledge of Latin prosody, and ability to write Latin prose.

A French instructor was listed in 1921. The yearbook for that year does not list an English faculty. In 1923-24 the English staff consisted of two instructors; one of them stayed only a year, and the other was the President Young's daughter. About this time a course in business English was developed for commercial-course students. The football coach, W. E. Anderson, became director of the Department of English in 1924. Miss Young, married S. L. Hargrove, dean and vice-president of the school, and both retained their positions.

As well as traditional grammar and literature courses, the 1920s brought such course offerings as debate, forensics, and playwriting. Public speaking, journalism, and literary criticism were also offered.

The Latin curriculum remained about the same, continuing to offer course readings in Caesar, Cicero, Vergil, Horace, and Livy.

In the meantime, the high school used state-adopted texts and followed the practical philosophy that English must be taught according to the rule that "usage is the law of language."

Beginning in September, 1925, the English Department started a program in remedial English. Students were both assigned to the course and promoted from it entirely at the discretion of the instructors.

In 1927 for the first time a course in Negro literature was offered. The required readings were W. E. B. Du Bois's *The Souls of Black Folk,* Walter F. White's *Fire in the Flint,* Booker T. Washington's *My Larger Life,* Paul Dunbar's *Lyrics of Lowly Life,* and Benjamin G. Brawley's *Six Negro Women of Achievement.*

Among the specific requirements of courses were such assignments as these: journalism students were required to work on the university bulletin staff; Shakespeare students wrote a technical analysis of *Othello;* students specializing in Victorian literature wrote a three-thousand word paper on the literary development of the period.

During the 1920s emphasis was on mastery of practical and vocational subjects. But the Latin faculty held out, deploring the trend away from the "old school" and deeming it "inadvisable to leave off altogether those subjects which have for their ultimate the cultural phase of education." Thus the Latin Department, under Dean Hargrove and Peter Meggs, continued to offer the full complement of classics courses all the way through Livy's *History of Rome.*

Ms. Hargrove resigned from the faculty in 1930 to devote her time to her three children. When Zachary Hubert became president of the University, the English staff was expanded to four. An instructor in public speaking was added in 1930-32. Three of the four staff members were replaced when Young became president of Langston for the second time in 1931. Dewey Batchelor was the sole holdover from the previous administration.

The curriculum in the early depression years of the 1930s required all freshmen and sophomores to take English, with remedial English for those who scored low on entrance exams. Foreign-language offerings were French and German. In 1934-35, Collins George became director of the Department of Foreign Languages. He designed a curriculum that offered four full terms of French and German, including required reading of German newspapers and conversational French and German.

Not until the wartime years of the early 1940s did the English and language department staffs increase in size. In 1941-42 there were five on the English staff, as well as a lab-school English instructor and a French teacher. Students who were required to take remedial English received no course credit. They were taught spelling, word usage, and sentence construction by the intensive-drill method. Altogether there were twenty-two English courses, six courses in French, and four each in Spanish and German. Beginning in 1941 all English majors had to take a final comprehensive written exam in English and American literature. Two years of English were required of all students in arts and science. An English major undertook twenty-four hours beyond the required courses.

For unknown reasons the course in the Negro in American literature was dropped from the curriculum in 1943.

Melvin B. Tolson, poet and playwright, joined the English faculty in 1947. He had studied at Fisk, Lincoln, and Columbia universities and received the A.M. from Columbia. Langston created a new title for him: Professor of Creative Literature. He came to Langston from Wiley College, in Marshall, Texas, where he founded the Little Log Cabin Theatre and became noted as "the radical little man who brought undying fame to Wiley as a debate coach, lecturer, author, instructor, and personality."

Joy Flasch, chairman, Communications Department. Courtesy of Joy Flasch.

Keith Slothower, who had charge of the Dust Bowl Players, the campus drama group, until his death in 1977.

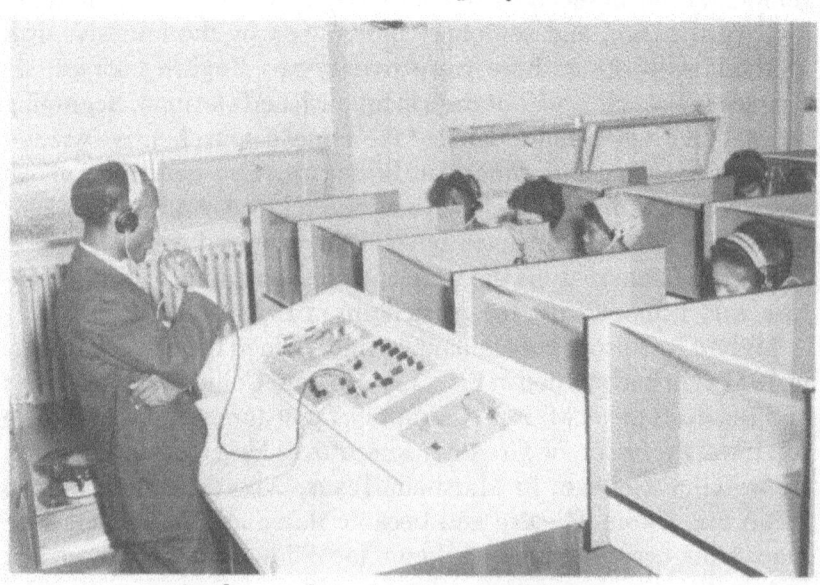

Study carrels in the Language Laboratory.

At Langston, Tolson founded the Dust Bowl Players. The theater group performed adaptations of such plays as Lorraine Hansberry's *A Raisin in the Sun,* James Hilton's *Lost Horizons,* and the popular mystery *Dial M for Murder.* Tolson contributed his own dramatization of White's *The Fire in the Flint.* This production was staged for the National Convention of NAACP before an audience of five thousand.

An excellent account of Tolson's life and work at Langston is given in the Twayne United States Authors' series biography *Melvin B. Tolson,* by Langston Professor Joy Flasch.

Upon his death in 1966, Tolson was succeeded by Keith Slothower, who remained in the position until his death in 1977.

Both faculty and course offerings expanded in the postwar years. With the drive for accreditation the requirements for English majors were upgraded. English majors had to pass departmental exams, at the end of the junior and senior years. The junior exam was written; the senior exam oral. If the student was found "deficient," he had to take additional course work and then take the exams again.

Youra Qualls became the first woman chairman of the English Department in 1955. Five instructors and two professors completed the department, which also offered courses in speech and French.

Between the 1950s and 1960s the courses remained the same, but the numbering system changed. Survey courses were begun. The greatest change came in the physical facilities available for language instruction. The school added a communications center with both reading and language labs. The Little Theatre complex housed the Dust Bowl Players with an auditorium (capacity 380) stage facilities, two rehearsal rooms, and costume storage.

A required freshman reading test was begun in 1961, and students who scored low took remedial reading. Two courses were offered, each of which carried a one-hour credit. The humanities curriculum was also established in the early 1960s.

Departmental organizations included the English Club, the Dust Bowl Players, the French and Spanish club and the Book Review Club. The chairman of the department was Moxye Weaver King. She was succeeded in 1965 by Elwyn Breaux Welch. During this

Elwyn B. Welch, chairman, Department of English.

time a more diverse faculty, including many non-Langston-trained instructors, was recruited. Joy Flasch, who had received her doctorate from OSU; Elizabeth Kendall, who was educated at Stanford University and in Germany; V. F. Pons, of Havana, Cuba; and Jan Rolland Lucien, from Haiti, all came to Langston during the period 1963-65. Homer Nicholson, who had been a Rhodes Scholar at Oxford and received the Ph.D. from Vanderbilt University, joined the faculty in 1965.

In the late 1960s a restructuring of the teacher's degree program in English was completed. New courses included human growth and development, audiovisual education, educational psychology, and measurement and evaluation. A student could major in either English or teaching of language arts. Minors were English, speech, and French, German, or Spanish. In another curriculum change Elmyra Davis, who had been with the library since 1943, transferred to the reading lab in 1963 and later to the English faculty. Other English faculty members in the late sixties included Joann Clark and Oletha Tolliver.

The Dust Bowl Theatre complex was enlarged to seat about one hundred. The Humanities courses expanded to four. The liberal-arts English degree required twelve hours of foreign-language credits. The Creative Writing Club and Alpha Mu Gamma were

Scene from the campus production of Hello, Dolly! presented by the Dust Bowl Players in 1976. Actors are Michael Vance Moore and Freddie Foshee Cudjoe. Courtesy of Public Relations Office, Langston University.

added to the department's organizations. All these changes were made before 1975.

In 1974 a new Communications Department was established, separate from the English Department. In the new department were courses in broadcast journalism, theatre arts, speech, drama, and humanities. This department was established through the help of the Oklahoma City Broadcaster's Association, whose members had visited the campus in 1972 and urged the erection of a campus radio station and training in its operation. This training would help supply broadcasters with qualified minority employees. A class D FM station was set up in the Young Auditorium with studios upstairs. The station, KALU, began operation on March 6, 1975. It broadcasts about three hours a day on 90.7 FM, using about $12,000 worth of equipment.

In its first years of operation the Communications Department under Joy Flasch has provided outstanding events for the Langston campus. In 1974, Julie Haydon starred in the Dust Bowl Players' spring production of the *Spoon River Anthology.* More than one thousand off-campus guests saw the production during its two-week run. Five matinee performances were given for high schools with the aim of recruiting more nonblack students for the school. The same production was presented as Langston's entry in the Oklahoma College Theater Festival.

The department is also the host for the Carl Albert Oratorical Contest. Another responsibility of the department is the school newspaper, the *Langston Gazette,* founded during the administration of President Harrison. By May, 1975, thirty students had passed the FCC third-class radio-telephone operator's test, and three had received broadcast endorsement.

The Humanities Department employs team teaching in cooperation with art and music instructors. The Communications Department has four full-time faculty members, five part-time staff members, and a special consultant. In 1978 the department had approximately seventy major students.

A renovation of the Theatre Arts Center in the basement of Young Auditorium was completed in 1976. Through 1977 four students had graduated with degrees in broadcast journalism and three with degrees in theater arts.

Melvin B. Tolson: The Subject Is Poetry

A member of the Langston faculty from 1947 through 1965, M. B. Tolson brought recognition to the school through his poetic achievements and through the creation of a strong Fine Arts Department. He became professor of English and drama at Langston in 1947, the same year in which he was appointed poet laureate of Liberia. These appointments climaxed a career that had already included publication of his Dark Symphony and "Rendezvous with America" and receipt of the Omega Psi Phi Prize for Creative Literature.

Tolson was a "natural" for the Langston environment. He left Wiley College in Texas to accept the job. He was forty-seven years old when he arrived in Oklahoma, having been born in 1900 in Moberly, Missouri, of Negro, Indian, and Irish ancestors. As a child he liked to play ball, play the mandolin, practice "weed" medicine on his brothers and sisters, and study. He attended high school in Kansas City, Missouri, where he worked with the Little Theatre Club, was captain of the football team, and was named class poet. After one year at Fisk, University, Tolson went on to complete his college work at Lincoln University in Oxford, Pennsylvania.

Before joining the Langston faculty Tolson had established a reputation as a debate coach: he had led debate teams to ten national championships for Wiley College. At the end of the 1930s Tolson's interest had turned to drama and playwrighting. Some of his short plays include those with Oklahoma settings, Bivouac on the Santa Fe and Transfiguration Springs.

In the 1950s, while teaching at Langston and overseeing the Dust Bowl Players, he wrote original full-length dramatic productions and adapted works for the stage. The Moses of Beale Street, and Southern Front concerned racial situations. He also produced Black No More, based on George Schuyler's novel and The Fire in the Flint, adapted from Walter White's book. He completed manuscripts of three novels, "Beyond the Zaretto," "The Lion and the Jackal," and "All Aboard."

The Dust Bowl Players, Langston's campus lab for speech

Melvin B. Tolson (left), with Karl Shapiro. Courtesy of Public Relations Office, Langston University.

courses, developed into a full ethnic-theater group in the 1950s. They appeared not only on campus but before such groups as the national Baptist Convention and the NAACP conclave. Among the presentations of the Dust Bowl Players directed by Tolson were A Raisin in the Sun, Lost Horizons, and The Heiress.

While he taught at Langston, Tolson customarily woke after midnight and devoted the rest of the night to writing poetry. The Langston years saw publication of Libretto for the Republic of Liberia in 1953 and the psychological poem "O. and O. E." in 1954. The last poem won a Poetry magazine prize.

Beginning in 1954, Tolson served four terms as mayor of Langston village. He lived in a white-frame house near Highway 33. He was in declining health when his masterpiece, Harlem Gallery, appeared in print in 1965. Long-overdue literary tributes began pouring in. He was invited to New York, Philadelphia, and Washington D.C. Langston dedicated the Fine Arts Festival to him, and Karl Shapiro shared the platform with him. The yearbook that year was dedicated to Tolson and Coach Zip Gayles.

From his retirement in 1965 until his death a year later Tolson had more speaking engagements than he could fill. He was honored at the Library of Congress, the White House, and the Tuskegee Institute. In May the American Academy of Arts and Letters presented him with the annual poetry award. In August, 1966, he died of cancer at the age of sixty-six. He was buried in Summit View Cemetery in Guthrie. Memorial services were held in Young Auditorium at Langston.

Tolson's bequest to the university, the Tolson Collection of black literature and art, part of the Langston Library holdings, is one of the most extensive collections of its kind in the country. It is an invaluable part of Langston's heritage from the poet.

Langston faculty member Joy Flasch has written a critical biography of Tolson. The book, Melvin B. Tolson, was published in 1972 by Twayne Publishing Company in its United States Authors Series.

In 1973 the Langston Creative Writing Club erected a stone monument to Tolson in front of the white-frame house near Highway 33. It says, simply, "A Black Poet Lived Here."

CHAPTER TWENTY

Home Economics

THE FIRST instructor of girls in "domestic economy" was Mary Lee McCrary, who taught at Langston from 1900 until 1913. During the early years the courses focused on sewing and millinery. The aim was to prepare girls to be housewives or to be self-supporting in "domestic" careers such as dressmaking. The students who enrolled in sewing had to pay a lab fee of 75 cents.

The first listing of cooking courses came in 1913-14. At that time the terminology was "domestic science" (food courses) and "domestic art" (clothing courses). Girls furnished their own notebooks and paid a lab fee of 35 cents for the cooking course. The domestic-art

A fitting demonstration in a home-economics class, 1923-24. Mrs. Emma Wells, left, was the instructor.

Mrs. J. West, *clothing instructor, 1923-24.*

course included instruction in hatmaking, dressmaking, and pattern drafting.

The terms "domestic art" and "domestic science" finally gave way to the over-all term "home economics" during the 1920s. Today the Department of Home Economics at Langston operates under the Division of Vocational and Technical Education, offering a teaching degree and a liberal-arts degree.

The teacher-education program leading to a degree in home economics that qualified the graduate to teach in Oklahoma schools (or elsewhere) really began in 1923. The first home-economics certificate was issued in 1924, and the first bachelor of science degree in home economics was granted in 1931. The university first qualified for teacher-education aid in 1926.

In 1923-24, under Dr. Young's first administration, a home-management house was built as the practical-living aspect of the home-economics curriculum. The state legislature appropriated the money for construction and equipment of a one-story frame cottage. An early-day picture shows front and side entrances with screened doors, two brick columns supporting the front porch, and a coat of white paint. There was no landscaping around the house.

From 1924 to 1930, Mrs. Garvis Sparks Ricks, teacher trainer in charge of the home-management cottage, lived on the premises. The house was only big enough to accommodate two girls at a time. They resided in the cottage for six-week periods, for which they received three hours' credit.

New sewing rooms were added to the women's dorm. The foods lab was in the annex of Phyllis Wheatley Hall. Practice teaching was done either in the university high school or the Langston public school from 1923 to 1937, when it was done it approved centers in the state. From 1927 annual home-economics conferences were sponsored.

In 1930, Lenouliah E. Gandy joined the faculty. Later she became vocational home-economics supervisor for departments in separate schools. She was also state adviser to the New Homemakers of America. She was a member of the home-economics faculty at Langston at the time of her death in 1963.

A new home-management cottage was built of native stone in 1930. This modern house, which cost $7,900, could accommodate four girls and a teacher as live-in residents. The house also had a guest room. After the new cottage was completed, home-economics students were required to live in it for nine or ten weeks for practical experience. The division director supervised the cottage man-

Garvis Sparks Ricks, chairman of the Home Economics Department and teacher trainer, 1923-27 and 1931-35. Courtesy of the late Garvis Sparks Ricks.

Senior normal home-economics class, 1927-28, shown inside the practice cottage.

agement, but the girls planned and prepared the meals and did the housekeeping.

Despite a new home-economics lab on the second floor of the Administration Building, the facilities for cooking and sewing remained inadequate. The late 1930s and 1940s brought a surge in enrollment in "home ec" courses. The same facility that had accommodated 30 girls enrolled in home economics teacher education in 1930-32 was severely strained by an enrollment of 154 in 1940. An appropriation of $2,300 was made in 1940-41 to enlarge and remodel the department. The improvements included two lecture rooms, a clothing room, a foods lab, a dining room, a lounge, and two offices. By this time the era of restricting home economics to "cooking and sewing" had passed. Training was provided in five different areas: child development and family relationships, consumer education, housing and home management, clothing and textiles, food and nutrition, and home-economics teacher education. In the 1960s the faculty included one specialist in each area, a standard necessary for maintaining accreditation.

The home-economics program had been accredited by the North Central Association during the 1950s, when it was under the direction of Sadie G. Washington. She had earned her master's degree at Columbia University, in New York City, and had come to the Home Economics Department at Langston in 1937. The department gained accreditation from the National Council for Accreditation of Teacher Education in the mid-1960s when it was under my direction.

In 1968 the Home Economics Department moved from the second floor of Moore Hall to new space on the third floor of Jones Hall. The new facilities included a suite of offices, a receptionist's office, two classrooms, a sewing and textile lab, a food lab, a curriculum library, and a living-dining area. There was office space for five professors. New equipment and furnishings were provided. This section was part of the ten-year development plan for Langston.

In a sign of the times, Langston enrolled its first male home-economics major in 1968. Odie Waller, of Memphis, Tennessee, who also played quarterback for the Langston football team, became a full-time student in diet and nutrition in the general home-

Lenoliah E. Gandy, state vocational home-economics supervisor for black high schools, state adviser for New Homemakers of America, and teacher trainer, 1937-63.

Sadie G. Washington, director of Home Economics Division, 1937-65.

Ella M. Washington, professor of clothing and textiles, 1946-60.

Odie Waller, the first male graduate of the Home Economics Department, 1971. Courtesy of Odie Waller.

economics program. He graduated in 1971. After working as a dietician at a Memphis hospital, he is now employed by the United States Postal Service.

Other faculty members in home economics from 1930 to 1975 included F. V. Greene, N. McGowan, Ruth Jason, Edith Tate, E. M. Washington, Clara Fisher, Wilma Holt, Dannie Keepler, Glenda Warren, Sharon Hunt, and Ann Day. In 1972, Annie A. West became acting chairman of the department. Doreatha Gaffney was named chairman in 1975, followed by Willia A. Combs.

CHAPTER TWENTY-ONE

The School of Law

A FASCINATING, if minor, chapter in the history of Langston University involves the School of Law, which was in existence for less than two years and enrolled only one student: The story behind the Langston Law School lay in the question of whether Negroes would have access to then segregated graduate schools within the state.

The test case for striking down Oklahoma's constitutional barriers was provided by a Chickasha girl and Langston graduate, Ada Lois Sipuel (later Fisher). She completed her undergraduate work at Langston in 1946 and declared her intention of enrolling at the University of Oklahoma School of Law in Norman.

Backed by the local and national NAACP chapters and with the editorial support of Roscoe Dunjee, of the *Black Dispatch*, Ms. Fisher arrived at OU and was promptly denied admittance. This touched off state and federal court cases that lasted for two years.

The state's reaction to the court case was to fund and organize a hastily established "separate but equal" School of Law at Langston University. This school, which used the library facilities of the state capitol, was financed out of the governor's contingency fund. A member of the state legislature from Lawton donated use of his offices as classrooms for the new department.

A bulletin issued in January, 1948, declared the Langston University School of Law in operation, established by the A & M Board of Regents on January 24, 1948. The location, 428 State Capitol Building, Oklahoma City, was said to be advantageous to students: they could observe trials before the State Industrial Court, the State Criminal Court of Appeals, and the State Supreme Court. Students were to have full access to the State Law Library. Under the plan the school would confer the degree bachelor of Laws upon graduates.

The school issued a publication listing classes for three years of work. The faculty consisted of the dean, Jerome Hemry, of Oklahoma City, and three professors: Arthur Ellsworth, Victor Kulp, and Wallace Robertson.

The admission requirements for the new school were a bachelor's degree at an accredited four-year institution or three year's work with a C average or status as a "special student." Special students must have completed high school and be over twenty-three years of age.

Tuition was to be three dollars per semester credit hour for Oklahoma residents and eight dollars for nonresidents. The schedule called for spring, fall, and summer sessions with an additional August intersession.

The bulletin stipulated that first-year required courses would be contracts, torts, property, procedures, agency and partnership, and moot court training.

One student enrolled, T. M. Roberts. He attended classes for one semester.

Ada Lois Fisher received a certified letter from Langston's President Harrison, informing her that the law school was officially open and substantially equal to the OU Law School. Ms. Fisher again went to Norman to the OU Law School campus and applied for admission there. Dr. J. E. Fellows, dean of Admissions and Records, again denied her admission and informed her of the Langston School of Law.

The result of this decision was an anti-Jim Crow rally at Langston that attracted nearly one thousand students. The demonstrators loudly denounced the OU administrative action, which by then had barred seven Negroes from entering Law School.

Attorneys for Ms. Fisher took the case to the United States Supreme Court. Attorneys Thurgood Marshall, of the NAACP, and Amos Hall, of Tulsa, conducted the case. The gist of their arguments was that the newly opened Langston School of Law was certainly not the equal of the well-established Norman school.

Interested parties made contact with lawyers and faculty members in Chicago, California, and the East. These men visited both the Langston School of Law and the University of Oklahoma facility.

Ada Lois Sipuel, photographed when she helped open doors for blacks to Oklahoma graduate and professional schools. Courtesy Ada Lois Fisher.

Earl G. Harrison, dean of the University of Pennsylvania Law School, declared in June, 1948, "The Langston law school cannot properly be called a law school." He adversely compared the hastily organized school with OU's Law School, which had been in existence for thirty-nine years.

There was a separation of cases in August, 1948, which made the arguments encompass both legal schooling for students like Ms. Fisher who wished to pursue a law degree, and those like G. W. McLaurin, who already held a master's degree from the University of Kansas and wanted to work toward a doctorate in school administration. This broadened the case to encompass the whole question of graduate education for blacks.

As explained earlier, until this time Oklahoma had paid out-of-state tuition of Negroes who wished to pursue professional degrees. The intent of the financial aid was to avoid opening state school facilities to blacks. In fact, the supplemental out-of-state aid was often insufficient even to pay train fare. At this time the state legislature made an attempt to double the amount of money available for out-of-state education.

Ada Lois Sipuel Fisher, chairman of the Department of Social Sciences.

In October, 1948, under pressure from the United States Supreme Court and the Circuit Court of Appeals, the Oklahoma State Board of Regents voted to admit McLaurin to classes at OU on a "segregated basis." At the age of fifty-four he entered the College of Education, thus ending fifty-six years of segregation at OU. Less than a month later he was back in court trying to end his peculiar status in the classrooms (he was seated in a section of the classroom roped off from the rest of the students). His case was denied by a three-judge federal circuit court. Again McLaurin appealed to the United States Supreme Court.

A stormy state legislative session in 1948-49 resulted in agreement by the Joint Educational Committee of both houses on a compromise bill that allowed Negroes to undertake graduate work at OU and OSU. In June, 1949, Ms. Fisher said, "I am certainly grateful to my legion of friends who have stood beside me during the past three and one half years." She made her speech following her official enrollment in classes at the University of Oklahoma Law School in Norman. She completed her law degree in 1951 and entered practice in Oklahoma City. Later she returned to Langston University as a staff member for public relations and then as head of the Department of Social Sciences.

In 1950 the United States Supreme Court struck down the last of the Oklahoma Statutes relating to the case of G. W. McLaurin. After five years of legal struggle on behalf of Ms: Fisher and McLaurin, a victory parade was held in Oklahoma City. Both Negro and white citizens paraded and sang in the streets in celebration.

The Langston University School of Law, having enrolled only one student for one semester, did not function after 1950.

CHAPTER TWENTY-TWO

Music

THE RECORDS of Langston University indicate that from the beginning music was an integral part of campus life. All students enrolled in "vocal music," and courses in instrumental music were offered to those who wished to participate. The daily chapel exercises included singing, and on at least two evenings a week there were services in the dorms that included singing.

Formal music instruction and formation of the Langston University Orchestra began under the leadership of Zelia Page, the daughter of the school's first president, Inman Page. Her first orchestra, which had seven members, began performing in 1902. A photograph in the 1902-1903 catalogue shows girls playing the piano, the violin, and a brass instrument, probably a cornet. Boys attired in stiff white shirts and dark suits and ties performed on bass, clarinet, french horn, and cornet. The orchestra sat on a bare wooden stage in a large room.

Under Miss Page's ambitious tutoring a choral society was formed and a department of music was set up for instruction in voice and piano. The vocal-music curriculum was a three-year course. It was not explained how long the piano course was to last, but advanced students were to play Bach, Liszt, Chopin, and Mozart.

The orchestra had grown to twenty-three members by 1904. An instructor in "pedagogy and vocal music," George Porter, joined the faculty. The number of instruments owned by the school had also increased. In the university orchestra photograph in the 1903-1904 catalogue are drums, violins, violas, flutes, a slide horn, a clarinet, saxophones, and bass instruments.

By 1907 Ms. Page, who had become Mrs. Breaux, had added a band and a glee club to the Department of Music. Her assistant was

MUSIC

The early-day university wagon and band. Courtesy of Marietta Cooper Bryant.

Luther L. Henderson. A photo postcard of the first band shows an elegant wagon drawn by two large white horses. The band members, apparently all but two males, wore military-style uniforms with five brass buttons down the front. Cadet-style brimmed caps were worn by the boys, while the two girls wore graduation hats complete with tassels. The bandmaster had a rounded top hat and a tasseled baton.

By 1912, Zelia Page Breaux's title had become director of music. During that year the band and orchestra met twice a week for practice, and the glee club and chorus practiced once a week. All instruction in vocal and instrumental music was free to students enrolled in the school, and the instruments continued to be furnished by the University.

The Department of Music became the Department of Fine Arts in 1923. The director was Bulah Douglas. The music section occupied the southeastern part of Attucks Hall. There were four studio rooms crammed with ten pianos, three of which were large cabinet-style grand pianos. Additional practice rooms were available in the dorms.

During the spring quarter before graduation from the piano course, a student had to give an examination performance. The exam included technical exercises and study pieces. In addition the candidate gave a graduation recital. During their course work, the piano students practiced three hours a day and had two private lessons a week. The curriculum advanced from major and minor scales in the first year to concertos by Mendelssohn, Rubinstein, and Schumann in the fourth-year.

The only admission requirement for the vocal-music course was graduation from high school. The student could enroll in a program that required a daily hour's practice in voice and another hour's practice on piano. The rest of the first-year curriculum included music history, harmony, Italian, French, and *solfeggio*. In the second year music theory and German were added. In the third year two hours' daily practice in both voice and piano were required. Students received credit for rehearsals and performances. In the senior year sixteen credits were allowed for the two public recitals.

Students who intended to teach music in the public schools took courses in conducting, community singing, folk dancing, and music notation. Six hours of observation in music classes were required each term. Beginning in 1924 students could earn a certificate that entitled them to teach public school music for five years. Life certificates were granted to those who did additional work equivalent to a bachelor's degree, and one-year certificates were issued to those who had studied out of state or had completed sixty hours of college work.

In 1926-27, the Fine Arts Department included music, art, and physical education. The piano instructor was Maude Cox. A course in violin was added. The following year the Fine Arts Department had a new chairman, Ms. S. W. Hughey, and the band director was P. M. Jones. Course work in cornet was added.

Any student who wanted to specialize in one instrument could do so for five dollars a quarter. Special courses were given in brass, reed, string, woodwind, and percussion instruments.

Othella Oglesby, who had studied at the American Conservatory of Music in Chicago, joined the faculty in 1931. John Killingsworth, who became chorus director in 1934, had also studied at the American Conservatory. Band and orchestra were directed by Lawrence Davis.

Students who were not majoring in music could join the musical groups. They could join the male glee club, the choral club, the ladies' glee club, the band, the orchestra, and the junior band.

During World War II, despite the decline in student body the school maintained the music department with sufficient course work to offer a B.A. in music. In the early 1940s Langston had a band, an orchestra, a chorus, quartets, an a cappella group, and a chapel choir. Students who participated in these extracurricular groups could receive 1 hour of credit. A new course in conducting and orchestration was established in 1943. Despite the offerings of the department, the music course of study did not lead to state certification.

The standards for admission to the music department as a major were changed after the war. In the 1948-50 biennium it was expected that students who pursued majors in voice, piano, or instruments would come to Langston with some degree of proficiency. The Music Education Club was organized to present lectures for liberal-arts students.

The Music Department was housed in Page Hall after the mid-1950s. It contained lecture rooms, teachers' studios, offices, and practice rooms. A music and record library, which had been organized in 1947, continued to grow. A $15,000 general-education grant enabled the department to purchase a sound mirror, a large phonograph-recorder, an organ, a concert grand piano, records, and more band instruments. The organ and the grand piano were installed in Young Auditorium.

Music students were not allowed to organize off-campus groups without the approval of the faculty. The same approval was needed for either on or off-campus performances by individuals. Students were not supposed to give private lessons to other students. A music major was to practice two hours a day. Smoking was prohibited in class and in practice rooms.

In 1961-62 music scholarships were available for the first time. Applicants had to audition for the music faculty, whose chairman was Thomas Anderson.

Professor William E. Sims, who had been the bandmaster, became chairman of the Music Department in 1963. Two years later he undertook the additional title dean of instruction. Five new staff members joined the Music Department in that year. Sims later became president of the University.

Under the direction of William B. Garcia the Langston University Choir expanded. In 1967 there were forty members from Oklahoma, Texas, Tennessee, California, Michigan, Pennsylvania, and Ohio. The concert choir presented programs with a wide range of musical styles. On the same program they sang selections from Bach's Cantata 47, Rodgers and Hammerstein's *Oklahoma!* and pop movie tunes such as "Moon River." Besides performances on Founder's Day in Langston the choir gave concerts at Wichita (Kansas) State University and in Chicago, Detroit, and Saint Paul. They traveled and performed for almost a week in March, 1967.

Under funds from the Title III higher-education program, Langston staged a fine-arts series in 1970-71. Visiting artists-in-residence conducted master classes on campus. Composer Eva Jessye was one of the visiting artists; another, George Shirley, gave lectures and demonstrations.

The Music Department undertook an ambitious project: presentation of a folk oratorio based on Milton's *Paradise Lost* and *Paradise Regained.* With Eva Jessye as composer-conductor and Omar Robinson, Jr., as associate conductor, the ensemble included the concert choir, the university instrumental ensemble, and soloists. Besides the Milton work, set in a framework of Negro music, Ms. Jessye's compositions included a folk drama, *The Chronicle of Job,* and *The Life of Christ in Negro Spirituals.*

A variety show entitled *Black Pride Demonstrated* was staged by the Music Department in December. The Christmas concert featured a ceremony of carols. Other participants in the fine-arts series included artist Mayhugh Sneed; jazz performers Julian ("Cannonball") Adderly and his brother, Nat Adderly; and the black drama troupe Concept East, from Detroit.

Alumni Band Day was held in April, 1971, as part of the ongoing series. A special outdoor concert honored former Langston bandsmen.

Amelia R. Taylor, professor emeritus of music, piano, voice, and choir. The Music Theater in Hargrove Music Hall is named for her.

Mitchell B. Southall, composer and musician, Langston graduate, and former Langston University faculty member. Courtesy of Mitchell B. Southall.

In 1971-72 the Music Department sponsored a marching band, a concert band, a pep band, a jazz band, a combo, a string ensemble, the university and concert choirs, a male glee club, a music theater, a brass ensemble, a woodwind quintet, and a clarinet choir. There was the Music Education Club; Kappa Kappa Psi, the honorary band fraternity; and Tau Beta Sigma sorority for women band members. A course in Afro-American music was offered both majors and to other interested students.

Formal jury examination of music majors began in the 1971-72 school year. Each student performed before a faculty committee and was evaluated at the end of each semester. A recital was required after six semesters of study. Band and choir members had to appear at commencement. The only way to avoid the required

The Langston University Band and Chorus in recital, directed by T. J. Anderson, chairman of the Department of Music.

recital was to develop "physical and emotional" problems — and the performance had to last at least forty-five minutes.

In 1971-72 all music majors had to enroll in secondary piano until they could pass a piano proficiency test. In that year the course numbers were changed from three to four digits, although the course offerings did not change. A new band director, Beray Thigpen, from Mississippi Valley State College, joined the faculty in 1972.

A student who wished to major in voice had to audition before members of the faculty. The prospective student had to sing two selections from a choice of six; one selection must be sung in Italian. The audition demonstrated the student's proficiency in breath control, interpretation of language, and general vocal ability.

Sam Sadler and His Song

The Langston hymn, "Dear Langston," was written by Samuel Levi Sadler. Born in Denison, Texas, in 1882, Sadler was reared by his grandmother in Muskogee, Oklahoma, where he attended Dunbar School.

During his years at Langston he developed a love of the fine arts, especially music and poetry. His poem "Dear Langston" was probably written during his sophomore year, in 1898. It was set to music by J. D. Work, of Fisk University.

After graduating from Langston in 1901, Sadler taught English at his alma mater. He married Martha Arelia Elliott, and the family lived in Langston community on the main street, across from Sutton's store. A daughter, Sammye Mae, was born there.

In 1924 the family moved to Muskogee, where, after teaching English in the Negro public school, Sadler was elected principal. He held that position for twenty-four years. During that time he received his master's degree from Iowa University, Iowa City, Iowa. He was a member of Omega Psi Phi fraternity.

For eight years he was principal of Wheatley Highschool in

Samuel Levi Sadler, author of "Dear Langston." Courtesy of Sammye Sadler Walker.

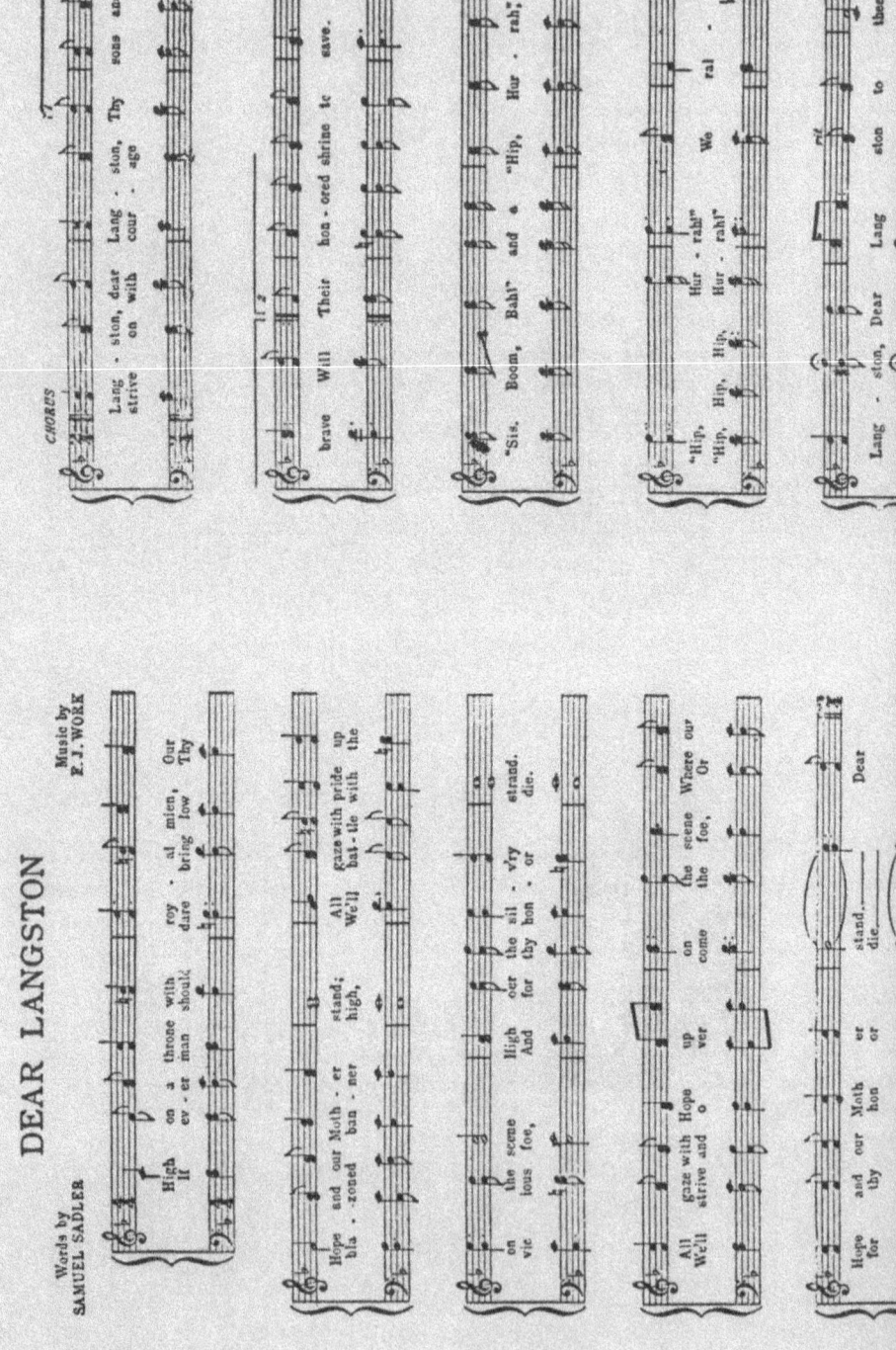

Boynton, Oklahoma. He retired there and became interested in farm projects. After retirement he again devoted time to writing poetry. "A Simple Request" was published in Poetry on the Air in 1963. That same year a junior high school in Muskogee was named in his honor. During the early integration years the schools and names were shuffled about, but the name Sam Sadler Junior High School was restored in 1975.

Besides poetry and farming, Sadler collected books as a hobby, counting many rare editions among his collection. He died in 1967.

Dear Langston

High on a throne with royal mien,
Our Hope and our Mother stand:
All gaze with pride upon the scene
High o'er the silv'ry strand.
All gaze with hope upon the scene
Where our Hope and our Mother stand.

If ever man should dare bring low
Thy blazoned banner high,
We'll battle with the vicious foe,
And for thy honor die.
We'll strive to overcome the foe,
Or for thy honor die.

CHORUS:
Dear Langston, dear Langston
Thy sons and daughters brave
Will strive on with courage
Their honored shrine to save.
With a "Sis, Boom, Bah!" and
a "Hip, Hurrah,"
With a "Hip, — Hur-Rah!"
We rally to Langston, Dear Langston,
to thee.

CHAPTER TWENTY-THREE

Research

UNTIL 1946 faculty members undertook all research projects independently. Mozell C. Hill established the Office of Institutional Research immediately after World War II. Hill submitted his proposal for the project in February, 1946, offering to serve as director of research. Research categories were established: (1) studies of physical, biological, and socioeconomic environments and (2) subjects involving the Langston faculty and student body. All faculty members were encouraged to undertake research through the research office, but only a few responded.

Some of the research projects conducted by the faculty included a study of racial attitudes among college students, social values of returned war veterans, and race relations in industry. In 1942-43 the University issued a bulletin containing a report prepared by the research unit. The title of the report was "Culture of a Contemporary All-Negro Community." It surveyed social and cultural aspects of life in Logan County and the city of Langston.

Scientific projects included research on chemotherapeutic agents and synthesis and pharmacology of local anesthetics. The leading scientific researcher during this period was Professor R. P. Perry.

During the 1940s most of the research results appeared in Langston's *Southwestern Journal*, which was first published in 1944. Some of the article titles give an indication of the range of interests: "Hiram R. Revels: First Negro Senator," "Studies in Iodine Metabolism," and "Some Problems Confronted in the Teaching of History in a Negro College." S. L. Hargrove contributed "A History of Langston University."

One project conducted by the Office of Institutional Research during this period was the preparation of an exhaustive bibliography of works by and about Negroes in Oklahoma. The office sought census records from 1790 onward, annotated materials, obtained photostats of rare documents, and accumulated maps, figures, and charts concerning the black population in Oklahoma.

The research office also conducted annual leadership conferences, beginning in January, 1946. The first conference centered on curriculum development.

A second research team formed in the mid-1960s during Hale's administration. Larry K. Hayes conducted a research seminar at Langston once a week for nine weeks. Acting in the role of consultant, Hayes taught faculty researchers methods of data documentation, organization of research materials, and research methods.

Soon after Professor Haye's seminar came the appointment of the second director of research, Richmond Kinnard. Glenda Warren and I became members of the research team, who worked with Professor Donald Allen, a consultant from OSU.

In 1968 the Oklahoma Consortium on Research Development provided pilot funds to Langston to encourage faculty members to prepare research proposals. The funding came to about two hundred dollars for each proposal. In addition to providing the pilot funds the consortium sponsored development seminars.

In 1971, Langston joined the OSU Agriculture Experiment Station in setting up a joint Research Advisory Committee. Three faculty members from each school served on the committee. The three members from Langston were R. E. Kinnard, James L. Mosley, and the author.

By the mid-1970s the Langston research faculty had grown to six, and by 1977 to twelve, plus two staff workers. The director of the research staff in 1977 was Steve B. Latimer. Today all faculty members of the research team hold doctorates, and approximately twelve students a semester work on the various research projects.

The projects completed by the second research team included a study of nutrition, family commensality, and academic performance of high school youth, published in the *Journal of Home Economics* in June, 1970, academic aspirations and financial preparations for college, published in the *Journal of Negro Education* in spring, 1971, and a study of rural life in Logan County.

In 1972, Congress passed a bill providing over eight million dollars in research funds for black land-grant schools and Tuskegee Institute. Langston's original grant from this program was $429,000. In 1978 the appropriation was $529,001. Current studies include research in such varied subjects as accumulation of nitrate in soil and water, selection and care of clothing by adolescents of low-income families in Oklahoma, and physical and chemical studies of glycosidases from barley. Twelve projects had been funded through 1977.

CHAPTER TWENTY-FOUR

Science

THE FIRST science courses Langston offered were for students enrolled in the "classical" college course. Although no students were pursuing this level of education in 1898, the course work was described as basic instruction in botany, physics, astronomy, geology, and chemistry. The first science faculty consisted of J. St. Cyr Tucker, who taught at Langston the first two years, and A. B. Whitby, who was professor of science from 1900 to 1901.

Students who planned to enroll in the "scientific" course enrolled in the same classical studies, as well as mineralogy, electricity, and zoology. The senior-year offerings were to be "meteorology, entomology, history of the inductive sciences, spherical astronomy, and vertebrate zoology." These courses were structured so that upper-division high school and normal school students could enroll in them.

The curriculum for early-day agriculture students was a practical one. The catalogue for 1900 listed with science courses such courses as animal surgery and sanitation. The grade-school section, which had the largest enrollment, taught youngsters geography, nature study, and physical geography under the science classification and also listed a special science reading course.

The early-day catalogues list many offerings under such titles as "electrical and mechanical engineering" and "civil architecture." It is hard to determine which of these courses were actually taught, and the enrollment figures are in doubt. The course offerings for 1898-1900 supposedly included surveying and mapping, steam engines and boilers, dynamo design, and applied mechanics.

At this time in its development Langston planned to offer five years of elementary work, four years each of classical and scientific college work, three years of either classical or scientific college-

251

preparatory work and four years each for students enrolled in the education, engineering, agriculture, home economics and music schools.

Some of the early-day textbooks included Boyer's *Elementary Biology*, which the ninth-grade English class read, and Cyr's graded readers. The scientific texts were Hinman's *Eclectic Physical Geography* and Blaisdell's *Physiology*. The course stressed use of the microscope and instruction in drawing internal organs. Eighth-graders studied Bert's *First Steps in Science*.

The bulletin for 1902 stated that the school possessed "an excellent laboratory" for natural sciences. There was also a "limited" lab for mathematics, domestic economy, and agriculture. The Department of Mechanical Arts had "more than $8,000 worth of machinery and tools."

By 1904-1905, additional science courses had appeared in the catalogue. Plant histology was offered in the spring term. The students were to meet for three class periods and two labs a week. The botany lab had many slides for the student to study under the microscope and an adequate supply of dissecting tools and tables. The physics lab had static machines, dynamos, motors, and electrical apparatus. Most of the labs were on the first floor of the east wing of the Main Building. The chemistry lab, which was in the basement, was equipped with "sinks, water, tables, cases, balances and chemicals."

A small natural-history museum served as a public-interest point and University service area. The museum, actually part of the Science Department, was contained in one large room, 25 by 32 feet. On display were agricultural products, home economics exhibits, and more than 150 different specimens of stuffed birds and animals. There was also a section of minerals with 150 specimens and "relics."

The science courses and labs had become more sophisticated by 1912, when biology courses had access to dissecting tools, compound and simple microscopes, microtomes, culture ovens, and sterilizers. By this time William A. Hinton had joined the faculty as professor of natural and physical sciences. The new inorganic chemistry course required five hours of lab a week and collateral reading

SCIENCE

The late Dr. H. W. Conrad, an early campus physician.

texts. The quantitative analysis course required seven lab periods a week. In the physiology courses students dissected frogs, dogfish, pigeons, and cats.

A prenursing program began in 1913. The three-year curriculum ended with a pin and a diploma. The course work consisted of lectures and practice in dispensary work. The requirements for entering the prenursing program were stringent. The prospective student had to apply in writing to the president of Langston and accompany her application with a letter of recommendation from her clergyman and one other character witness. In addition the girl had to present a doctor's certificate that she was in "sound health" and had "unimpaired mental faculties." Students in the nursing program were to be between twenty and forty years old, of average height and weight, and able to read and write. They had to be able to do fractions and figure percentages. After three months' probation, student nurses were allowed to wear the school "duty dresses." They were dark-blue checked gingham with white collars and cuffs, white aprons, and caps. No costume jewelry was allowed.

The prospective student was to bring to the campus with her "comfortable rubber-heeled shoes, a warm wrapper, a waterproof, a pair of rubbers, and an umbrella." Her supplies should include scissors, a watch with a second hand, ten white aprons, and a napkin ring. She also had to deposit with the president of the school the amount of her return fare in case she was dismissed for "inefficiency, misconduct, or any other reason."

The nursing texts, which covered anatomy, physiology, practical nursing, and materia medica, were accompanied by a pocket medical dictionary. Some of the courses in the last year included nursing of the ear, nose, and throat; hydrotherapy; obstetrics; special tuberculosis nursing; and first aid.

Practical work for the first-year student nurse included duty in the clinic and infirmary wards (described below). The second-year practicum consisted of work in the wards, the operating room, the clinic, and the diet kitchen and duty in contagious cases. The third-year students had charge of the wards, worked in the operating room and diet kitchen, and did some private nursing.

Twenty-two girls enrolled in the nurse's training department in 1913. Five of them (including two from outside the state) were in the "regular" nursing courses. Seventeen took the "special" course. All of the special enrollees were from Langston city.

In the early twenties the science faculty consisted of R. N. Pyrtle, director, Paul McCree, and Ida Wade. Pre-medical courses were part of the school's curriculum in 1922-24. The catalogue recommended completion and at least two years of college work before entering medicine. A basic course for future doctors, dentists, and pharmacists included English, French, German, mathematics, physics, chemistry, botany, zoology, and embryology.

The Chemistry Department expanded in the mid-1920s to include agricultural chemistry and home-economics chemistry. In 1925, when LeRoy Moore was appointed director of science, he revised all the course offerings except the premedical curriculum. Science was required from freshman through senior years. All science majors must take fifteen hours of either physics or chemistry. High school students took required courses in both physics and chemistry.

An interesting aspect of the history of the Science Department concerns the use of students as nurses' aides. The following account was told to me by a woman who served as nurse's aid in 1926-28, while she was a high school student. Her story demonstrates that, despite lack of training, the students performed well.

The first clinic was housed in an old frame building north of the football field. Today Sanford Hall stands on the site of Attucks Hall, the site of another clinic staffed by the dean of women, who also served as nurse. North of the football field was still another house used to isolate the contagious cases. This last building was called the Infirmary. There major diseases such as smallpox were treated.

My informant recalled that one case she was called to attend was a girl with acute appendicitis. The year was 1927; the month was February. On a cold, dark, windy night, after lights and heat had been turned off, the patient grew much worse. The student aide tended the girl by the light of a flickering kerosene lamp until morning, when the patient was taken to a Guthrie hospital.

When the women's dorm was built, the nursing section moved there. Patients who were not seriously ill were cared for in their rooms. Other rooms were set aside on the second floor, southwest, for girls who were deemed seriously ill. During the year, my informant said, three girls became so ill that they were sent home. All of them later died of tuberculosis.

The nurse's aide, generally addressed as "nursie," was allowed to supervise the patient's dinner trays. As a result the student nurses had access to the best food the kitchen had to offer, a decided benefit of the job in those days.

When Dean Baker left Langston, she was replaced by Dr. Wilhelmena Bowles, and the clinic closed. During President Young's tenure, students who became seriously ill were sent home. Later a campus infirmary was established.

In 1927-28, the faculty of the Chemistry Department was Dean

R. P. Perry, chairman of the Chemistry Department, in the classroom.

L. G. Moore, chairman; Ida Wade, associate professor; and A. J. Lee, assistant professor. The major program in chemistry required thirty-six hours, a minor in mathematics, and two semesters of physics. Under Moore's leadership the course was further upgraded on the college level, and Ida Wade became principal of the high school in 1929-30. When Moore retired in 1961, he had served as head of the Department of Natural Science, dean of instruction, and director of the College of Arts and Sciences. Serious efforts were made to obtain well-qualified teachers: all the new faculty members of the Science Department in 1928 were graduates of such universities as Iowa State, Kansas State, and Florida A&M. Course requirements were also upgraded. The only students exempt from science requirements were majors in manual training and public school music.

Even during the depression years of the 1930s the Science Department continued to grow, with five on the faculty in 1933. Course offerings included animal ecology, entomology, parasitology, and bacteriology, in addition to the basic biology courses. Optics and radio theory were offered in the mid-1930s, as well as molecular physics and community hygiene.

A strong Chemistry Department began to develop in the prewar years and maintained research programs during World War II. The number of chemistry courses increased from nine to eleven. At war's end the department boasted a dean, R. P. Perry, with a Ph.D. and eight faculty members.

The Department of Natural and Physical Science was divided in 1944. Astronomy and geology were restored to the curriculum. New advanced chemistry courses were added, such as semi-microqualitative analysis. Chemistry students had to complete ten courses in their major and thirty hours in biology and physics or mathematics. The first course in chemistry research was offered in 1948-50. In the mid-1950s, Langston was still requiring entering freshmen to take both biology and chemistry.

Moore was succeeded by William M. Collins in 1962. Collins was named dean of instruction and director of the Divisions of Arts, Sciences, and Agriculture. Head of the Department of Biology was Walter Jones. Acting chairman of the Chemistry Department for 1961-62 was James Simpson. Gomez C. Hamilton retired from the biology staff that year, after serving at the university for thirty-nine years. Ernest Holloway, who joined the biology staff the next year, later became interim president of the University.

Training in the sciences was geared to prepare students to enter medical or dental schools or other preprofessional training programs. A major in medical technology was available, although it did not lead to professional certification upon completion.

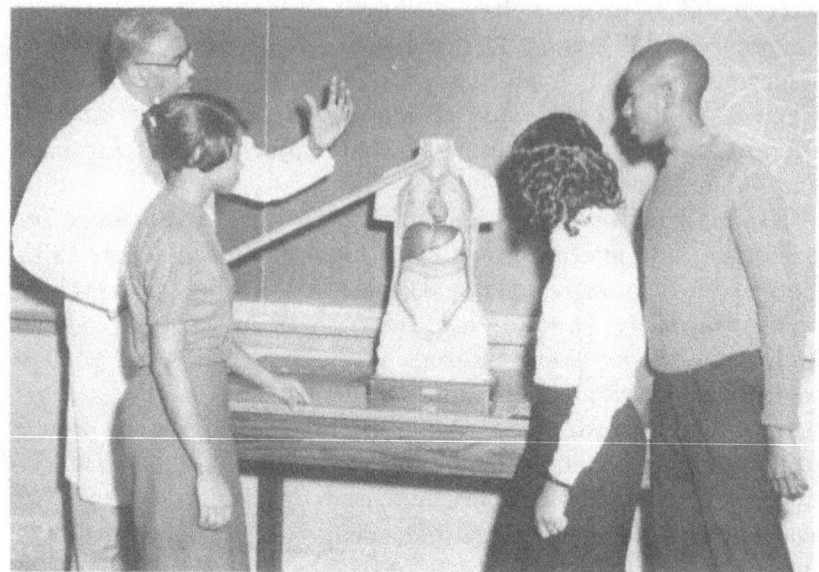

The late Gomez C. Hamilton instructing a biology class.

In 1966, Ephraim Wall joined the physical sciences faculty, and Steve B. Latimer was appointed director of the department.

In the 1970s Langston's science curriculum included a two-year prenursing program. Degrees were offered in chemistry and chemistry teacher education. Scientific German was added as a course offering in 1973, along with integral calculus. Other faculty appointments in the 1970s included William Willingham as chairman of the Chemistry Department and James Simpson as director of development. Sarah Thomas headed the Biology Department. In 1974, William Franks became chairman of the Department of Physical Science.

The Dean: LeRoy G. Moore

LeRoy G. Moore devoted thirty-seven years of service to Langston University. He came to the institution in the fall of 1925 as a chemistry teacher and chairman of the Department of Natural Sciences. In 1940 he was appointed dean of instruction and remained in that position until his retirement in May, 1962.

Moore was born in Pratt, Kansas, in 1893. He attended the public schools of Medicine Lodge, Barber County High School, and Southwestern College, Winfield, Kansas. He earned his master's degree at the University of Kansas, in Lawrence, and did further graduate study in 1937-38 at Cornell University, Ithaca, New York, and at the University of Kansas in 1944-45.

LeRoy G. Moore, professor of chemistry, 1925-62 and dean of academic affairs, 1940-62.

Before joining the Langston faculty, Moore taught in Little Rock, Arkansas, and served in the armed forces. He taught at Arkansas A&M in 1920-21 and at the Manual Training High School in Muskogee from 1921 to 1925.

Moore married Theresia Amanda Bolden in 1922. They had two children, LeRoy, Jr., and Jane Frances. Since retirement Moore has assisted in efforts to obtain accreditation for Texas College (Tyler, Texas).

Despite his many professional honors and academic and administrative achievements, Moore remained above all a dedicated chemistry teacher. Many former students remember him as the teacher who introduced them to science in their high school years. His classroom was a model of discipline. Students who arrived late were not permitted to enter the class and received a zero for the day. He stimulated home study by conducting class quizzes from a set of index cards that he flipped at random, selecting questions, and calling on students for answers. He would shuffle the cards several times during a class period, pouncing upon the prepared and the unprepared. Students called him by his nickname, "Smiley," behind his back, but never to his face.

He was chemistry professor throughout his years at Langston, even during his tenure as dean of instruction and while he was chairman of the Chemistry Department, from 1925 to 1946. He directed summer sessions from 1940 to 1962. He is listed in Who's Who in American Men of Science and in 1968 was named a fellow of the American Institute of Chemists. Moore Hall, on the Langston campus, is named in his honor.

During his time at Langston there were few hats that Dean Moore did not wear. He served on diverse committees, such as the committee that studied whether to establish a branch campus in Oklahoma City in 1954; he was a discussion leader for the Conference on Religion and the State University, held at the University of Michigan in 1958; he hired students for summer jobs. Among his many awards was the Sigma Xi key for research in chemistry.

The Moore family was loyal to Langston throughout the years. Ms. Moore, an alumna of the school, was assistant professor of education for seventeen years. Both of the Moores' children at-

tended Langston and went on to obtain advanced degrees. LeRoy Moore Jr., joined the faculty of Southern University, Baton Rouge, Louisiana. Jane married a Los Angeles surgeon, C. N. Shropshire, Jr. Many of Dean Moore's students who went on to obtain advanced chemistry or medical degrees keep in touch with him.

When Moore retired in 1962, he was honored by the faculty for his long service. After retirement he made his home in Guthrie.

CHAPTER TWENTY-FIVE

Trades and Mechanical and Industrial Arts

THE NAME by which industrial education has been known at Langston has varied through the years. It has been called industrial arts, manual training, mechanical and technical education, and trades — all more or less interchangeably. By whatever name, what was meant was "practical education," in distinction from the liberal-arts curriculum. Through the years it was structured as a degree-granting program and then restructured as a two-year (or less) training program offering a certificate. In the earliest years there were "departments" of electrical and mechanical engineering and a program called "civil architecture," but no enrollment or graduation statistics are available to indicate how many students pursued these courses or at what level. Over the years the curriculum was revised; architecture was dropped in 1912, and "carpentry mechanics" was changed to "manual training" in 1913.

Langston has provided some form of industrial training every year since its founding. The peak enrollment in such courses came before World War II. Beginning in the 1950s and continuing to the present day, the enrollment in teacher-education, professional and preprofessional, and liberal-arts courses has exceeded that of the traditional industrial-arts courses. Many of the manual-training courses have been dropped. Currently, under the Division of Applied Science, the school offers work in industrial education, (a degree program) industrial technology, data processing, preindustrial engineering and electronics technology.

The first superintendent of the mechanical-arts section was William A. Jackson. Under his direction the school offered such courses as heating and ventilating, surveying and mapping, strength of materials, forging and tool design, and machine shop. Jackson, whose title was later changed to professor, remained on the faculty until 1906.

TRADES AND MECHANICAL AND INDUSTRIAL ARTS

The early-day campus blacksmith shop.

Apparently there was sufficient enrollment in the industrial classes by 1902 to warrant hiring additional faculty. Charles Brown is listed as assistant along with Newton Trout in the Langston catalogue for 1902-1903.

Along with expansion of the faculty the course work changed somewhat. In the college section, where work in the mechanical arts led to a B.S. degree, Latin instead of French was required in the freshman year, algebra replaced trigonometry, and physics was dropped altogether. A minimal number of general-education courses such as history and literature was required.

The trades courses were open to students as early as seventh-grade level. In 1904 students at the eighth grade level could enroll in machinist courses, seventh-graders could sign up for carpentry and steam engineering, and sixth-graders could take blacksmithing. The program ended with the equivalent of a ninth-grade education and a certificate. Instructors in carpentry and in blacksmithing were on the staff.

Those who wished to pursue a college degree in industrial education had to meet the following requirements: they must be at least sixteen years old; must know arithmetic (both metric and standard), algebra, and geometry; and must have some knowledge of history, grammar, and the classics. Among the works with which the students had to be familiar were *Macbeth, As You Like It, Evangeline, The Legend of Sleepy Hollow, Twice-Told Tales,* and Thomas Macauley's *Life of Johnson.*

Shopwork during the early years consisted of such projects as welding steel and iron, tempering tools, boring, drilling, milling and turning simple cylinders, joining core boxes, casting original designs, and solving an art problem in stonecutting. Additional course work included chemistry, political economy, English and American literature, and three terms of "rhetoric." A student could expect to learn welding and tool making during his first year, wheelwrighting in the second year, and carriage building and horseshoeing in the final year. Along with this practical knowledge he would pursue sixth-, seventh-, and eighth-grade studies. At "graduation" he was entitled to a certificate of proficiency in blacksmithing. The programs in carpentry and mechanics were similar. Special instructors with the titles instructor of woodworking and instructor in machine work were on the staff in 1905.

Courses in mechanical and architectural drawing were transferred to the math department in 1912. The manual-training courses centered around joinery, wood turning, forging, machine work, and physics. Students had to buy a set of drawing instruments costing seven dollars and must be available for a half day of work on Saturdays.

In those years the machine shop was equipped with a Flather twelve-inch-swing engine lathe, a Draper eight-inch-swing engine lathe, a Cincinnati six-inch lathe, a Bath universal grinding machine, a twenty-inch-stroke geared shaper, a 36-inch radial drill and upright drill, a Flather planer, and a universal milling machine.

The machine shop as it looked in the 1930s.

In addition the shop had a complete assortment of hand tools, vises, and cutters.

The shop had two woodworking rooms equipped with twelve training benches. Each table had a complete set of tools and some power tools, such as sanders and borers. In the blacksmith shop were six Buffalo draft forges, a tire shrinker and benders, a blast blower, and a hand forge. The foundry had a capacity of one and a half tons of iron per hour. Later the students also worked in the power, electric-lighting, and central heating plants.

In the early twenties the school became embroiled in a dispute over whether it should be primarily a trade school or a liberal-arts and teacher's college. The Mechanics Department had broadened by this time to include instruction in auto mechanics and "applied electricity," which taught, among other things, how to build radios. It was suggested in the 1923-24 catalogue that students who finished the applied-electricity course would be able to find jobs in house wiring, telephone work, power plants, and general repairing.

In addition to the three-year courses, there was a special short course in auto mechanics designed primarily for "car owners and

Class in tailoring for both men and women. S. G. Code (center, wearing suit) was the instructor in 1923-24.

chauffeurs." There was also a two-years teacher's course in manual training. Students in this course had to be high school graduates and take courses in both woodwork and mechanical drawing. Manual training in high school spanned all four years. It was a continuation of manual training given to grammar-school students.

In 1924 the program was designated the Trades and Industrial Program (T&I). C. B. Hutchinson was designated "director — engineering and head of trades and industrial." Three instructors taught manual training, auto mechanics, blacksmithing, plumbing, steam engineering. The college courses were also available in the high school and were taught by the same staff. A later member of the T&I staff taught tailoring. It was a two-year course in which boys learned to construct bib overalls, suspenders, and pockets and use sewing machines. The first-year project was a vest, and the second-year project was a coat. All home economics majors were required to take tailoring, too. The girls made coats, skirts, and suits. Shoemaking and printing were added in 1925.

The late E. A. Miller, chairman of the Trades and Industrial Arts Department, 1927-30, and instructor, 1935-62.

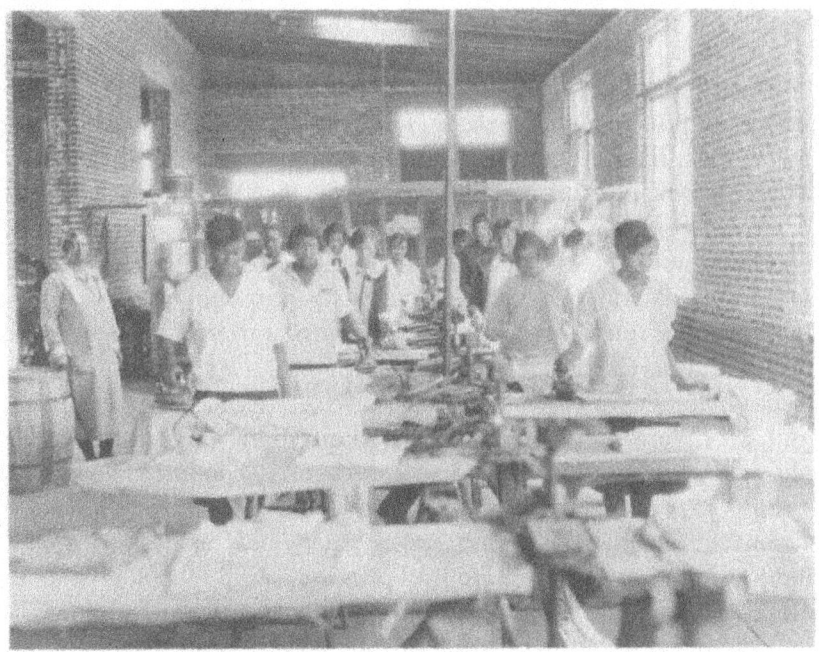

Mrs. A. B. Cotton, laundry instructor, and a class in the 1920s.

Throughout the 1920s the enrollment in industrial arts continued to grow, and by 1929 the department had a faculty of nine. The head of the department, E. A. Miller, held a B.S. degree from Pennsylvania State College. In 1929 there was even a "laundering" instructor. The three-year course of study included "soaps, sodas, chlorines, starches, blues, machines, belts, mildew and washroom management."

A special certificate was required to teach industrial arts in high schools. Langston prepared students to earn either five-year renewable or lifetime teaching certificates. Candidates must be at least eighteen and finish such courses as psychology, educational methods, American history, and practice teaching. The suggested course of study was a major in industrial arts and a minor in mechanical drawing plus twenty-one hours in education and psychology.

From the 1920s Langston was ahead of its time in recruiting women faculty members for the industrial-arts section. Mayme Weaver taught printing during this period, and Nelle B. Dillon was head of vocational-technical education from the late 1930s to the 1960s.

Courses for high school students in the early 1930s included tailoring, laundering, shoemaking, leatherwork, printing, radio, auto mechanics, manual training, carpentry, and mechanical drawing. There was a big turnover in the faculty in 1930, with only one holdover from the previous staff. The new head of the department was Legolian Gude, from Tuskegee Institute. An instructor in brick masonry was added. A former Langston graduate, Odell Gilyard, took over the farm shop. As a sign of the times harness making was dropped from the curriculum in 1941.

Few changes occurred in the industrial-training courses during and after World War II. Printing was omitted for a two-year period, and woodwork was combined with carpentry. The instructor in the cosmetology department was Thelma J. Arterbery. Majors included such fields as barbering, cosmetology, household maid service, and laundering. Langston offered a pilot's ground-school course in 1941-42. Students, employees of the school, and nonstudent civilians could take the flight training. The catalogue for that year did not state what facilities were to be used.

Nelle B. Dillon, head of the Vocational-Technical Division.

A radio class in 1923. The instructor was H. Hendricks.

During the war some of the T&I faculty members taught part time in other departments on the campus. During World War II the department was a civil-service training center, and provided special training to help students get jobs at such places as Tinker Air Force Base, in Midwest City. The school participated in the National War Production Program and set up a special aircraft shop to teach machine-tool operation, riveting, motor repair, and welding. The shop accommodated twenty-four students at a time, and the demand grew so great that three shifts met for instruction each day. In 1943-44 there were 488 full-time students on campus and an additional 35 civil-service trainees. More than six hundred students completed the course.

The industrial-arts faculty grew to its largest size just after the war. In 1953 came revisions in industrial training: two-year certificate courses were offered in only four areas, woodworking, auto mechanics, tailoring, and shoemaking. Teachers who wanted to obtain certificates in industrial-vocational education could attend courses on campus, summer sessions, weekend seminars, or inservice conferences throughout the state.

Raymond Johnson joined the faculty of the Mechanical Arts Department in 1956, following the death of Odell Gilyard. Johnson, a Langston graduate, later received his master's degree from Oklahoma State University and his doctorate in education from North Texas State. During his tenure at Langston the curriculum for the bachelor of science degree in industrial arts was revised again.

The industrial technology section added an electronics course in 1961. It was a two year course leading to a certificate. At that time students could enroll in the special trades courses as full-time, three-quarter, or half-time students. These special courses, designed for adults with nonstudent standing, included cosmetology and tailoring, woodworking, and shoe repair. The fee for each course was twenty-five dollars a week. Auto mechanics was offered for the last time in 1961-62. Cosmetology phased out in 1969. The department acquired a new name in 1967, when it became known as the Department of Technology. In 1969 associate-degree programs were established in electronics technology and data processing. The first instructor in data processing was James Cash.

TRADES AND MECHANICAL AND INDUSTRIAL ARTS

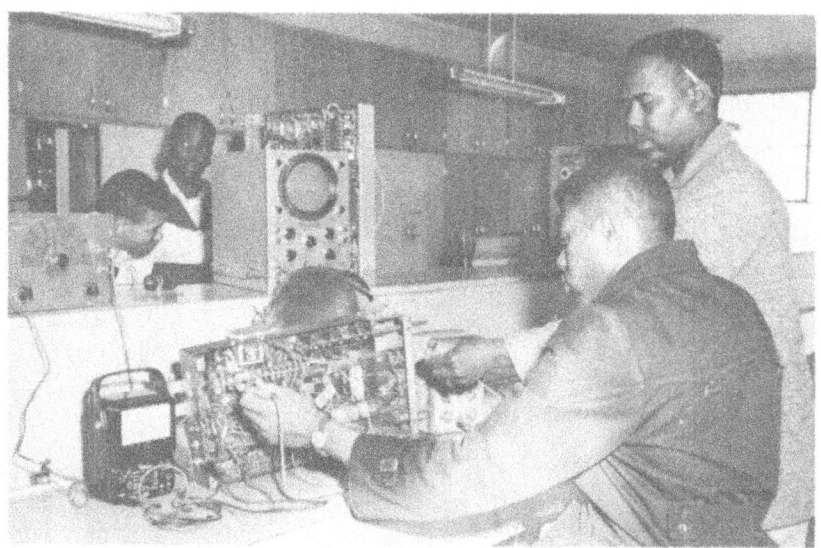

Practical training in the electronics technology lab under the supervision of T. G. Green (standing, right).

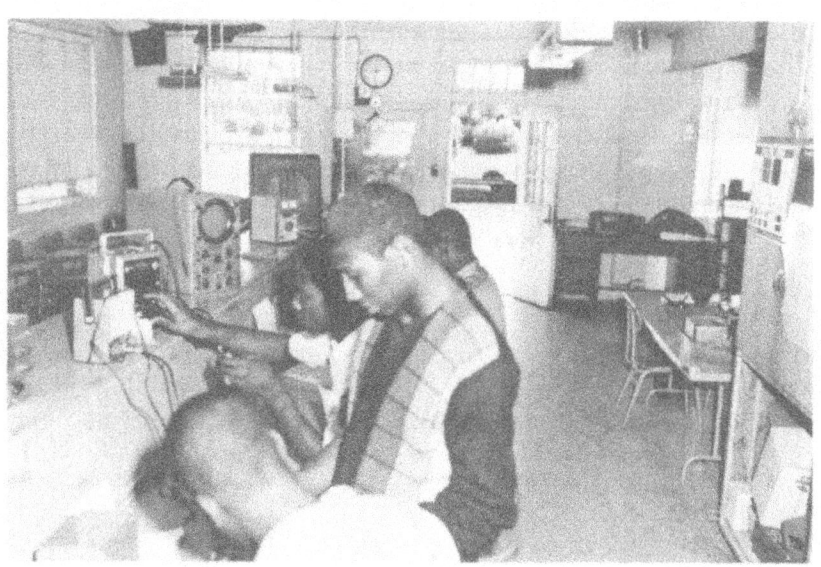

An electronics class, 1968.

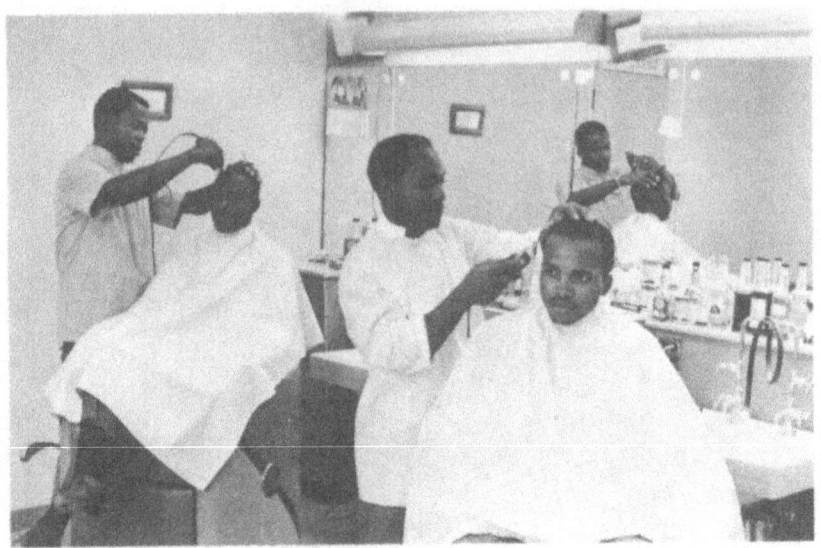

John Grayson (standing, center) instructing students in the Langston University barbershop, in the Student Center.

Course additions in the early 1970s were driver's education, photography, preindustrial engineering, and electronics technology. The department continued to offer the bachelor of science degree leading to a teacher's certificate. To teach in grades 7 through 12, a prospective teacher had to take sixty-two hours of general-education course work, twenty-two hours in professional education and fourty hours in industrial arts.

CHAPTER TWENTY-SIX

Langston Today — and Tomorrow

THROUGH THE YEARS since its founding Langston University has struggled for existence, plagued by political pressures, insufficient budget, lack of facilities, equipment, and supplies. At times it has been hampered by lack of adequate, qualified faculty and staff.

The early-day Negro settler who homesteaded on the plains of Oklahoma saw the need for an institution of higher learning. Those who settled in and around Langston had a spirit of determination to reach such a goal. They worked toward their goal, giving of their time, energy, and money to help lay the groundwork for the education of their children and generations to come. It was their desire to make the town of Langston the Negro educational center of Oklahoma. While they were striving to build homes out of hewn logs and native stone, they were also struggling to find resources to build schools and establish a college. They were still living in tents and dugouts as the schools went up.

In February, 1892, a common school was completed in Langston. Six months later the residents built a boarding high school. Besides the two public schools there was a short-lived Roman Catholic school, open to any child regardless of race, color, or creed.

But these schools did not satisfy the Langston citizens' determination to provide educational opportunities for the Negro youth of Oklahoma. On November 9, 1895, the *Langston City Herald* spoke for the town's settlers:

There is nothing we admire more than a high standing well regulated school, and there is no reason why Langston should not have as good a school as any town in Oklahoma. There are two things every successful town or city must have and these are good schools and good churches. Without them it is vain to hope for success. It is folly to expect an energetic and progressive people to live in a town where both the spiritual and educational interests are dead.

Such was the philosophy of early-day Langston settlers. In 1897 the determination and efforts of Negro leaders and politicians culminated in the establishment of Langston University by an act of the Oklahoma Territorial Legislature. Its purpose was to give the black people of Oklahoma normal, college, industrial, and agricultural education.

It was stipulated in the act that Langston citizens must donate the first forty acres of land on which the school would be built. It was not an easy task for the people of Langston to purchase the land. They worked together, prayed together, and pulled together until they achieved their goal. The group was small in size but great in courage and determination.

The Negro politicians and other leaders who had worked hard to get the school established also took the lead in helping the citizens raise the money to purchase the land. Much of the money was raised at community picnics and public meetings. There the citizens met the politicians and heard their speeches and their promises, many of which were never fulfilled. The rest of the money was raised by women in the community through the sale of cakes, pies, sandwiches, and dinners and monetary donations.

After they purchased the land, the citizens of Langston continued to give — this time the labor of their hands, as they helped erect the first building. I recall my father telling us how he drove his team and wagon eight miles to Langston to volunteer his services in helping dig the foundation for the first building on the university campus. Along the way he met his neighbors bound on the same mission.

The major obstacles to establishing a school of higher education for Negroes were thus overcome by legislative means bolstered by products of the human spirit — the citizens' determination, stamina, and ingenuity. Those obstacles gave way, only to be succeeded by others that down through the years have hindered the development of the university to its fullest potential — and even threatened its continued existence. These problems can be summarized as adverse political influence; adverse publicity; frequent change of presidents, resulting in frequent turnover of faculty and staff members; insufficient facilities, equipment, and supplies; low faculty and staff salaries and thus underqualified personnel; overburdening of faculty and staff members who at times had to wear too many hats to do a good job; lack of graduate-school education for blacks in Oklahoma before 1952- and lack of job opportunities in the Langston community so that students could earn money to help pay their way through school. The last problem became acute after 1950, when farming gave way to livestock growing and the farms became mechanized, thus eliminating farm jobs for students.

Yet through all the years of trial, Langston provided an invaluable good. Until 1952 few black students would have had an opportunity to attend college had it not been for Langston University. Families with several children to educate could send them all to Langston. They could not have afforded to send them out of state for education. For many, the only alternative was to grow up in ignorance. Because Langston endured, its graduates can be found all across the United States, making outstanding contributions in every field of endeavor.

Some of the problems of the past remain with us today. Yet despite the concerns and tensions of the present, I forsee a bright tomorrow for Langston University. I do not anticipate the demise of this educational institution, founded in courage and sustained by faith in the future. It continues to fill a need — for students of all races, not only those in Oklahoma but also young women and men from other states and foreign countries. Langston will survive because there remains an obvious need for the institution, and because it has become an integral part of the culture of Logan County and the sister towns Langston, Coyle, and Guthrie.

Langston has the capacity to become an economically and educationally viable institution. Many of the problems can be overcome if all concerned — legislators, regents, and university leaders — will think of Langston as a *state* school, not a black school. Langston's days as a black school ended in 1954. Freed from the chains of politics, aided by improved facilities, increased enrollment, and a healthy share of federal and state funds, Langston can soar to new educational heights. It can achieve the reality dreamed of by that courageous band of pioneers who sold pies and mortared stones to build a university on forty acres of Oklahoma prairie.

Aerial view of the Langston campus, 1969. Courtesy of Donald E. Allen.

Langston University of the future — an artist's conception.

Appendices

APPENDIX A

Chronology

1897 Oklahoma Territorial House Bill 151 passed, establishing Colored Agricutlural and Normal University of Oklahoma
1898 University opens; Inman Page, president; grades 5-8 meet in Presbyterian Church
1901 First two students graduate: J. I. Hazelwood, Langston; Ellen Strong, Guthrie
1905 Library holdings reach 900
1907 Main Building destroyed by fire
1909 Page Hall constructed
1914 Summer sessions begin
1926 University-owned land increased to 320 acres, with nine principal buildings
1927 First Founder's Day Celebration
1928 New girls' dormitory, accommodating 100, and new boys' dormitory, accommodating 50, constructed
1932 Two-year Normal School closed
1934 Operates (until 1940) branches at Muskogee, Ardmore, and Tulsa
1936 End of free tuition for Oklahoma students
1943 *Southwestern Journal* begins publication
1946 Campus high school closes; veterans total almost half of student body
1948 Accredited by North Central Association of Colleges and Secondary Schools; campus streets paved
1949 G. Lamar Harrison Library and new stadium, accommodating 4,000, completed
1953 Kappa Delta Pi, national educational society, establishes third black-college chapter at Langston
1955 Public Relations Office opens
1960 Harrison retires after twenty years as president; succeeded by Hale, first alumnus to return as president
1962 Electronics and technology courses added to curriculum

LANGSTON UNIVERSITY

- 1965 Accredited by National Council for Accreditation of Teacher Education
- 1968 All-time high enrollment: 1,336; special Black Heritage Collection is begun
- 1969 Largest class graduates: 207
- 1972 Tolson Collection housed in Page Library Annex
- 1975 Communications Department established; elementary lab school closed
- 1978 Campus size: 1,262 acres

APPENDIX B

Oklahoma Governors and Langston University Presidents

Dates	Governors	Dates	Presidents
1897-1901	Cassius M. Barnes	1898-1915	Inman Page
1901	William M. Jenkins		
1901-1906	Thompson Ferguson		
1906-1907	Frank Frantz		
1907-11	Charles Haskell		
1911-15	Lee Cruce		
1915-19	Robert Williams	1915-16	I. B. McCutcheon
		1916	R. E. Bullitt*
1919-23	James Robertson	1916-23	J. M. Marquess
1923-27	Martin Trapp	1923-27	I. W. Young
1927-29	Henry Johnston	1927-31	Zachary Hubert
1929-31	William Holloway		
1931-35	William Murray	1931-35	I. W. Young
1935-39	Ernest Marland	1935-39	J. W. Sanford
1939-43	Leon C. Phillips	1939	B. F. Lee*
		1940	Albert Turner
1943-47	Robert S. Kerr	1940-60	G. L. Harrison
1947-51	Roy J. Turner		
1951-55	Johnston Murray		
1955-59	Raymond Gary		
1959-63	J. Howard Edmondson	1960-69	William Hale
1963-67	Henry Bellmon		
1967-71	Dewey Bartlett	1969-74	William Sims
1971-75	David Hall	1974-75	James Mosley*
1975-78	David Boren	1975-77	Thomas English
		1977	Ernest Holloway*
		1978	Samuel J. Tucker
1979-	George Nigh		

*Interim president.

APPENDIX C

Presidents

Inman E. Page, First President (1898-1915)
In 1898, Page opened the doors of Langston University in the Langston Presbyterian Church, with a $9,000 budget. His tenure was marked by the following accomplishments:
1. Acreage increased from 40 to 320 acres
2. Construction of fourteen-room Main Building
3. Construction of the president's home
4. Construction of two dormitories, Attucks Hall (frame) and Phyllis Wheatley Hall (brick)
5. Construction of stone dormitory for men
6. Construction of fully equipped industrial plant
7. Construction of steam heating plant and securing of appropriations for electric lights and water works
8. Addition to College Department
9. Construction of $5,000 barn
10. Construction of infirmary
11. Construction of museum
12. Construction of twenty-seven room Main Building (the first Main Building had been destroyed by fire)

Isaac B. McCutcheon, Second President (1915-16)
During McCutcheon's short tenure, electricity was installed, running water was provided, window shades were installed in the dormitories, dishes and silverware were provided in the dining hall, and songbooks were purchased for the music hall.

R. E. Bullitt, Interim President (1916)
Bullitt served as acting president until John Marquess became president. No further data are available.

John M. Marquess, Third President (1916-23)
During Marquess' administration installation of electricity, running water, and steam heat was completed. Two dormitories, Marquess Hall (for men)

and Phyllis Wheatley Hall (for women) were completed, and the gymnasium, laundry, and president's home were built. Marquess was the first president to make the Boarding Department a source of revenue for the university. He often boasted that he built the gymnasium from those funds. Marquess Hall housed 100 men and cost $40,000.

Isaac W. Young, M.D., Fourth President (1923-27) and Sixth President (1931-35)

During Dr. Young's two terms the student body increased to 500, and the Correspondence and Extension departments were established. Dr. Young was successful in obtaining the first substantial appropriation for building and construction — for constructing and equipping the University Men's Dormitory, the University Women's Dormitory, the new Administration Building, the dairy barn, and the poultry plant and completion of the gymnasium, the Mechanical Building, and the steam laundry. He established departments for laundry, tailoring, auto mechanics, plumbing, printing, shoemaking, and landscaping.

Zachary T. Hubert, Fifth President (1927-31)

The University Men's Dormitory, the University Women's Dormitory, the Administration Building, and six teachers' cottages were completed during Hubert's administration (appropriations for the dormitories and Administration Building had been obtained during Dr. Young's tenure).

J. W. Sanford, Seventh President (1935-40)

Sanford Hall and the University Men's Annex were completed during Sanford's administration. He also improved the Administration Building (through appropriations secured during Dr. Young's administration). Sanford secured the appropriations for the Agricultural Building (Jones Hall) and the dairy barn.

B. F. Lee, Interim President (1940)

Albert Turner, Eighth President (1940)

G. L. Harrison, Ninth President (1940-60)

Harrison completed the Science and Agriculture Building (Jones Hall), the dairy barn, the pasteurization plant, the Agricultural Engineering Building, an arena, a meat laboratory, a twenty-four-room addition to the dormitory for men, a two-room addition to the Trades Building, and the brick infirmary building. Extensive repairs were made to Phyllis Wheatley Hall, and the first floor of Page Hall was converted into a college and high school library. Other improvements were a stucco garbage house; rooms for cosmetology classes, a radio shop, and a barbershop; and the enlargement of the shoe shop.

For aircraft mechanics' training Harrison secured $5,000 worth of equipment and an airplane motor appraised at $10,000. The university published its first catalogue in the university printing shop in the spring of 1940. Many revisions were made in the curriculum. Four faculty members who had earned doctoral degrees were employed. Harrison was responsible for changing the name to Langston University.

Under Harrison's administration the University was (1) accredited by the North Central Association of Colleges and Secondary Schools, (2) accredited by the Oklahoma State Board of Education, (3) approved by the U.S. Department of State for the exchange of foreign students, and (4) accredited with the Veterans Administration, operating under a contract enabling veterans to obtain educational benefits under the G.I. Bill of Rights.

William H. Hale, Tenth President (1960-69)

During Hale's administration a three-phase building and renovation program was completed:

Phase 1 (begun 1964): Construction of Gandy Hall, Brown Hall, William H. Hale Student Union, and three faculty apartment buildings and remodeling of Sanford Hall dining area into residence space

Phase 2 (completed 1968): Construction of Science and Technology Building, Library Annex (Page Hall) and Hargrove Music Hall and renovation of Young Auditorium and Harrison Library

Phase 3 (completed 1969): Construction of two air-conditioned dormitories accommodating 300 students and thirty-six student apartments and renovation of Moore Hall and Jones Hall, including air-conditioning

A coordinated ten-year plan of improvement was outlined in 1965 and updated in 1969 to project plans through 1975.

The university was accredited by the National Council for the Accreditation of Teacher Education during Hale's tenure. The College-Industry Cluster, the University Development Foundation, and the Cooperative State Research Program were established.

William E. Sims, Eleventh President (1970-74)

During Sims's tenure the Five College Curriculum Innovative Thrust Program was established, the Cooperative Extension Service (1890 program) was broadened, and the Cooperative Education Program was founded. Kerr-McGee Plaza and Fountain were built, and the dairy barn, pasteurization plant, and lab school were torn down.

PRESIDENTS

James L. Mosley, Interim President (1974-75)
Mosley was instrumental in obtaining a $400,000 appropriation from the Oklahoma Legislature to help pay off Langston University indebtedness.

Thomas E. English, Twelfth President (1975-77)
During English's administration the gymnasium was remodeled, the swimming pool was constructed, and a campus cleanup and beautification campaign was launched.

Ernest Holloway, Interim President (1977-78)
During Holloway's tenure the Legislative Support Campaign for securing financial aid for the physical plant and student scholarships was launched, the fiscal-accountability program was begun, and an information program to regents concerning strengths of the university was prepared.

Samuel J. Tucker, Thirteenth President (1978)

APPENDIX D

Vice-Presidents and Academic Deans

Dates	Name	Position
1920-23	John Buford	Dean of Agriculture
1921-22	J. Wilson Pettus	Dean of Arts, Sciences, and Education
1922-23	J. D. Elsberry	Dean of the High School
1922-24	Ralph Tyler	Dean of the Mechanical Division
1922-27, 1931-35	Byron K. Armstrong	Dean of Education
1923-24	W. B. Jones	Vice-President and Director of Extension
1923-28	S. L. Hargrove	Dean and Vice-President
1923-25	Sadie B. Davis	Dean of Women
1925-27, 1935-41	Allie B. Jones	Dean of Women and Nurse
1927-29	Ella P. Baker	Dean of Women and Nurse
1928-33	W. E. Anderson	Acting Dean
1930-32	Wilhelmena Bowles	Dean of Women and Physician
1933-35	Edna B. Kinchion	Dean of Women
1934-38	John C. Tinner	Dean of College
1934-44	J. J. Seabrook	Dean of Men and College Chaplain
1934-35, 1938-40	B. F. Lee	Dean of College of Arts Sciences
1940-41, 1941-62	LeRoy G. Moore	Dean of Instruction and Dean of Arts and Sciences
1941	Ann Brock	Dean of Women
1942	Josephine Berry	Dean of Women
1943-60	R. Patterson Perry	Vice-President and Administrative Dean
1943-44	Lena Brown Work	Dean of Women

VICE-PRESIDENTS AND ACADEMIC DEANS

Date	State-appropriated Funds	Non-State-appropriated Funds	Revolving Funds
1948-51	Mary S. B. Lee	Dean of Women	
1948-52	Julius H. Hughes	Dean of Men	
1951-53	Jean L. Noble	Dean of Women	
1952-53	Edwin Edmonds	Acting Dean of Men	
1953-55	Emma Bragg	Dean of Women	
1955-58	Marjorie Pearson	Dean of Women	
1958-59	Susan Haywood	Dean of Women	
1959-63	Rosa L. Wigley	Dean of Women	
1960-61	William Parker	Dean of Men	
1960-69, 1967-79	Inman A. Breaux	Vice-President, Dean of Administration, and Dean of Student Affairs	
1961-62	Eugene E. Brown	Dean of Men	
1961-63	Flora N. Swafford	Dean of Women	
1962-65	William Collins	Dean of Instruction	
1961-71, 1971-74	Booker T. Morgan	Assistant Dean of Student Affairs, Dean of Men	
1962-65	Eddie Strong	Dean of Men	
1962-67	W. A. Simpson	Dean of Women, Associate Dean of Students	
1965-69	William E. Sims	Dean of Instruction, Dean of Academic Affairs	
1965-72	L. R. Austin	Dean of Men	
1969-	Walter L. Jones	Dean of Academic Affairs	
1970-71	Myrtle Elliot	Dean of Women	
1970-77	Ernest Holloway	Dean of Student Affairs and Vice-President	
1972-78	Leslie Austin	Dean of Men	
1974-	Sylvia A. Lewis	Associate Dean of Students	

APPENDIX E

Enrollment, 1898-1978

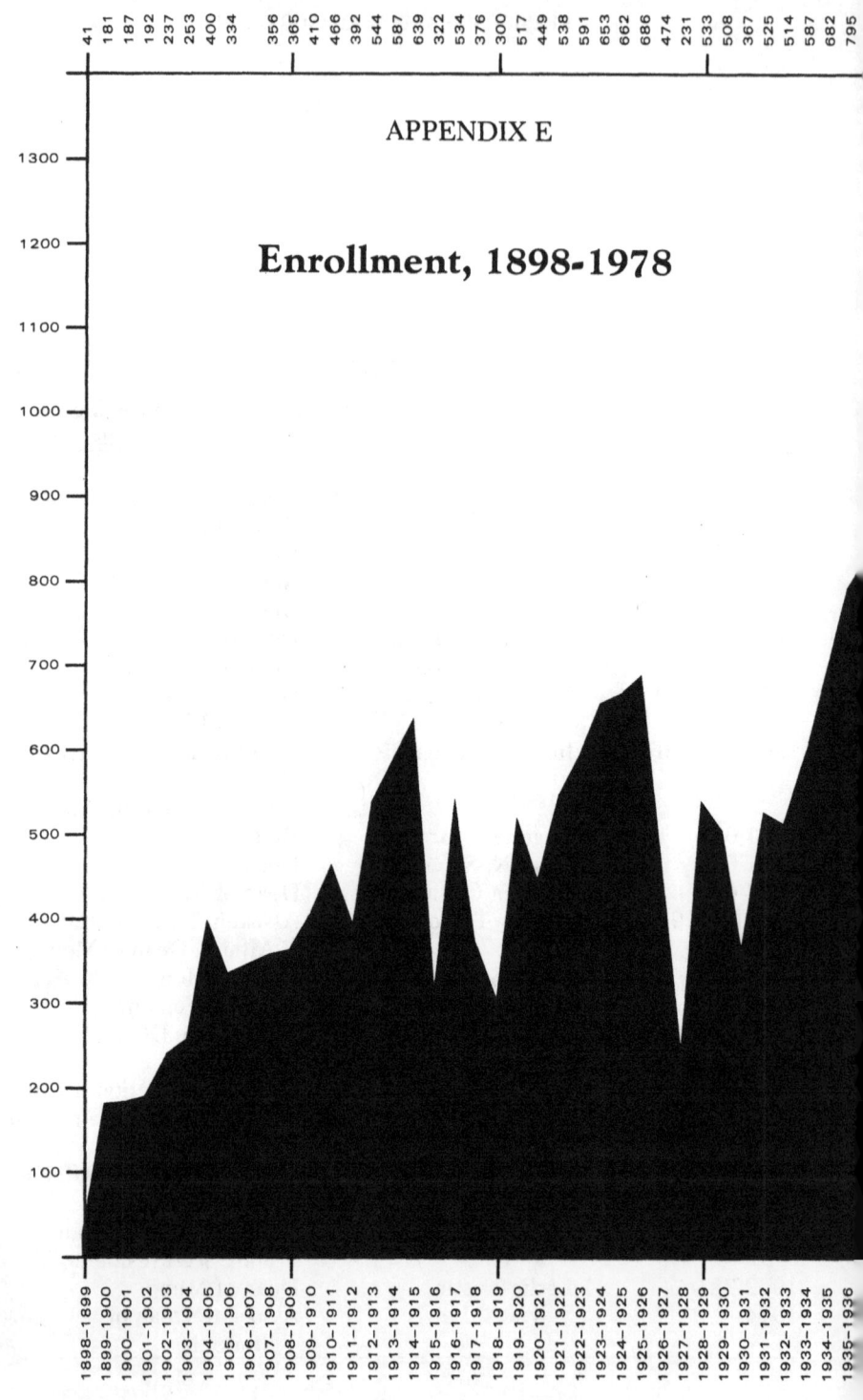

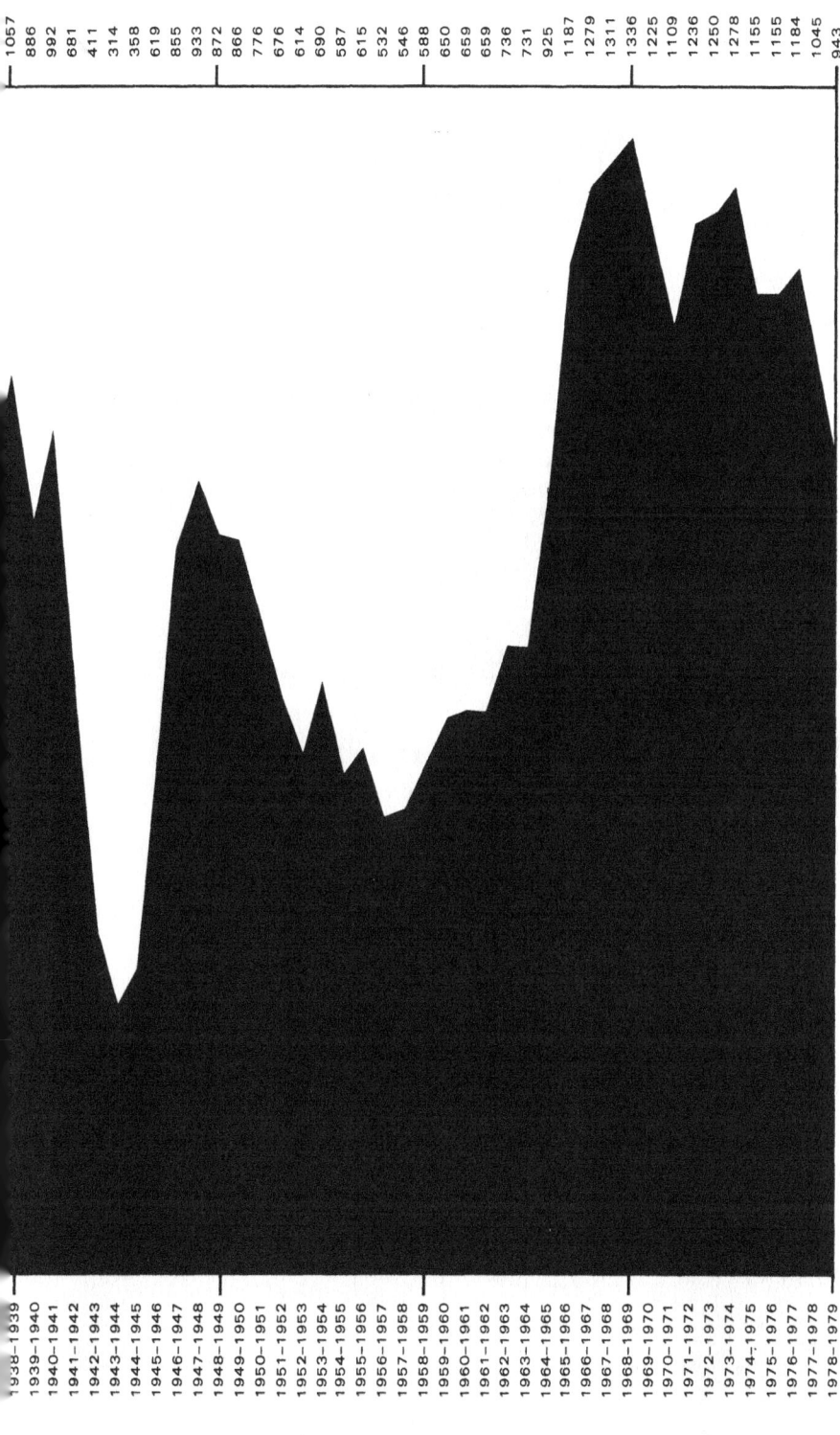

APPENDIX F

Appropriations to Langston University 1897-1975

Date	State-appropriated Funds	Non-State-appropriated Funds	Revolving Funds
1897-98	$ 5,000.00		
1898-99	4,000.00		
1899-1900	10,000.00		
1901-1902	85,000.00		
1903-1904	90,000.00		
1905-1906	95,000.00		
1907-1908	185,294.00		
1909-10	92,142.00		
1911-12	77,600.00		
1913-14	90,300.00		
1915-16	90,000.00		
1917-18	81,035.00		
1919-20	90,000.00		
1921-22	104,749.00		
1923-24	185,000.00		
1925-26	106,900.00		
1927-28	265,000.00		
1929-31	390,346.04		
1931-33	259,771.53		
1933-35	205,817.86		
1935-37	225,169.53		
1937-39	383,863.75		
1939-41	569,498.00		
1941-43	365,644.40		
1943-45	344,562.00		
1945-46	292,933.33		
1946-47	391,170.83		
1947-48	290,050.00		
1948-49	300,050.00		
1949-50	383,295.00		

APPROPRIATIONS, 1897-1975

1950-51	368,818.00		
1951-52	368,648.00	$	15,000.00
1952-53	342,240.00		
1953-54	501,681.00		15,000.00
1954-55	501,681.00		
1955-56	460,367.00		
1956-57	472,643.00		
1957-58	506,861.00		
1958-59	509,934.00		
1959-60	529,918.00		
1960-61	451,411.00		
1961-62	529,918.60		
1962-63	449,547.10		
1963-64	563,477.44		
1964-65	492,761.93		
1965-66	948.250.28		
1966-67	720,169.28	$	335,278.50
1967-68	768,632.00		486,492.00
1968-69	804,819.00		590,685.00
1969-70	849,860.00		595,000.00
1970-71	884,022.00		551,000.00
1971-72	898,144.00		441,779.00
1972-73	938,116.00		510,049.00
1973-74	1,112,375.00		690,620.00

Source: Biennial reports of the Oklahoma State Regents for Higher Education, 1897-1974.

APPENDIX G

The Land-Grant College

When the land-grant college system started with legislation sponsored by Justin Morrill in 1862, the law had little significance for black people in America. They were still enslaved, and higher education was a distant dream. Higher education for blacks came through passage of the "second Morrill Act" in 1890, when the original colleges could no longer operate on endowment income and inadequate state support. The second Morrill Act, termed the "1890 Program," provided annual appropriations based on formulas to create new land-grant schools for blacks. Seventeen southern states established schools for Negroes as a result. All these schools have been closely involved with the United States Department of Agriculture from the passage of the Smith-Lever Act in 1914. More recent involvement with the federal government came about through funding from the Higher Education Act of 1965.

Thus over a quarter of a century before Oklahoma became a state, the government of the United States had established the policy of making land grants to the individual states for the purpose of endowing both common schools and institutions of higher learning.

The Oklahoma Organic Act provided a form of government for Oklahoma before it became a state. Oklahoma Territory set aside Sections 16 and 36 of each township for the benefit of the schools. The First Territorial Legislature gave counties the right to decide whether they would provide separate or mixed schools for their white and black children. Most counties established separate schools. In 1891, Territorial Governor George Steele reported enrollment of 20,085 white and 1,252 black children in territorial schools. The first black school opened in 1891 in Oklahoma City at the intersection of California and Harvey streets. The first school term lasted four months.

The pattern that firmly established segregation resulted from the United States Supreme Court decision in *Plessy* v. *Ferguson* in 1896. The decision stated that "separate but equal" facilities were constitutional. The decision was not reversed until 1954.

Under the Enabling Act for Oklahoma statehood Section 13 of each township was set aside for the benefit of higher education. The income from these lands is known as Section Thirteen and New College funds. It is credited directly to particular institutions, as opposed to other land-grant income, which goes into a general operational fund. Langston was one of the institutions named to share proportionately in the Section 13 funds.

Congress passed the Enabling Act in June, 1906, making Oklahoma the trustee of the land. Generally Sections 16 and 36 of each township were to be used for common schools, Section 13 for colleges, and Section 33 for charitable or penal facilities.

Langston received 100,000 acres under the 1906 act. Most of the land is situated in western Oklahoma, with a portion in Logan County and a small amount in New Mexico. The good faith of the state was pledged to preserve the land and use the money derived from it for the benefit of the school.

Through the years most of the land has been rented through agricultural leases. Such leases are executed for up to five years, while commercial leases do not exceed two years. The net rental income is disbursed among the six trust funds, of which Langston's is one.

Beginning in 1906, specific lands were assigned to Langston. Most of the 100,000 acres was secured by 1911, although the final tract of 37 acres (in New Mexico) was not listed until 1969. Some of the approved lands included 3,700 acres around Guthrie (approved in 1908), 90,000 acres in the Woodward District (also approved in 1908), several smaller tracts in the Woodward District (approved in 1908-1909), and a final 2,200 acres in western Oklahoma (approved in 1911).

As of June 30, 1974, Langston University's pro rata share of surface acres was 19,528.1, with a value of $455,211.92. The Department of the Commissioners of the Land Office is administered under the supervision of the commissioners by a secretary appointed by the governor.

The state of Oklahoma, as trustee owns approximately 760,000 acres of land. Of the money derived from the leases of the land, 45 percent is set aside to run the department. The excess, if any is disbursed periodically to the recipients of the trusts.

Each lease is separately appraised at least once every five years. Such factors as soil type, location, contour of the land, and availability of water determine the amount charged for the lease. After the estimate of the productivity of the land is made, the state determines what a fair "landlord's share of the rent would be. In other words, the land is rented on a "share-crop" basis. Consideration is given to the uncertainty of weather, crops, market prices, and production. Thus the rentals are conservative.

There are approximately 3300 leases in effect at the time of this writing. Of these about two-thirds are "preference" leases, which means that if the land is put up for sale the leaseholder has the option to purchase it. There are 72 grazing leases, some of which run as large as 17,000 acres. Most agricultural leases are in the amount of 160-acre tracts.

Information concerning these leases can be obtained in the annual lease reports issued by the state through the Department of Commissioners of the Land Office.

The Land Grant Centennial was celebrated in 1962. The university honored the occasion with a dinner at which Oklahoma's United States Senator Mike Monroney was guest speaker. The school also entertained W. M. Q. Halm, ambassador from Ghana, at the annual meeting of land-grant colleges in Kansas City that year.

APPENDIX H

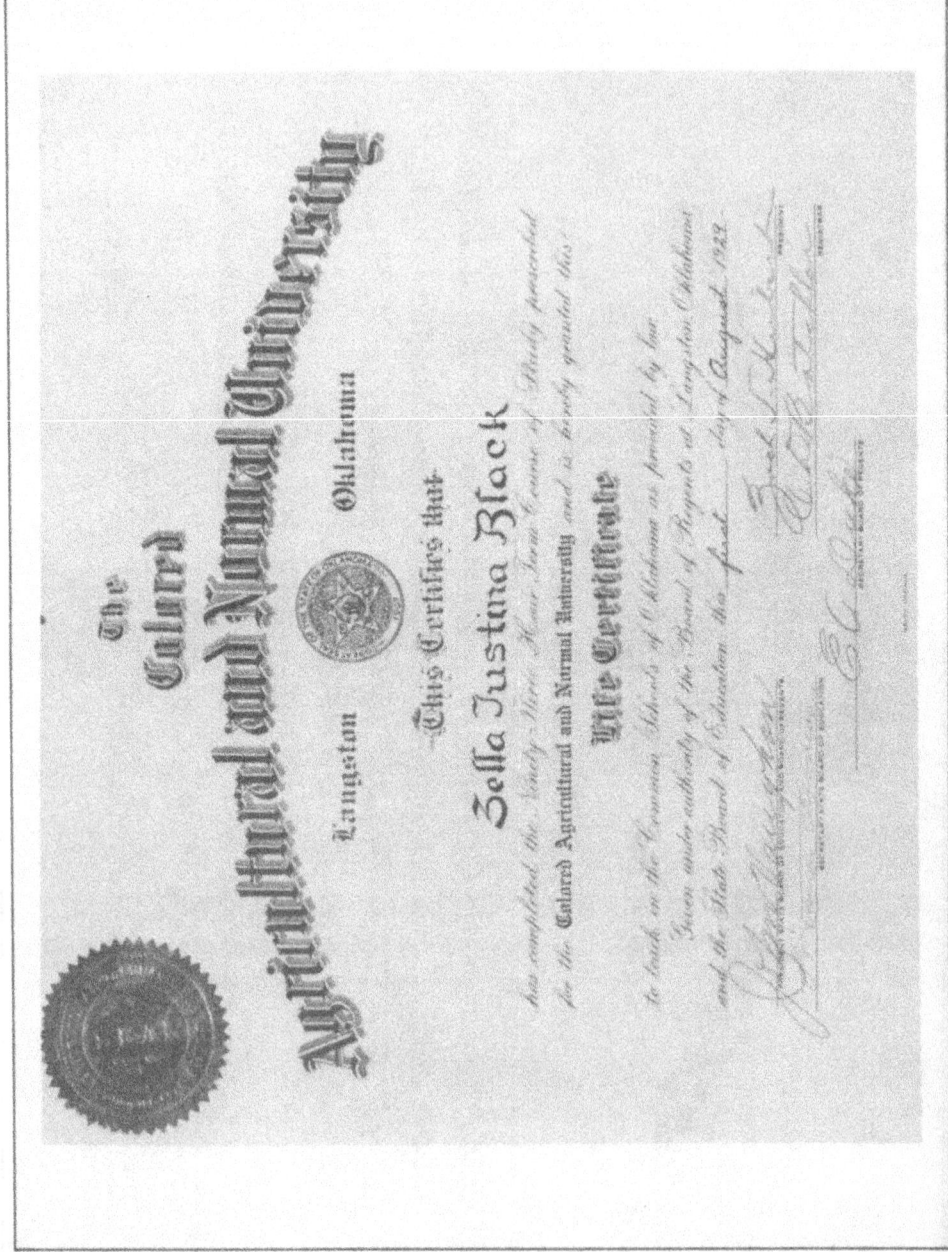

The Colored Agricultural and Normal University

By authority of the Board of Regents and upon recommendation of the Faculty hereby confers upon

Zella Justina Black

the degree of

Bachelor of Science in Home Economics

with all its honors, rights, and privileges.

Given under the Seal of the University at Langston, Oklahoma, on the twenty-ninth day of July, nineteen hundred and thirty-seven.

Richard Elgin, President of the Board of Regents
J. W. Sanford, Secretary of the Board of Regents
B. F. Lee, President of the University
Dean of the University

APPENDIX I

University Publications, 1898-1978

Langston University catalogues, 1898-1978.
Langston University annuals or yearbooks, 1921-78; known as *The Langstonian* in 1921 and 1922, *The Claw* in 1927; and *The Lion* from the 1930s to 1978.
Agricultural and Normal University *Bulletin — Agricultural and Home Economics Number.* Founded 1923; issued monthly.
Reflector, 1927-40.
LU Review, 1939-1950.
Langston University Gazette, founded 1951, during Harrison's administration, and still published.
Southwestern Journal, research journal published four times a year. First published June, 1944; publication suspended during the 1950s.
Langston Newsletter, bimonthly publication. First published October 1, 1960, during the first year of Hale's administration, and still published.
Langston University handbooks:
  Faculty and Staff Handbook, 1940-.
  Student Handbook, 1940-.
  G. Lamar Harrison Library Handbook, 1957-.
  Handbook of Directions for Preparing Research Papers, Department of English and Modern Languages, 1966.
Langston University Alumni News Notes, 1968-.
Projection, newsletter published bimonthly by Cooperative Extension Service in cooperation with Oklahoma State University and the U.S. Department of Agriculture, 1974-.
Helpful Hints for the Home, by Ruby King, Cooperative Extension Services in cooperation with Oklahoma State University and U.S. Department of Agriculture (one-year project).
Self-Study of Langston University and Provisional Report Teacher Education Program Submitted to the North Central Association of Colleges and Secondary Schools and to the National Council for the Accreditation of Teacher Education, 1969.

UNIVERSITY PUBLICATIONS

From 1927 to the early 1940s, Langston University owned and operated its own printing press. My youngest brother, William W. Black, earned his room and board working in the print shop during the years 1927 to 1935. He informed me that the Langston University catalogues were printed on the campus in the early 1940s. Printing jobs in the years 1927 to 1935 included meal tickets, football tickets, programs for various occasions, calling cards, and letterheads and envelopes for various departments. Virtually all of the university's printing was done on campus during those years.

At first all printing was done by hand on an old-fashioned printing press. Later a Linotype machine was purchased and then a more modern press. Mrs. E. E. Weaver (Mayme) was the first printing teacher and supervisor. C. C. Mack succeeded her in the early 1930s. During the postwar years industrial education gradually faded from the Langston curriculum, and the printing press fell into disuse. President Sims donated the printing equipment to the Okmulgee School for Disadvantaged Children in 1973.

APPENDIX J

Degrees Conferred by Oklahoma Institutions of Higher Education, 1975-76

Percentage Distribution of Degrees by Race					
	Associate	Bachelor's	Master's	First Professional	Doctor's
White N-Hisp.	87.2	89.6	84.7	92.8	84.7
Black N-Hisp.	6.2	4.5	3.5	2.0	3.5
Hispanic	0.9	0.5	0.3	0.6	0.3
Asian-Pac.	0.5	0.5	0.8	1.1	0.8
Am. Ind. Alask.	4.0	2.3	2.1	3.5	2.1
N. Res. Alien	1.2	2.6	8.6	0.0	8.6
	100.0	100.0	100.0	100.0	100.0

Percentage Distribution of Degrees by Age							
	Under 20	20-24	25-34	35-44	45-54	Over 54-	
Associate	2.3	51.2	28.6	13.3	3.9	0.7	=100.0
Bachelor's	0.2	72.6	22.0	3.9	1.1	0.2	=100.0
Master's	0.0	31.1	51.3	11.7	5.1	0.8	=100.0
First Professional	0.0	62.6	35.9	1.4	0.1	0.0	=100.0
Doctor's	0.0	22.6	47.6	23.3	5.5	1.0	=100.0

Source: Oklahoma State Regents for Higher Education, *Oklahoma Higher Education Report,* vol. 3, no. 9 (May 31, 1977), p. 4.

APPENDIX K

Organizational Chart, 1978-79

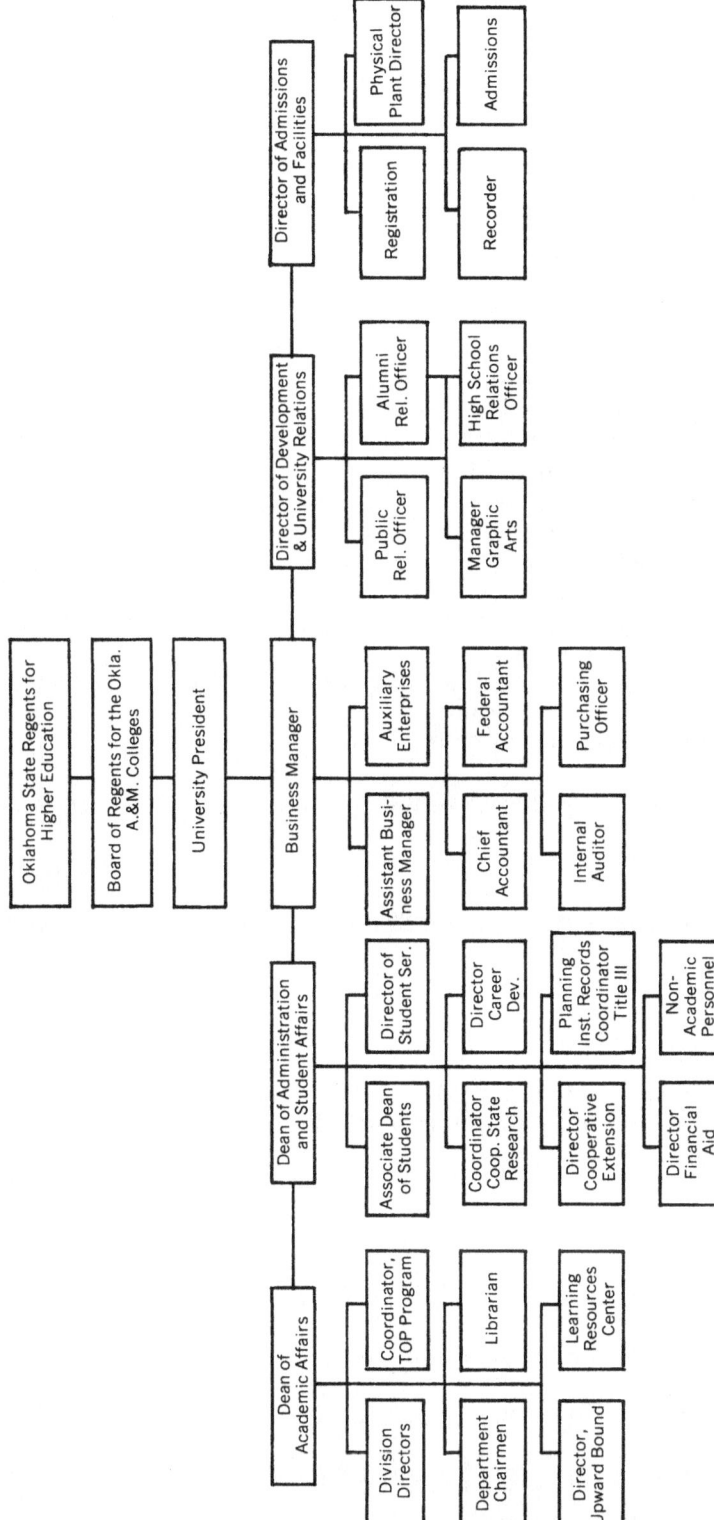

APPENDIX L

Faculty and Research Staff, 1978-79

Faculty:
    Total full-time teaching faculty: 64
        Professors: 12
        Associate professors: 13
        Assistant professors: 14
        Instructors: 25

Total nonblack full-time teaching faculty: 19
    Professors: 3
    Associate professors: 4
    Assistant professors: 3
    Instructors: 9

Part-time white faculty: 3
Part-time Iranian faculty: 1

Distribution of black faculty:
    American: 43
    Ethiopian: 2

Distribution of nonblack faculty:
    Whites: 16
    Korean: 1
    Cuban: 1
    Indian (Oriental): 1

Total research staff: 20
    Nonblack staff (professional): 12 (60 percent)

Notes on Sources

Chapter One

Kaye M. Teall, ed., *Black History in Oklahoma: A Resource Book* (Oklahoma City: Oklahoma City Public Schools, 1971), pp. 157ff. See also the Fred S. Barde Newspaper Collection, *Bureau*, March 3, 1890; *Langston City Herald*, December 19, 1891; January 16, March 30, May 28, July 2, 27, 1892. White-backlash fears reported in the *Hennessey Clipper* were reprinted in the *Langston Herald*, January 16, 1892. Further commentary can be found in Mozell C. Hill, "The All-Negro Communities of Oklahoma," *Journal of Negro History*, July 31, 1946, p.25. A WPA Writer's Project compiled a journalistic history of the early community but should be consulted with care. See *New York Times*, April 9, 1891. McCabe sold the *Langston Herald* in 1892.

Chapter Two

On raising money for the school: *Langston City Herald*, May 8, 1897. Standards and regents set by *Session Laws of Oklahoma*, April 12, 1897, pp. 40-41. Financing is reviewed in a thesis by Oliver Hodge. For details on land leasing see annual reports of the Commissioners of the Land Office (Oklahoma City: State Capitol Building, various years). Land-grant tracts are recorded in U.S. Department of the Interior, General Land Office, CA&NU lists (Washington, D.C., 1907, 1908, 1911, 1969). All other pertinent data are published in the biennial reports of the Oklahoma State Regents for Higher Education. The 1977 Legislative Committee recommendations were published in the *Daily Oklahoman*, December 6, 1977.

Chapter Three

For Inman Page, see especially *Langston University Alumni Association Bulletin*, 5th ed. (Muskogee, Okla.: Lewis Printing Co., 1941), p. 11; and W. Sherman Savage, *The History of Lincoln University*, (Jefferson City, Mo., 1939) pp. 40-78. The alumni bulletin cited above also outlines conditions under McCutcheon and the conflict with Hogan. The *Black Dispatch* article, dated March 11, 1916, was quoted in *Harlow's Weekly*, January 31, 1917. Additional biographical material on Harrison is included in *Eyes* (Iowa City, Iowa), June, 1946. For data concerning the Hales, see *Langston University Gazette* 10 (May, 1961). For the ten-year plan see *Sunday Oklahoman*, December 22, 1968. The quotation on guidance is taken from an interview in the *University of Chicago Magazine*, October, 1966. Hale's firing is documented in the *Daily Oklahoman*, October 28, December 6, 1969. A résumé was provided by Larzette Golden Hale. Professional data sheets were provided by Mosley, Holloway, English, and Tucker. The information on the firing of Tucker was taken from the *Guthrie Daily Leader*, December 21, 1978. The appointment of Holloway as interim president was reported in the *Black Dispatch*, December 21, 1978.

Chapter Four

The history of the Normal Department is contained in the Langston catalogues, issued in the early days as *Colored Agricultural and Normal University Bulletins*; see issues for 1902-1903, 1904-1905, 1912-13, 1923-24, 1926-27, 1930-31, 1934-35. Other information in author's files.

LANGSTON UNIVERSITY

Chapter Five

Information on the College Preparatory Department was taken from yearly bulletins, catalogue editions, and Langston yearbooks. Excerpts from the senior-class history appear in the annual, *The Langstonian* (Guthrie, Okla.: Cooperative Publishing Co.,), p. 38.

Chapter Six

The memories of A. H. Fuhr are contained in an address entitled "Seventy-seven Years in Retrospect," delivered at the Founder's Day observance on March 10, 1974. The description of early-day family outings is based on the author's personal recollections. Catalogue E, issued at Langston in 1923-24, contains some data on this era. The visit of Langston Hughes to the campus is documented in "Poetry and Life," *"Southwestern Journal* 1 (May, 1944): 53. See also details in Langston University Alumni Association Bulletin, 5th ed. (Muskogee, Okla: Lewis Printing Co., 1941), pp.7-8.

Chapter Seven

Enrollment statistics are drawn from university records. Special attention should be given to the CA&NU Bulletin (Langston, Okla.: Age Print, 1904-1905) and the 1898-99 and 1899-1900 editions (Guthrie, Okla.: State Capitol Printing Company). For other early-day notes see *Oklahoma State Capitol,* art ed., May 26, 1900. See also James S. Buchanan and Edward Everett Dale, *A History of Oklahoma* (Evanston, Ill.: Row, Peterson and Company, 1935) p. 304. "Summary of Resident Enrollment" is contained in the *First Biennial Report* of the regents, issued in 1942, and in succeeding reports. "Langston University Enrollment Trends" was issued by the Office of Admissions and Records of Langston University on September 16, 1975. See also *Daily Oklahoman,* September 22, 1977.

Chapter Eight

Data on student expenses are taken primarily from CA&NU catalogues, 1898-1975. The brochure entitled *Financial Aids Program* was issued by Langston University in 1976. The Kerr-McGee program is described in the *Langston Gazette* 15 (November, 1964). A self-survey of the teacher education program was submitted to NCATE in 1968; see pp. 21, 36. The preliminary report, "Self-Study Task Forces for the Seventies," was issued at Langston University on August 22, 1972. The State Regents' report "Trend in Average Salaries Paid All Full Time Faculty by Academic Rank" was issued in December, 1963. See "Regents Scuttle Raises for Langston," *Black Dispatch* 64 (June 19, 1975); *Guthrie Daily Leader* 84 (June 19, 1975; "LU Pay Increases Tabled by Regents" and "Increase of Faculty Salaries at Langston," *Black Dispatch,* August 4, 1977. All material drawn from regents' reports is prepared by the Division of Fiscal Affairs and published at the State Capitol Building, Oklahoma City. See especially the Annual Report for 1976-77: *Faculty Salaries in the Oklahoma State System of Higher Education.*

Chapter Nine

Data on student organizations are documented in the annuals issued by the school under the titles *Langstonian, Claw,* and *Lion.* Information was also obtained from Sadie Waterford Jones.

NOTES ON SOURCES

Chapter Ten

Data on the vice-presidents and academic deans were obtained from the Langston University records.

Chapter Eleven

Information on the strike was obtained from the following original documents in the President's Office, Langston University: communication dated November 1, 1928, from student body to President Hubert; list of monetary contributions to student strike, and minutes of Student Council. The minutes of the Committee on Student Rights contain the names and apologies of students who did not participate in the strike. The personal recollections of Roosevelt Gracey and Moxye Weaver King substantiate the account of this event. See also minutes of the special meeting held November 19, 1928, and the first Constitution and By-Laws of CA&NU, and the original ledger of the student council, kept by the secretary, Theresa Black. "The Other Side of the Question at the CA&NU" was distributed not only on campus but across the state. See *Black Dispatch*, January 29, 1929, and *Guthrie Daily Leader*, January 25, 1929. The results of the strike and the leaders' later lives and careers were recalled by Ira Hall. Neither the student council minutes nor the ledger of 1928-29 is paged.

Chapter Twelve

See catalogues of CA&NU for 1898, 1900, and 1902. Young's statement is contained in the *Agricultural and Home Economics Bulletin*, 1923-24. See also the Alumni Association Bulletin for that year. The CA&NU report "Expenditures" (February 27, 1939), p. 109, documents the financial status of the library in 1939. The annual library reports issued after 1944 are also available. The historical brochure was issued in 1950 on the opening of the G. Lamar Harrison Library.

Chapter Thirteen

"A Self-Study of Langston University" was issued by the school in 1965; see especially pp. 9-12. "A Plan for the Seventies" was issued by the Oklahoma State Regents for Higher Education in 1970. See also the Task Force report of Langston, issued in August, 1972. "Higher Education for Negros" is contained in the state regents' *Third Biennial Report*, pp. 41-43. The accrediting visit of 1944 was reported in *Black Dispatch*, February 12, 1944, p. 11. The section "Concerning Graduate and Specialized Education for Negroes in Oklahoma" is taken from a regents' report, p. 291.

Chapter Fourteen

Data are taken from the early CA&NU bulletins (catalogue edition), issued at Langston in 1902-1903, 1904-1905, 1923-24, and 1934-35, and, later, from the catalogue for 1961-62. Material concerning the New Farmers of America in Oklahoma is contained in a thesis by James Monroe Jenkins.

LANGSTON UNIVERSITY

Chapter Fifteen

Descriptions of courses and faculty are taken from university catalogues. Students of Eugene Brown provided personal data. See also the program of the exhibition, December 11-19, 1931. Wallace Owens and Juanita Cotton provided professional data sheets.

Chapter Sixteen

A. H. Fuhr provided data on early-day athletics at Langston. See also the university bulletin of 1912-13. Booker T. Robinson furnished reminiscences of early-day football and pictures of the 1924 "Wonder Team." Thomas Black, Jr., was also interviewed. See annual issues of the *Langstonian* for athletic records of the twenties. World War II teams featured in *Applause* 2 (1945). See also the Arkansas-Langston football program for November 15, 1947. Gayles's record appeared in *Oklahoma Today* 22 (Spring, 1972). The Langston track team received notice in the *Langston Gazette* for June, 1965; and in the *Guthrie Daily Leader*, April 28, 1974. See the Schoats interview in the *Daily Oklahoman*, August 30, 1977.

Chapter Seventeen

The Committee on Community Service was an internal committee of the university. Its report was part of the task force report for the 1970s, issued in the self-study report of May, 1972. Mozell Hill and Thelma Ackiss, *Culture of a Contemporary All-Negro Community* (Langston, Okla.: Social Science Department, Social Research Unit), July, 1943. Much of the material on the city of Langston today was supplied by Kenneth Hamilton.

Chapter Eighteen

Much of the material concerning cooperative extension work can be found in *Agriculture and Home Economics,* CA&NU Bulletin 1 (July, 1924). See also J. A. Evans, *Extension Work Among Negroes,* Circular no. 355 (Washington, D.C.: U.S. Department of Agriculture), September, 1925. *A Decade of Negro Extension Work,* Miscellaneous Circular no. 72 (Washington, D.C.: U.S. Department of Agriculture), covers the period 1914-24. See also annual reports of the Extension Division, Oklahoma Agricultural and Mechanical College (now OSU), Stillwater. Hazel O. King and James L. Mosley also provided data. Cooperative extension work between land-grant colleges and the U.S. Department of Agriculture is authorized under the Smith-Lever Act, 7 U.S.C. 341 et seq.

Chapter Nineteen

See CA&NU bulletins from 1898 to 1913 for documentation on language courses offered in those years. For Tolson see Joy Flasch, *Melvin B. Tolson,* United States Authors Series (New York: Twayne Publishers, 1972). Ms. Flasch also contributed data concerning the Communications Department. Elwyn Welch provided curriculum data for the 1975-76 English and foreign-language courses.

NOTES ON SOURCES

Chapter Twenty

CA&NU catalogue, 1902-1903, p. 22; Zella J. Black [Patterson], "Development of Homemaking," *Southwestern Journal* 3 (1947). The story on Waller appeared in the *Langston University Gazette*, 1969.

Chapter Twenty-one

See "Graduate Education for Blacks," in the Oklahoma State Regents' *Fifth Biennial Report* (1948-50), pp. 83-84. The history of the Ada Lois Sipuel Fisher and G. W. McLaurin cases is given in *Black Dispatch*, April 9, 1965. Ms. Fisher also provided personal interviews. See also *Issue of the School of Law*, Langston University Bulletin (Oklahoma City: State Capitol Building, January 26, 1948); and "Professor Recalls Brealing Law School Barrier," *Guthrie Daily Leader*, March 1, 1971.

Chapter Twenty-two

Sources for information about music at Langston are the CA&NU catalogues, Langston University bulletins, programs of the Department of Music, and Sammye Sadler Walker.

Chapter Twenty-three

Titles of research projects are listed in issues of *Southwestern Journal*, beginning in 1943; see especially vol. 1, no. 1. (May, 1944). Data on current research funding were provided by Steve Latimer.

Chapter Twenty-four

Leroy Moore provided information about the Department of Chemistry. Information about the early-day student-nursing program is based on a 1977 interview with Ira B. James, who worked her way through school as a student nurse in the 1920s. The CA&NU bulletin of 1912-13, p. 143, lists nursing-school requirements. Changes in structure were recorded in the Langston University catalogue of 1954-55, p. 34.

Chapter Twenty-five

See text and pictures in early-day Langston University bulletins, especially those for 1900-1901 (pp. 18-19); 1904-1905 (pp. 12-14); and 1912-13 (pp. 103, 104). Flight training is mentioned in the bulletin for 1941-42 (p. 121).

Chapter Twenty-six

"The Early Development of Langston City," data contained in a research paper by Kenneth M. Hamilton (1977); "Langston Must Have a Good School," *Langston City Herald*, November 30, 1895; "Raising Money for School," *Langston City Herald*, May 8, 1897; Langston University Alumni Association *Bulletin*, 5th ed., pp. 7-8.

Index

Academic Department: 112
Accreditation: 146-50
Ackiss, Thelma: 196-97
Administration Building: 40, 46, 146, 230
Afro-American Heritage Center: 54
Aggie Club: 128
Agricultural Appropriations Act of 1972: 202
Agriculture Club: 162
Agriculture Department: early emphasis on, 154; and school farm, 154-58; courses in, 154-55; scholarships in, 156; curriculum changes, 154; buildings and equipment of, 160; personnel of, 163
Agriculture Division: *see* Agriculture Department
Agriculture Experiment Station (OSU): 249
Allen, Donald: 249
Allen, Mizura: 203
Alston, A. J.: 15
American Association of Colleges for Teacher Education: 52
Anderson, Marian: 85
Anderson, Thomas: 241
Anderson, W. E.: 134; as football coach, 175, 216; as director of English Department, 216
Appropriations, 1897-1975: 292-93
Art Department: established in 1927-28, 164; exhibitions of, 165, 169; chairmen of, 166-68; faculty of, 169
Arterbery, Thelma J.: 268
Association of American Colleges: 52, 148
Athletics Department: beginning of, 172; and early days of football, 172-75; coaching staff of, 173-76, 181; women in, 173, 175; and football teams played, 174; and football players, 175; and championship teams, 176-77; in World War II, 176-77; and postwar years, 177; and track and field, 178, 180, 182; and discus championship, 180; instructors in, 181; and professional football, 181-82; and football team of 1924, 185-90
Attucks Hall (dormitory for women): page 18, 34

Bailey, Joseph: 77
Baker, Ella P. (dean of women): 133, 136-37, 139-40
Barnes, Cassius M.: 16, 80
Basic Educational Opportunity Grants: 120
Batchelor, Dewey: 217
Bell, William: 136
Bellmon, Gov. Henry: 115
Bethune, Mary McLeod: 85
Biology Department: 257-58
Black, Theresa: 136
Black, Thomas H., Jr.: 156
Black Dispatch: 47, 223
Black Minister's Alliance: 212
Black People's Union: 130
Board of Regents (first) of Langston University: 16; early action of, 17; *see also* under names of members
Board of Regents of Oklahoma Agricultural and Mechanical Colleges: 23, 36, 47, 61-63, 68-69, 71-72, 117, 138, 150
Boren, Gov. David: 140
Bowles, Wilhelmena: 255
Boys' Glee Club: 127
Brazile, Ed: 180
Breaux, Zelia Page: 238-39
Brooks, Paul: 211
Brown, Charles: 263
Brown, Eugene E.: 165-66
Brown, E. J.: 95
Brown, Joseph: 136
Buford, C. R.: 153
Buford, E. John: 73, 155
Bullitt, R. E. (Langston University president): 36, 113
Byrd, Syble E.: 78

311

Campbell, T. M.: 209
Camp Gruber: 129
Carry, George: 215
Carver, George Washington: 210
Cash, James: 270
Cement, Ella: 203
Central State University (Edmond, Okla.): 169, 180
Chancelor Club: 127
Chemistry Department: 254-58
Chicago Conservator: 4
Chronology: 281-82
Clark, Joann: 220
Claw, the (college annual): 126
College Department: 31-32, 40
College of Arts and Sciences: 46
College Preparatory Department: 75, 110-12
Collins, William E.: 257
Colored Agricultural and Normal University: 10, 13, 50, 110; purpose of, 15; site of, 15; founding of, 15, 31; *see also* Langston University
Combs, Willa A.: 232
Commencement, 1927: 107-109
Communications Department: 222
Control and Education Board: 23
Corrado, Anna: 181
Cotton, Irabell Juanita: 169-70
Cox, Maude: 240
Coyle, Okla: 96, 196, 202
Crisp, T. M.: 176, 178, 180-81
Crowell, Bernard G.: 178, 181
Crowell, Virginia: 144
Cruce, Gov. Lee: 22
Cunningham, Larry: 182

Davis, Elmyra Richardson Todd: 144-45, 220
Day, Ann: 232
Delta Gamma Alpha (club): 128
Department of Development and Public Relations: 58
Department of Natural and Physical Science: 257-58
Department of Technology: *see* mechanical and industrial arts, trades courses

Depression: 113-14, 118, 196, 210, 217, 257
Derricotte, Juliette: 126
Desegregation: 57, 116
Division of Vocational and Technical Education: 228
Dixon, Willie: 180
Douglas, Beulah: 239
Dunjee, Bessie Floyd: 125
Dunjee, Roscoe: 47, 233
Dust Bowl Players: 130, 219-23

Edmondson, Gov. J. Howard: 115
Education Department: 77
Elsberry, J. D.: 73
Ellsworh, Arthur: 234
Enabling Act land grant: 17
English, Thomas E. (Langston University president): 67, 115; background of, 67-68; and school financial troubles, 68-69, 122; discharged, 69, 117
Enrollment: in 1898, 110; in 1900, 110; counties, states represented in, 110-11; decline of, in 1904, 111-12; seesaw pattern of, 112-13; in World War I, 112-13; during Depression, 113-14; in World War II, 115; under Pres. William H. Hale, 115; for 1975-76, 117; for 1977 and 1978, 117, 140; 1898 to 1978, 290-91
Esoteric Club: 126; *see also* Phyllis Wheatley Club
Expenses, student: 118-24
Extension Service, Agriculture and Home Economics: early history of, 206; in Oklahoma in 1910, 206; Negroes in, 206-12; women in, 207-208, 211-12; and boys' clubs, 207-208; at State Fair of Oklahoma, 208; and Negro community fairs, 208-209; funding of, 210; Langston University-Oklahoma State University programs merged, 212

Faculty and research staff, 1978-79: 304
Federal Credit Union: 202
Federal Higher Education Act of 1965: 22, 144; Title I, 22; Title III, 22, 60, 61, 242; Title V, 22; Title II, 144

INDEX

Federal Housing and Home Finance Agency: 149
Fellows, J. E.: 234
Fine Arts Department: *see* Music Department
Fisher, Ada Lois Sipuel: 233
Fisher, Clara: 232
Flash, Joy: 219-20, 222
Football: *see* Athletics Department
Football team of 1924: 185-90; *see also* Athletics Department
Fort Sill, Okla.: 129
Fortune, T. Thomas: 6
4-H Clubs: 160, 208-209
Franks, William: 258
Frantz, Frank: 21
Freedmen's Bureau, U.S.: 13
Fuhr, A. H.: 82-84, 114, 153, 172
Funding: from land-lease money, 16-17; through Morrill Act of 1890, 17; from Enabling Act land grant, 17; and legislative appropriations, 17, 18; and Smith-Hughes Act, 19, 20; and George-Reed Act of 1929, 20; and George-Deen Act of 1937, 20; changes in, 20-22; and Federal Higher Education Act of 1965, 22, 60-61, 144, 242; and scholarships and loans, 58; and fund-raising drives, 66; and student loans, 120-21; and grants, tuition, 120-21; for library, 141-45

Gaffney, Doreatha: 232
Gandy, Lenoliah E.: 228
Garcha, B. S.: 163
Garcia, William B.: 242
Gary, Gov. Raymond: 115
Gayles, C. Felton ("Zip"): 176, 178, 180, 191-94
George, Wilnard: 136
George-Dean Act of 1937: 20
George-Reed Act of 1929: 20
G. I. Bill of Rights: 52, 115, 120
Gilyard, Odell: 268, 270
Girls' Glee Club: 127
G. Lamar Harrison Library: 143-45; *see also* Langston University library
Glover, William: 153

Goodie, John: 182
Governors of Oklahoma; 283
Gracey, Roosevelt T.: 131, 135-36, 140
Greene, F. V.: 232
Gregory, Dick: 140
Gude, Legolian: 268
Guthrie, Okla.: 7-9, 42, 48ff., 96, 202-205
Guy, William E.: 213, 215

Hale, Larzette Golden (Mrs. William Henri Hale): 53-54, 58
Hale, William Henri (Langston University president): 33, 148, 200; tenure, 52; integration problems of, 53-54; biography of, 54; "ten-year plan" of, 54-60; and desegregation, 57; dismissal of, 61; death of, 62; philosophy of, 115
Hale Student Center: 34
Hall, Abraham T.: 4
Hall, Amos: 234
Hall, Rubye M.: 23
Hamilton, Gomez C.: 257
Hargrove, Mrs. S. L.: 216-17
Hargrove, S. L.: 126, 216
Harkins, Clarence: 176
Harrison, G. Lamar (Langston University president): 26, 114-15; background of, 48-49; accomplishments as president, 48, 50-52; and Langston accreditation, 52, 147; resignation of, 52, 115; service of, under five governors, 115
Hart, Benjamin F., Jr.: 182-84
Hawes, Ada: 215
Haydon, Julie: 222
Hayes, Frances M.: 78
Hayes, Larry K.: 249
Haynes, Marques: 176-77
Hazelwood, J. I.: 76
Head Start program: 58
Hemry, Jerome: 234
Henderson, Luther L.: 239
Henderson, Thomas ("Wild Man"): 181
Hennessey Clipper: 6
Heweltt, Helen Fowler: 211
High School Department: 75, 77-79
Hill, Mozell C.: 196-97, 248
Hill, W. A.: 207
Hill-Ackiss study: 196-97, 202-203

313

Hinton, William A.: 252
Hodge, Erma: 181
Holloway, Ernest L. (Langston University president): tenure of, 69, 72, 74, 116; background of, 70; other Langston posts held by, 70, 257
Holloway, Gov. William J.: 22
Holman, Fred: 47
Holt, L. H. 16; *see also* Board of Regents (first) of Langston University
Holt, Wilma: 232
Home Economics Department: 165, 227; first instructor in, 226; first cooking courses in, 226; and home-management house, 228; faculty of, 232
Hooks, B. F.: 8
Hopkins, S. N. (on first Board of Regents): 16; *see also* Board of Regents (first) of Langston University
Hornbeak, Joe: 181
Howell, W. C.: 80
Hubert, Zachary T. (Langston University president): tenure of, 42, 217; biography of, 42; accomplishments of, 44; and student strike of 1928, 44, 131-40; and enrollment, 113
Hughes, Langston: 85
Hughey, Ms. S. W.: 240
Humanities Department: 222
Hunt, Sharon: 232
Hutchinson, C. B.: 266
Hyperion Club: 127

Indian Affairs Bureau grants: 120
I. W. Young Auditorium: 51
Jackson, William A.: 262
Jason, Ruth: 232
Jessye, Eva: 242
Johns, Calvin: 153
Johnson, J.W.: 15
Johnson, Mordecai Wyatt: 85
Johnson, Moses J.: 213
Johnson, Raymond: 270
Jones, Cornelia: 78, 175
Jones, D. C.: 158
Jones, Gilbert: 173, 214-15
Jones, P. M.: 240
Jones, Sadie Waterford: 129-30

Jones, Walter: 257
Jones, W. Bruce: 74
Jones Hall Science and Agriculture building: 51
Journal of Home Economics: 249
Journal of Negro Education: 249

Kansas City Times: 6
Keepler, Dannie: 232
Kelley, William V.: 126, 174
Kendall, Elizabeth: 220
Kerr, Gov. Robert S.: 115
Kerr-McGee Oil Corporation: 121
Ketchum, Edwin: 117
Killingsworth, John: 240
King, Hazel: 212
King, Moxye Weaver: *see* Moxye Weaver
Kinnard, Richmond E.: 163, 249
Knapp, Bradford: 210
Knapp, Seamon: 210
Kulp, Victor: 234

Land Grant Act of 1890: 202
Land-grant colleges: 294-96; *see also* funding
Langston, John Mercer: 3, 11-13
Langston, Okla.: 13, 205; location of, 3; founding of, 3; as Negro city, 3; black migration to, 5-7; and Jim Crow legislation: 6; and anti-immigration efforts, 6; population of, in 1891, 6; development of, 7-10; political alignment of, 8; and petition for college, 9; establishment of Colored Agricultural and Normal University at, 10; and town-university relations, 195-205
Langston Alumni Council: 61
Langston Board of Trustees: 198
Langston City Herald: 5, 9, 10, 15, 110, 273
Langston Gazette: 222
Langston Lions Lettermen's Club: 176
Langston University: official name of, after 1941, 13, 50; first Board of Regents of, 16; funding of, 16-23, 58, 60-61, 120-21, 144-45; opening of, 17; and land grant of 1906, 21-22; and Board of Regents for Oklahoma

INDEX

Agricultural and Mechanical Colleges, 23, 36, 47, 61-63, 68-69, 71-72; financial problems of, 23, 63, 65-66, 68-69, 116; College Department of, 31-32, 40; presidents of, 26-72, 283-87; Science Department of, 40; student activism at, 44, 51, 58, 112, 116, 131-40, 141-45; upgrading of physical plant of, 54, 150; and desegregration, 57, 116; and Normal (Teachers) Department, 75-76; memories of early days at, 80-109; enrollment at, 110-17, 290-91; student expenses of, 118-24; student organizations at, 125-30; and protests of March, 1978, 140; accreditation of, 146-50; and Task Force Committee report of 1972, 150; and proposed campus in Tulsa, 150; Athletics Department of, 172-94; and university-town relations, 195-205; and Cooperative Extension Service, 206-12; language studies at, 213-25; home economics at, 226-32; music at, 238-47; research at, 248-50; science studies at, 251-55; mechanical and industrial arts at, 262-72; trades studies at, 262-72; future of, 273-75, *see also* Colored Agricultural and Normal University

Langston University Alumni Association: 50, 83, 114; and Frederick D, Moon, 151-53

Langston University Club of Chicago: 130

Langston University Cooperative Extension Service: 206-12

Languages in curriculum: English, 213, 215-23; ancient, 213-14; modern, 213-15, 217; and faculty, 213, 215-17, 219-23; and Negro literature, 216-17; and clubs and organizations, 219, 222; and communications, 222

Latimer, Steve B.: 249, 258

Law School, Langston: 233; and case of Ada Lois Sipuel (Fisher), 233-37; established in 1948, 233; faculty of, 234; closed after 1950, 237

Lee, Benjamin Franklin (Langston University president): 46, 114

Lee, D. W.: 156, 158

Liberty, Okla.: 4

Library: 51, 58; holdings of, 141, 143-45; funding of, 141-45, 147; staff of, 142; new building for, 143-44; and Melvin Tolson Black Heritage Center, 144; grants for, 144-45; *see also* G. Lamar Harrison library

Lioness Club: 127

Roberts, T. M.: 234

Robertson, Wallace: 234

Robinson, Edward: 9

Robinson, Omar, Jr.: 242

Sadler, Samuel Levi: as instructor in English, 215; as composer of "Dear Langston", 215, 245-47

Salone, A. M.: 77

Sanford, J. W. (Langston University president): tenure of, 44; biography of, 44-46; popularity of, 46; resignation of, 46; and federal relief programs, 114; and study for State Board of Education, 146

Sanford Hall: 34, 46, 255

Schoats, Albert: 181, 184

School Days, 1915: 123-24

Science Department: 40; first courses in, 251-52; in grade-school section, 251; additional courses in, 252, 257; and museum, 252; faculty of, 252, 254, 256-58; prenursing program of, 253-55

Second Annual Oklahoma Farm and Home Congress, Langston University: 209

Shirley, George: 242

Simpson, James: 257-58

Sims, William E. (Langston University president): tenure of, 62-63, 115; on land-grant schools, 63; resignation of, 63-65; earlier roles of, at Langston, 158, 163, 242

Sipuel, Ada Lois: 233

"Six-Graders Day": 60

Slaughter, Thomas: 17

Slothower, Keith: 219

Smith, Donald Lee: 181

Smith, Mary: 126

Smith-Hughes Act for vocational training: 19
Sneed, Mayhugh: 168
Social Uplift Club: 129
Southern Education Report: 57
Southwestern Athletic Conference: 176
Southwestern Journal: 248
Spartans (club): 126
Spaulding, M. F.: 158, 197
Starks, Rev. W. J.: 78, 95
State Board of Regents for Higher Education: 22-23, 121-22, 146-47, 236
State Department of Education Board: 23
State Negro Chamber of Commerce: 160
Stewart, R. E.: 9
Strike, student, of 1928: 44, 131-40
Strong, Ellen Cockrel: 76
Student Center: 54
Student loans: 21, 120
Sulcer, Charles Henry Williams Murce: 13
Lions Club: 126-27
Literati Club: 125, 127
Little Star of the Black Belt (Roman Catholic newspaper): 9
Locan County: 3-4, 7, 8, 15, 110, 196-97
Long, H. J. ("Little"): 175
Lucas, Paralee V.: 215
Lucien, Jan Rolland: 220
Lynce, J. R.: 6

McCabe, Edward P.: 3-8
McCrary, Mary Lee–227
McCree, Paul: 79, 254
McCutcheon, Isaac Berry (Langston University president): tenure of, 34, 112; biography of, 34; and discord, 34-36; resignation of, 35
McDaniel, Mayme: 142
McGowan, N.: 232
McLaurin, G.W.: 235-37
Main Building: construction of, 18-19; destroyed by fire, 18, 33, 80-82, 112, 141
Marland, Gov. E. W.: 46, 114, 152-53
Marshall, Thurgood: 234
Marquess, John Miller (Langston University president): tenure of, 36, 113, 145; biography of, 36-37, 126; accomplishments of, as president, 37-39; resignation and death of, 39; as promoter of football, 174; and Community Fair, 195
Marquess Hall: 34, 137
Mathis, B. M.: 158
Mechanical and Industrial Arts Department: curriculum changes in, 262, 265-66, 272; early courses in, 262-63; faculty of, 262-63, 268, 270; requirements in, 264; shopwork in, 264-65; drawing course in, 264; flight training in, 268; cosmetology in, 270
Meggs, Peter: 216
Memphis Commercial: 6
Memphis Free Speech: 6
Midwest City, Okla.: 205
Miller, E. A.: 268
Miller, Moses F.: 176-77
Mixed Glee Club: 127
Monroe, Benjamin: 163
Montgomery, John: 117
Moon, Frederick D.: biography of, 151; and Langston Alumni Association, 151-53
Moore, Eugene: 158
Moore, LeRoy G.: as dean of instruction in 1940, 73-74, 176; as football coach, 176; as director of science, 176, 254-56; other roles of, 256-57, 259-61
Morrill Act of 1890: 17, 28, 31
Mosley, James L. (Langston University president): tenure of, 65, 115, 122; biography of, 65; accomplishments of, as president, 66; on Research Advisory Committee, 249
Moten, Eta: 85
Mozart Musical Choral Club: 127
Murray, Gov. Johnston: 115
Murray, Gov. William H.: 22, 40, 113
Music Department: role of Mrs. Zelia Page Breaux in, 238-39; orchestra of, 238, 241; choral society of, 238, 241; vocal-music curriculum in, 238, 240; bands and glee club in, 238-39, 241, 243; faculty of, 238-42, 244; changed to

INDEX

Fine Arts Department in 1923, 239; choir of, 242; and Sam Sadler and "Dear Langston", 245-47
Music Education Club: 241, 243

National Association for the Advancement of Colored People (NAACP): 6, 219
National Association of Intercollegiate Athletics: 181
National Council for Accreditation of Teacher Education: 60, 121, 148-50, 230
National War Production program: 270
National Youth Administration: 165
New Farmers of America: see Agriculture Club
New Homemakers of America: 228
New York Age: 6
New York Times: 9
Nicholson, Homer: 220
Normal (Teacher's College) Department: 16; see also Normal (Teacher's) Department
Normal (Teacher's) Department: purpose of, 75-76; first graduates of, 1906, 76; enrollment in, 112; see also Normal (Teacher's College) Department
Norman, Okla.: 129
North Central Association of Colleges and secondary Schools: 52, 143, 148, 150, 230

Octette (Club): 126
Oglesby, Othella: 240
Oklahoma Agricultural and Mechanical University: see Oklahoma State University
Oklahoma Art Center: 169
Oklahoma Association of Colored Women's Federated Clubs: 212
Oklahoma Baptist University: 180
Oklahoma City, Okla.: 202
Oklahoma Collegiate Athletic Conference: 178
Oklahoma governors: 283
Oklahoma Immigration Society: 4

Oklahoma Industrial School and College Commission: 9
Oklahoma State Board of Agriculture: 23
Oklahoma State Board of Education: 248
Oklahoma State University: 23, 147, 169, 212; Agriculture Experiment Station of, 249
Oklahoma Territorial Convention of 1894: 13
Oklahoma Territory: 3
Organizations, Langston University: 125-30
Owens, Wallace, Jr.: 169

Page, Inman Edward (Langston University president): 80, 83, 110, 112-13, 121, 195; tenure of, 26; biography of, 26-31; accomplishments of, as president, 31-34; resignation of, 34, 36; death of, 34
Page Hall: 33, 131, 141-42, 169
Parker, L.: 180
Patterson, Zella J. Black: 249
Payne, John D.: 166
Payne, Kenneth: 182
Perry, R. P.: 248
Peters, Annie: 207
Pettus, J. Wilson: 73
Philips, Gov. Leon: 115
Philomathean Club: 125-26
Phyllis Wheatley Club: 125-26; see also Esoteric Club
Phyllis Wheatley Dormitory: 26, 34, 228
Physical Education Department: see Athletics Department
Pinchback, P. B. S.: 6
Pons, V. F.: 220
Popular Orchestra (Langston orchestra): 127-128
Porter, George: 238
Presidents of Langston University: 248-87
Prince Hall Grand Lodge: 212
Publications 1898-1978: 300-301
Pyrtle, R. N.: 79, 254

Qualls, Youra: 219

317

Ray, V. N.: 126
Reed, Wylma Frances: 125
Renfrow, William Gary: 13, 15
Research Projects: of faculty, 248-49; and Office of Institutional Research, 248-49; subjects of, 248-50; and seminar, 249; funds for, 249-50; and Research Advisory Committee, 249; current, 250
Ricks, Mrs. Garvis Sparks: 228
Ritzhaupt, Louis: 48
Robbins, Charles H., role of, in founding of Langston, Okla.: 3, 6
Roberts, Joseph: 17, 80-81
Task Force for the Seventies (report): 121
Taylor, J. E., Jr.: 216
Taylor, R. R.: 112
Tecumseh, Okla.: 6
Thatcher, James: 182
Thigpen, Beray: 244
Thomas, Prof. (Langston teacher): 131, 133
Thomas, Sarah: 258
Thompson, Francis (on first Board of Regents): 16; *see also* Board of Regents (first) of Langston University
Tillman, George: 153
Tillman, William: 86
Title III funds: *see* Federal Higher Education Act of 1965
Tolliver, Oletha: 220
Tolson, Melvin B.: 217-19, 223-25
Trade and Industrial Building: 51
Trades courses: 262-64, 272; faculty for, 263-64, 268, 270; for seventh-graders, 263; in carpentry, 264; in blacksmithing, 264; in auto mechanics, 265-66, 270; in shoemaking and printing, 265-66, 268; in masonry, 268; in woodworking, 268
Trades and Industrial Program (T&I) *see* mechanical and industrial arts, trades courses
Trapp, Gov. Martin Edward: 113
Treble Clef Club: 126
Trout, Newton: 263
Tucker, J. St. Cyr: 251
Tucker, Samuel J. (Langston University president): tenure of, 71, 116, 140; background of, 71-72; dismissal of, 72
Tulsley, J. W.: 15
Turner Albert Louis (Langston University president): 26, 114; appointed in 1940, 46; resignation of, 47; death of, 48
Turner, Gov. Roy: 115
Tyler, E. O. (on first Board of Regents): 16; *see also* Board of Regents (first) of Langston University
Tyler, P. F. (on first Board of Regents): 16; *see also* Board of Regents (first) of Langston University

Unassigned Indian Lands: 3
United States Department of Agriculture: 195, 206, 210, 212
United States Department of Housing and Urban Development (HUD): 203
United States Department of State: 148
University Band: 127
University Choral Club: 126
University-community relations: in early years, 195-96; during economic decline of town, 196-97; and rural decline, 196-97; disharmony in, 196; and housing problems, 197-98, 203; and town businesses, 198; guidance clincis in, 199-200; surveys of, 199-200; and Upward Bound program, 200; and Head Start program, 201; and University self-study report, 201-202; and churches, 203; and new town homes, 203-205
University Concert Band: 126
University of Oklahoma: 147, 169-70; College of Law of, 233-36
University Orchestra: 127
University Quartette: 127
Utopia (club): 127

Veterans Administration: 21, 52, 115, 148
Vice-presidents and academic deans: 73-74, 288-89
Vinci, Carl: 180-81

INDEX

Wade, Ida: 79, 254, 256
Wall, Ephraim: 258
Wallace, Arthur: 17
Wallace, D. J.: 8, 9
Waller, Odie: 230
Walton, Gov. John C.: 113
Warren, Glenda: 232
Washington, Booker T.: 206, 208
Washington, E. M.: 232
Washington, Mrs. E. M.: 143
Washington, Sadie G.: 230
Watlington, J. M.: 156
Weaver, Mayme: 268
Weaver, Moxye: 140; as chairman of English Department, 219
Welch, Elwyn Breaux: 219
Wells, Ida B.: 6
Wells, W. M. T.: 158
West, Annie A.: 232
Western Age: 172
White, Jimmie L.: 163, 203
White Cappers (offshoot of Ku Klux Klan): 6
Whitby, A. B.: 251
Whitby, Banter: 73
Williams, A. A.: 10
Williams, Gov. Robert L.: 112
Williams, John T.: 176
Willingham, William: 258
Woodson, Carter: 85
World War I: 112-13, 207; Langston entertainers in, 129
World War II: 115, 119, 241, 268, 270; Langston entertainers in, 128-29; football during, 176-77; agriculture during, 210-11
Wright, Henrietta (Beasley): 142

Young, Isaac William (Langston University president): two terms of, 39, 95, 141, 153, 175, 255; biography of, 39-40; accomplishments of, as president, 40-41; death of, 42; and Langston enrollment, 113
Young, Leonelle: 78
YWCA, on Langston campus: 126

www.ingramcontent.com/pod-product-compliance
Lightning Source LLC
Chambersburg PA
CBHW020737160426
43192CB00006B/221